PHILOSOPHY
OF THE
ARTS

PHILOSOPHY
OF THE
ARTS

MORRIS WEITZ

New York
RUSSELL & RUSSELL

1964

For Kiki

ACKNOWLEDGMENTS

I wish to acknowledge my gratitude to the following who kindly gave me permission to quote passages from their publications: Appleton-Century-Crofts, Inc., *Principles of Aesthetics*, by DeWitt Parker, copyright, 1946; Chatto and Windus, *Art*, by Clive Bell, *Transformations* and *Vision and Design*, by Roger Fry; The Clarendon Press, *Philosophy and History: Essays Presented to Ernst Cassirer*, edited by Raymond Klibansky and H. J. Paton; Harcourt, Brace and Company, *The Art in Painting*, by Albert Barnes, *Collected Poems 1909–1935*, by T. S. Eliot, copyright, 1936, by Harcourt, Brace and Company, Inc. and *Selected Essays 1917–1932*, by T. S. Eliot, copyright, 1932, by Harcourt, Brace and Company, Inc. and *Abstract and Surrealist Art in America*, by Sidney Janis; Harper and Brothers, *The Understanding of Music*, by Max Schoen, and *Native Son*, by Richard Wright; The Hogarth Press, Ltd., *The Artist and Psycho-Analysis*, by Roger Fry; Henry Holt and Company, Inc., *Understanding Poetry*, by Cleanth Brooks and R. P. Warren; International Publishers, *Selected Works of Karl Marx and Frederick Engels*; The Macmillan Company, *Wild Swans at Coole*, by W. B. Yeats, copyright, 1917, by Margaret C. Anderson, 1919 and 1946 by the Macmillan Company and used with their permission; the *New Republic*, "The 'Difference' of Literature," by Clive Bell, in their issue of November 29, 1922; Novello and Company, Ltd., *The Beautiful in Music*, by Eduard Hanslick; Oxford University Press, *What Is Art?* by Leo Tolstoy, translated by Aylmer Maude; Oskar Piest and The Liberal Arts Press, *Art, the Critics, and You*, by C. J. Ducasse; and Yale University Press, *The Analysis of Art*, by DeWitt Parker.

PREFACE

This is an essay in aesthetic inquiry in which certain very definite problems are dealt with in an attempt to offer some solutions of them. Like a number of other books which have appeared in the last decade, it is concerned with some few aesthetic issues that are being discussed in contemporary theory. It shares with these works the conviction that aesthetics ought to consider, in an analytic manner, very concrete problems that have arisen in discussions about the nature of the arts and its relation to appreciation.

C. I. Lewis is undoubtedly correct in his recent reflection that "In the whole area of philosophical studies there is probably no other topic which is marked by so much unclarity and so little unanimity as is exhibited by the subject of esthetic theory." [1] Whatever the final merits of Lewis's claim, there is one way in which this situation may be remedied. We can begin with those problems that are already extant in contemporary aesthetic theory, practical criticism of the various arts, and the writings of some of our best living artists.

The situation in aesthetics is somewhat analogous to that which prevailed in the philosophy of science some quarter of a century ago. The dominant mode of philosophizing about science at that time was to take it as one great, total body of knowledge and to interpret it in some overbearing, ontological manner, usually to the detriment of science in relation to other kinds of human activity. Russell, Whitehead, and certain of the members of the Vienna Circle promoted a quite different conception of the philosophy of

[1] C. I. Lewis, An Analysis of Knowledge and Valuation, p. 434.

science. Essentially it consisted in digging into some of the crucial, much-discussed questions with which practicing scientists were concerned. In some cases, in the extreme positivists, for example, this piecemeal approach, in which philosophical problems were determined by scientists, led to the repudiation of any aspects of philosophy of science which were not a direct outcome of practical scientific questions or which were oriented toward some metaphysical synthesizing of materials. But this did not occur in all cases, certainly not in Russell and Whitehead, both of whom, in different ways, to be sure, offered as integral parts of their philosophies of science, ontological and cosmological categories and systems.

In contemporary aesthetic theory, I suppose, we are at the beginning of a new era in which we must also dig into extant issues which are being disputed by all people interested in the arts and not only by aestheticians. Some aestheticians who have already dug in seem to manifest the same tendencies as their over-zealous confrères in philosophy of science in their insistence upon discarding any aesthetic nugget that sparkles a little too dazzlingly with speculative suggestion or synthesis. In so far as their injunctions will keep us from treating the arts "from above," to paraphrase Fechner, it is a healthy thing; but if their work should create undue fear in the formulation of new ideas, most of which, let us even grant, will probably be invalidated, their basic contribution will have been not in the promotion of clarity but rather in the sterilization of aesthetic inquiry.

There is, I think, too much fear of being wrong and too much desire to be right in the whole of contemporary philosophy. As a reaction to previous bad philosophizing, it is salutary; but as an ultimate criterion, it is regrettable. Philosophy, after all, is nurtured as much by the mistakes that it sows as it is by the truths that it reaps. Indeed, cannot one safely assert that much which is vigorously and challengingly valid in contemporary philosophy has been the result of the stimulation and reactions afforded by the most speculative of modern philosophical systems, that of early logical positivism?

The positivists are quite correct in their insistence upon the verbal, specious character of many philosophical disputes, including aesthetic ones. And in this book I shall try to expose some of these. But one must not conclude from any such initial success that all philosophical problems are rooted in differences in or abuses of language. Philosophy in the main is still the quest for real definitions; it is still concerned, as it was for Plato, Aristotle, Descartes, even as it is for Russell today, with the understanding of reality in all of its many categorial features.[2] In philosophical aesthetics this means that at least one of its central problems remains the definition of the nature of art; and I shall have much to say about that in this essay.

The nature of art is our main problem. Around it we shall deal with such related questions as those of the meaning of form and content, representation versus nonrepresentation, the meaning of music and abstract art, the special importance of the medium in art, the conception of art as a language and the nature of appreciation. These problems are considered in relation to the arts themselves: painting, poetry, music, the motion picture, etc. Throughout, there is no insistence upon finality in the solutions offered; nor do the answers to all the questions stand or fall together. Rather, in typical "Cambridge analytic" fashion, we shall focus upon certain crucial issues that, when taken together, relate quite systematically, in an attempt to bring a little more clarity into the field of aesthetics.

M.W.

[2] See my article, "Philosophy and the Abuse of Language," *The Journal of Philosophy*, XLIV, No. 20 (September 25, 1947), for a refutation of the view that all philosophical differences are linguistic or rooted in any abuse of language.

CONTENTS

1

AESTHETIC FORMALISM

2

THE CRITIQUE OF FORMALISM

3

RESOLUTION: THE ORGANIC THEORY

4

THE ARTS: PAINTING

1

AESTHETIC FORMALISM

Introduction

Let us begin our inquiry with an exposition of an aesthetic theory that has engendered a great deal of dispute among aestheticians, critics, and artists. This is the theory of formalism. During the last hundred years, there have been a number of formalist aesthetics developed. Two of these are the German school, initiated by Herbart, systematized by Zimmermann, and supposedly championed in musical criticism by Hanslick; and the British group, consisting primarily of Clive Bell and Roger Fry. Because of the stringency of their views, and because they lend themselves to clear, systematic presentation, we shall start with the formalism of Bell and Fry. They were primarily practicing critics who were intent upon coming to grips with modern painting; their aesthetic theory was the result of their attempt to think through and get clear about the implications of the revolution that was going on in France after the hegemony of Cézanne had been established. The concepts they developed, the rejections they cultivated, and the issues they inspired make them extremely valuable models upon which to initiate our aesthetic analysis.

In the exposition that follows, we shall be concerned mainly with the presentation of the views of Bell and Fry and, in so far as possible, within their own terminology and set of assumptions. The critical examination of their basic concepts and doctrines will be offered in later chapters.

Bell's Theory of the Art Object

Both Bell and Fry regard the concrete work of art as the essential object of aesthetic analysis. And yet they begin their inquiries with what they consider to be a fact about their appreciation of art. "The starting-point for all systems of aesthetics must be the personal experience of a peculiar emotion." [1] This emotion is taken to be an unique one, in that it is evoked only by art, or by nature when it is seen in a certain formal way.

It is rather interesting that Bell and Fry, who are avowed formalists, place themselves also in the emotionalist tradition in aesthetics. Like Tolstoy, they regard art as the efficient cause of an emotional experience. They differ from Tolstoy in that they find this experience to be qualitatively distinguishable from other emotional experiences and unrelated to the emotions communicated by the representations of the work of art. It is important to recognize that Bell and Fry can be classified as both formalist and emotionalist because we can realize even this early in our study the ambiguous character of the dispute between formalists and emotionalists (e.g., C. J. Ducasse) in contemporary aesthetic theory; we can also recognize that many of the terms that refer to prevalent aesthetic views, like voluntarism, intellectualism, emotionalism, formalism, or hedonism, are treacherous and to be employed with extreme care, since some of these terms refer to theories concerning the art object whereas others apply to theories of the creation of art or the appreciation of art. Many unnecessary disputes could be avoided if aesthetic labels were not pasted in one piece on aesthetic theories, but rather were applied separately to different views about the various constituents of the aesthetic experience.

In Bell, the first problem of aesthetic analysis is *what* in the art object causes one to have the unique aesthetic emotion? This is also the central problem of aesthetics for him, and its solution the revelation of the essential quality of art. Bell's answer, of course, is that significant form is the essential, the distinguishing feature of art, that which initiates the aesthetic emotion.

In painting, Bell finds that significant form is constituted by certain combinations of lines and colors that move us in a certain ecstatic way. But this does not render significant form subjective; this ecstatic aesthetic emotion is a clue to the presence of significant form. Bell insists that significant form is an objective quality of a work of art and inheres in it in the way that the material elements do. One may ask if a painting is in tempera or oil. In the same way one may inquire whether or not a painting has significant form. The objectivity of significant form is all-important for criticism since the function of the critic is "to be continually pointing out those parts, the sum, or rather the combination, of which unite to produce significant form." [2]

Like Tolstoy, Bell denies the identity of beauty and art. Significant form is not the same as the beautiful. The beautiful is the pretty, the pleasing, and often the sexually attractive; but flowers and birds and lovely girls do not possess significant form since their combinations of line and color do not evoke the aesthetic emotion but rather move us, when they do, to nonaesthetic emotion.[3] In painting, we apply the term "beautiful" to those pictures which contain representations of objects that would be considered beautiful (i.e., pretty, attractive) outside of art. Thus we say that a picture which represents a pretty girl is a beautiful picture.[4]

Significant form is the essence of art. It can move us aesthetically, to rapture and ecstasy. But painting can evoke nonaesthetic emotions, too, through elements other than the right combinations of line and color. Narrative, religious, or social art — Bell calls these "descriptive art" — utilize line and color only to induce ordinary emotions. The essence of descriptive art is that it sacrifices significant form for representation. Bell offers no detailed analysis of representation in art, but what he means is clear enough from his examples. He means by it those elements that look like certain events or psychological states which exist outside of art.

Our ordinary attitude toward representation is that it can play a positive role in the total work of art. This Bell denies: representation is never beneficial. It is either harmless or downright harmful. It is harmful when it diverts our attention from the lines and colors to the associations of the representational elements. It is harmless when it is resolved or dissolved into the plastic elements of colors and lines, that is, into significant form. "If a representative form has value, it is as form, not as representation." [5] "If the representative element is not to ruin the picture as a work of art, it must be fused into the design . . . It must be simplified into significant form." [6] There are many examples that bring out Bell's point here. Consider Seurat's "Sur La Grande Jatte" or Brueghel's "Peasant Wedding Dance" or Cézanne's "Italian Girl." Each of these contains some representational elements — of people, trees, water, animals. In order that we may not allow these elements to evoke the emotions that people or animals or trees do, we must interpret these elements as combinations of line and color, and refuse to see them as anything more.

The problem arises, why have representation at all, then? Painting must be specified, made concrete, "canalized," to use Bell's term; significant form is *this* combination of line and color, or *that* combination, not merely an abstract universal. Consequently, the artist must particularize his significant form; he must solve what Bell calls the "technical problem" of art.[7] The representational elements constitute a specific mode of significant form. One artist depicts a single girl resting on a couch; another, a group of peasants making merry; a third, a crowd of people resting quietly in the sun on a beach. Their representations are necessary as *foci* of significant form, but that is their sole aesthetic importance.

Bell's Theory of Art Appreciation

There are two kinds of art object for Bell — the descriptive and the significantly formal. Corresponding to them, there are two kinds of appreciation, "impure" and "pure." [8] Impure appreciation is the indulgence in the representational elements and the emotions that attend them. Pure appreciation is the indulgence in the significant form of the work of art. This indulgence is of a special sort and is characterized by certain rare qualities. First, it involves the transcendence of our ordinary activities and the entrance into a Platonic realm of nonordinary experiences.

Art transports us from the world of man's activity to a world of aesthetic exaltation. For a moment we are shut off from human interests; our anticipations and memories are arrested; we are lifted above the stream of human life. [9]

A good work of visual art carries a person who is capable of appreciating it out of life into ecstasy. [10]

The contemplation of pure form leads to a state of extraordinary exaltation and complete detachment from the concerns of life. [11]

Be they artists or lovers of art . . . those who achieve ecstasy are those who have freed themselves from the arrogance of humanity. He who would feel the significance of art must make himself humble before it. Those who find the chief importance of art . . . in its relation to conduct or its practical utility . . . will never get from anything the best that it can give. Whatever the world of aesthetic contemplation may be, it is not the world of human business and passion; in it the chatter and tumult of material existence is unheard, or heard only as the echo of some more ultimate harmony. [12]

In its exalted character, the appreciation of art resembles the experience of the religious person, the philosopher, and the mathematician. The mathematician and the pure spectator of art feel emotions for their objects of study which do not arise from any relation between the objects and their ordinary experiences with other human beings, but only from the objects themselves. Both respond to what Bell calls the valid combinations of forms presented to them. Like pure appreciation, the mathematical experience is a rapturous one, generated specifically by the examination of proofs. The mathematician's experience, qua mathematician, is not rooted in human relationships and values — "life" — but in mathematics itself. The mathematician, like the pure appreciator, brings nothing from life, no knowledge of its affairs or emotions.[13]

The pure spectator resembles the philosopher in that both "inhabit a world with an intense and peculiar significance of its own; that significance is unrelated to the significance of life. In this world the emotions of life find no place. It is a world with emotions of its own." [14]

By the religious experience, Bell means the expression of the individual's sense of the emotional significance of the universe. This expression also involves emotions that are different from and transcendent of the emotions of ordinary life. It also transports us to the ecstasies of unearthly states of mind. "Art and religion belong to the same world . . . The kingdom of neither is of this world." [15]

Pure appreciation possesses other characteristics: It is independent of any body of facts, historical or psychological. "To appreciate a work of art we need bring with us nothing from life, no knowledge of its ideas and affairs, no familiarity with its emotions." [16] The traditional cognitive attitudes of belief, disbelief and make-believe are all irrelevant since they are responses to the representative aspects of art.

Like Münsterberg, Bell proclaims the "isolated" character of the appreciation of art. "The only way to appreciate perfectly a work of art is to see it as though it were the only thing of its sort in existence. To see it in relation to anything else is to see it impurely." [17] And like the aesthetic hedonists, Bell affirms the pleasure principle of appreciation. "Connoisseurs in pleasure — of whom I count myself one — know that nothing is more intensely delightful than the aesthetic thrill." [18]

To sum up: Bell finds in the true appreciation of art an exalted, rapturous, nonpractical, disinterested, pleasurable, contemplative experience, the essence of which is that it is a response to significant form. By the "unique aesthetic emotion," he means the totality of these characteristics.

Bell's Theory of Art Creation

The distinction between the impure and the pure appears also in Bell's discussion of artistic creation. Most artists, Bell contends, are woefully impure. Incapable of creating aesthetically moving combinations of line and color, they aim at the evocation of ordinary practical emotions and attitudes through the embodiment of and the emphasis upon the representational in their work. The whole of descriptive art, which is essentially art in which representations have not been dissolved into line and color, is the product of these artists who are unable to achieve significant form, and who consequently aim at something else.

Pure artistic creation, on the other hand, is tied to significant form. It is primarily, Bell asserts, a function of *vision*, of seeing reality in a certain way: as pure form. All of us may look at a landscape. Most of us will see it as a complex of hill, cows, barns, and trees. But not the true artist, who will visualize it rather as colors and lines in relation to each other. The artist is seeing reality, or rather a portion of it, as significant form; and his vision possesses all the characteristics of the true spectator's view of art: It is rapturous, nonutilitarian, disinterested.[19] The artist transforms his unique vision of reality into his art object.

Bell's theory is rather similar to that of many modern aestheticians and artists, in his distinguishing between two ways of looking at things, the practical and the aesthetic. Ontologically, the more revealing is the aesthetic since it is taken as a *truer* vision than the practical. This notion that artistic creation is a metaphysical enterprise, a revelation of certain ultimate characteristics of reality, has been advocated by artists of all sorts in our era, by artists as diverse as Kandinsky, Dali, Chagall, and Picasso, to mention but a few.

The question arises, *Why* do certain combinations of line and color move us, the spectators, aesthetically? Bell proposes as a "metaphysical" (he really means a psychological) hypothesis that we are moved because basically spectators share in the artist's unique vision of reality as significant form.[20] Even those of us who are not able to transcribe our visions upon the canvas can see reality as line and color and can react to nature in a non-practical, disinterested, rapturous way.

Bell's Special Theory of Literature

In his various writings, Bell has touched upon some of the arts other than painting, mainly music and literature. His musical aesthetics parallels his aesthetics of painting. The essence of music is also significant form, that is, certain combinations of sound which evoke the peculiar aesthetic emotion that takes us out of our humdrum everyday world.[21]

Literature, however, presents a much more serious problem. Most aestheticians, naturally enough, I suppose, like most philosophers, are monists, and are constantly striving to explain all the arts by one principle. But not Bell, who, with candor and perspicacity, recognizes what he regards as the irreducible differences between literature and painting. In an essay that was published in the *New Republic*, called "The 'Difference' of Literature," Bell enumerates these. Literature is basically informational and cognitive in its content, the embodiment of ordinary emotions; and consequently appeals to its readers by means of the associations that it calls up.

All I am sure of is that literature is an art altogether different from the arts of painting and music, and that to appreciate it a man need not possess that peculiar sense of abstract form — "pure form," if you will — without which he can get little or nothing from the other two.

. . . We all agree that there is in literature an immense amount of stuff which is not purely aesthetic, which is cognitive and suggestive, and which an intelligent bourgeois can understand as well as anyone else.

Literature, I cannot help thinking, must be something very different from painting — a less pure art I should say, an art with more body in it and, I will add, an art of far more importance to the human race. I am persuaded that people can genuinely appreciate literature though they lack that strange power of reacting intensely to abstract form which is essential to a comprehension of the visual arts. And this I account for by supposing that formal significance, without which a picture is utterly worthless, is not the essential quality, is not even the most important quality, in a book. If, indeed, I rightly understand what formal beauty is, I believe that you can have good literature without it and good literary criticism without much appreciation of it.[22]

In *Art*, Bell claims that literature can never be pure art, since it is concerned with facts and ideas, and is consequently primarily intellectual. Even Shakespeare's sonnets are impure because the form, which ultimately reduces to musical tones in melodic and rhythmic relations, "is burdened with an intellectual content, and that content is a mood that mingles with and reposes on the emotions of life." [23] Poetry becomes pure only when it is resolved into music, and we are then able to regard it as the stimulus of our aesthetic beatitude.

Bell completes his aesthetic theory with a discussion of the function and value of the aesthetic experience. His theory *seems* to be an escapist one. "Because the aesthetic emotions are outside and above life, it is possible to take refuge in them from life." [24] But this is a superficial interpretation of his views since it does not consider adequately the role he assigns to the aesthetic experience in relation to man's total experiences. The experience of art, because it involves the presence of significant form, gives man the assurance of at least one "absolute good"; and this is sufficient to make of our lives a momentous and harmonious whole. Life has little enough to offer, but in its best moments, in the aesthetic experience, for instance, which is so very different from our ordinary activities that Bell designates it as "above life," life can justify itself and in its own terms: "Rapture suffices. The artist has no more call to look forward than the lover in the arms of his mistress. There are moments in life that are ends to which the whole history of humanity would not be an extravagant means; of such are the moments of aesthetic ecstasy." [25]

Fry's Psychological Views as the Basis of His Aesthetics

The aesthetic theory of Fry has much in common with that of Bell, but it is developed with greater detail and awareness of the difficulties posed by aesthetic formalism. Fry's aesthetics is rooted in certain psychological doctrines, the basic one being the principle of polarity. Man is essentially bipolar, according to Fry: it is the instinctual as against the imaginative.

> We see a wild bull in the field; quite without our conscious interference a nervous process goes on, which, unless we interfere forcibly, ends in the appropriate reaction of flight . . . The whole of animal life, and a great part of human life, is made up of these instinctive reactions to sensible objects, and their accompanying emotions. But man has the peculiar faculty of calling up again in his mind the echo of past experiences of this kind, of going over it again, "in imagination" as we say. He has,

therefore, the possibility of a double life; one the actual life, the other the imaginative life.[26]

Our bipolarity, Fry maintains, manifests itself in a number of ways. Consider vision. Our vision, when we are responding instinctually to our environment, is partial, transient and utilitarian. What we see is determined as much by our practical needs as by our eyes. But when we are responding imaginatively, our vision is lingering and consequently more complete. Not being tied to the life of action, we can now focus upon and attend fully to our perceptual experiences.

Our emotional life, too, is bipolar. On the instinctual level, we are indulgent creatures, participating, strongly and overwhelmingly, in our emotional experiences. Fry takes this to mean that we are therefore unable to comprehend our experiences, being too much involved in them. Experienced imaginatively, however, our emotions become more meaningful in the sense that we understand their characteristics better. The jealous lover, for example, can hardly survey the complete character of his experience, especially in those moments of its greatest ascendancy; but let him relinquish the force of his experience, look upon his jealousy, survey it in a detached and spectatorial way, and although his experience will of course be weaker, he will, compensatorily, comprehend the meaning of jealousy better than he did while in its throes.

Our evaluations differ, too. Instinctually, we are practical moralists toward our environment. That is to say, we must make choices, and they must be responsible ones. But when we swing to the imaginative pole, we abandon this sense of responsibility and as a result attain a complete tolerance toward our total environment. We now evaluate it in an amoral way, accepting everything for the sake of contemplative experiences.

Finally, our purposes are bipolar. The goal of instinctual experience is adjustment or survival; whereas the purpose or function of our imaginative life is the enrichment of our experience.

Fry's Theory of Art Creation

Fry, like Bell, distinguishes between pure and impure aesthetic experience. The pure is a function of the imaginative pole in man; the impure, a product of his instinctual side. All artistic creation, art objects, and art appreciation can be classified in one of these two ways. Fry has expressed clearly the difference between the imaginative and the instinctual, so far as the artist is concerned, in his rejection of the Freudian theory of artistic creation:

> I believe that two distinct aims and activities have got classed together under the word art, and that the word artist is used of two distinct groups of men. One of these groups into which I would divide artists is mainly preoccupied with creating a fantasy-world in which the fulfillment of wishes is realised. The other is concerned with the contemplation of formal relations. I believe this latter activity to be as much detached from the instinctive life as any human activity that we know; to be in that respect on a par with science. I consider this latter the distinctive esthetic activity.[27]

Fry's views on the nature of pure creation constitute a sustained development. Like his great compatriot, Bertrand Russell, Fry never hesitated to change his ideas to meet the challenge of new facts. In neither of these men's works is there to be found the fitting in of the facts to meet the demands of obsolete theories.

There are in Fry's work, so far as I can make out, three separate theories of pure artistic creation. At first, Fry claimed that artistic creation is the communication of the artist's detached attitude toward *any* aspect of the instinctual life or our surrounding world of nature.[28] Dramatic, associational, representational, and all emotional values he considered to be legitimate vehicles in artistic communication. In fact, the artist may deal with anything: love, hate, tables, battles, coronations. The function of the artist is to interpret these things imaginatively.

It is difficult to understand why Fry rejected this theory which has many contemporary supporters. In his essay, "Retrospect," he states only that Bell's aesthetics and Cézanne's paintings convinced him that pure creation is a more limited endeavor.

In his second period, Fry regarded pure artistic creation to be the communication of man's instinctual biological life in so far as his experiences reduce to certain *plastic* elements, like line, color, rhythm, mass, space, light and shade. These the artist presents as an ordered and varied whole.[29] On this view, artistic communication is limited to the plastic-emotional components of human experience in the world of nature.

Further study of the Post-Impressionist movement in painting led Fry to abandon this second view for an even more severe and limited doctrine. True or pure creation, on this third view, becomes the communication of the artist's vision of the world as a compositional, spatial structure. All of the elements that Fry accepts as legitimate are reduced to the compositional. Color is now rejected in the way that representation was characterized as illegitimate on the second view.[30] Artistic creation is also characterized as a function of vision, of seeing the world as significant form, as a relational, structural, compositional affair.[31]

Fry's Theory of the Art Object

Fry advanced three different theories of the nature of pure art, which correspond to his three theories of pure artistic creation. The earliest of these conceives art as an enhanced representation of *any* aspect of reality, human or "nature." Representation of emotions, life situations, historical or psychological narrative are all legitimate and acceptable. All have their own contribution to make to the total work of art.[32]

Corresponding to the second theory of creation, the pure art object is taken to be an imaginative embodiment of the sensuous and relational — that is, the *plastic* — characteristics of reality.

Color, line, rhythm, volume, space, light and shade, in their unity and variety, are the essential qualities of art. Representation is considered illegitimate; which makes pure art nonrepresentational in character and essentially plastic in conception. The paintings of the Post-Impressionists, especially of Cézanne, are singled out as the creative realization of these aesthetic principles. In their work, Fry submits, we find the conscious repudiation of the representational and, in its place, the emphasis upon the plastic in art. Their work is a constant challenge to the imagination, not to the instinctual and its ordinary emotions.

In his last period, Fry offers the most stringent of conceptions of the nature of the pure art object. It is now interpreted as the embodiment of significant form, i.e., compositional space-structure, rather than combinations of color and line. Pure art becomes almost puritanical in that all color and decorative qualities of line are repudiated.[33]

Throughout these three periods, it is important to see, Fry maintains what he construes to be a formalistic theory of the art object. At first, though, form is interpreted as the detached reorganization of the instinctual life; as the *manner*, the way in which ordinary experiences are treated.[34] Cézanne and Bell offered Fry a more plastic conception of form.

> It became evident through these discussions [of Post-Impressionist aesthetics] that some artists who were peculiarly sensitive to the formal relations of works of art, and who were deeply moved by them, had almost no sense of the emotions which I had supposed them to convey . . . It was, I think, the observation of these cases of reaction to pure form that led Mr. Clive Bell in his book, "Art," to put forward the hypothesis that however much the emotions of life might appear to play a part in the work of art, the artist was really not concerned with them, but only with the expression of a special and unique kind of emotion, the aesthetic emotion. A work of art had the peculiar property of conveying the aesthetic emotion, and it did this in virtue of having "significant form." [35]

In the final period, form becomes mathematical in conception. Fry's analysis of Raphael's "Transfiguration" reveals in a clear way this narrowing conception. The painting is discussed in terms of its form and content. The content is said to comprise the representation of two episodes in the Christian story that occurred simultaneously at different places according to the Gospels, namely, the Transfiguration and the attempt of the Disciples to heal a lunatic boy. As spectators, we may react to this content and its associated ideas of suffering, dependency of man upon God, the diversity of experience, or even the metaphysical theme of Perfection as that which is inclusive of everything. The content is such that only a Christian or student of Christianity could understand it.

The form of the picture Fry designates as the compositional structure; specifically, the coördination and integration of masses, and the equilibrium of the many directions of line. The entire canvas is now *one* plastic whole, no longer two intellectual halves, as it is so far as its content is concerned. It is one spatial structure, with certain added attributed emotional properties that arise from the recognition of the delicacy of line and the power of the masses of the painting. Our reaction now — and this is the true aesthetic response — is to the pure significant form and not to the emotions of suffering, dependency, or the inclusiveness of the universe.[36]

This distinction between form and content, and the insistence upon form as the essence of art, are claimed by Fry for music, too. When we listen to a musical composition, say "God Save the King," to use Fry's example, we are immediately struck by some formal relations of melodic and harmonic design. Hearing it for the first time, we are told, we would derive from the mere recognition of the musical relations an emotion that would be untainted by images and ordinary emotions like that of patriotism which we associate with the words of the song. Fry agrees with Bell that pure music is pure form — that is, significant combinations of sound that move us in an aesthetically unique way.

It was the problem of representation that provided Fry with

the greatest difficulty in his aesthetic reflections throughout his career. In his first period, he held that representation does not necessarily conflict with but can actually make a contribution together with the plastic elements to the work of art.[37] Further study caused him to give up this theory. In "Some Questions in Esthetics" Fry investigates the problem in an extremely penetrating way. His main burden is to refute the general critique leveled against him by I. A. Richards, who had asserted in his *Principles of Literary Criticism* that formal and representational factors may conflict in some paintings; or may be stressed one above the other; but may also coöperate, and if they do, the fact that they do will constitute a refutation of the pet notions of an unique aesthetic emotion and pure art values.[38] One can readily see that there is much at stake here for Fry. If representation can be defended as a contributing factor in painting, as aesthetically legitimate, there is no pure art, no significant form; and if these things are no more, then there is no place for the pure aesthetic emotion, either.

Fry's reply to Richards and his defense of the thesis that representation does not contribute to the aesthetic worth of a painting consist in thorough analyses of four works of art: Brueghel's "Christ Carrying the Cross," Daumier's "Gare St. Lazare," Poussin's "Achilles Discovered by Ulysses Among the Daughters of Lycomedon," and Rembrandt's "Christ before Pilate." In none of these, Fry contends, is there to be found any real coöperation between the representational and the formal elements. The first of these pictures is thoroughly oriented toward the narrative and the literary; and the formal factors of space, light, and mass are all subordinated to the dramatic, psychological values of the historical event being depicted. As painting, Fry finds it trivial and without any emotional power, an example of what he calls "illustration," i.e., painting in which the plastic elements are *used* as accessories to the narration.[39]

The Daumier Fry considers to be better than the Brueghel,

plastically speaking, but still as constituting a basic conflict between the representational and the formal. He takes the whole picture to be more akin to certain nineteenth-century novels, with their emphasis upon the panorama of life, than to true painting. Plastically, the spatial elements are also subordinate to the psychological.[40]

In the Poussin, the formal values have precedence over the psychological and narrative ones. Psychologically, the picture is trivial, almost ludicrous in its artificiality, Fry asserts; but throughout the picture, the gestures or simulated movements of each figure are directed by some formal quality of rhythm or line and volume relation. The aesthetic value of the picture lies in its construction of fugal forms and not in the supposed coördination of the representational and formal elements.[41]

Only in the Rembrandt is there some appearance of coöperation. But upon analysis, this coöperation vanishes, for the analysis reveals the psychological inability of the spectators to integrate the spatial character of the plastic formal elements with the spaceless character of the emotional psychological elements:

> Indeed I cannot see how one is to avoid this. How can we keep the attention equally fixed on the spaceless world of psychological entities and relations and upon the apprehension of spatial relations? What, in fact, happens is that we constantly shift our attention backwards and forwards from one to the other. Does the exaltation which gratification in one domain gives increase our vigilance and receptiveness when we turn to the other, as would be implied by true co-operation? In this case [Rembrandt] I incline to think it does, although I doubt whether this more than compensates for a certain discomfort which the perpetual shifting of focus inevitably involves.[42]

Fry's conclusion, which he derives from this extended empirical investigation, is that pictures in which representations are subordinated to dramatic ends and are not liquidated or dissolved into the plastic elements are not simple works of art but mixtures of the art of narration and painting. They are to the whole art of painting what the song is to music, a hybrid, impure art.[43]

Unlike Bell, who distinguishes between the aesthetics of painting and literature, Fry tries to explain all the arts by means of the principle of significant form. And this is no easy matter, Fry recognizes:

> I cannot deny that the position I am trying to maintain is dangerously exposed. If it is to be held at all it must be held with regard to works of art of all kinds . . . The idea of a special kind of experience . . . may seem plausible enough with regard to our experience of certain peculiarly abstract musical constructions or even of certain kinds of architecture. It becomes far less plausible the moment representation of actual forms comes in, as in painting or sculpture, still less when, as in poetry, the novel or the drama, the very stuff of which these are constructed, namely words, calls up images and memories of things and emotions of actual life.[44]

Fry's theory is a simple one. The essence of literature is not certain single figures (characters) or collections of events (plot), but the *relation of inevitability*.

> It became evident to me that the essential of great tragedy was not the emotional intensity of the events portrayed, but the vivid sense of the inevitability of their unfolding, the significance of the curve of crescendo and diminuendo which their sequence describes, together with all the myriad subsidiary evocations which, at each point, poetic language can bring in to give fullness and density to the whole organic unity.[45]

Fry's Theory of Art Appreciation

Fry's theory of the appreciation of art is on the whole a reiteration of Bell's. Like the latter, he distinguishes between the pure and the impure modes. In the impure (or instinctual), the spectator interprets art as if it constituted ordinary life situations to which one ought to respond practically or morally. Here our reaction is one of simple indulgence in the emotions exhibited in the art object and, in the case of painting, in the content of the work. In pure (imaginative) appreciation, we respond in a detached, contemplative manner to art and our total response is to the form. It is an unique experience, which we may refer to as the aesthetic emotion.

Once again, Fry tangles with Richards: this time specifically on the issue of the uniqueness of the appreciation of art. Richards had written: "When we look at a picture, or read a poem, or listen to music, we are not doing something quite unlike what we were doing on our way to the Gallery or when we dressed in the morning." [46] The experiences are similar except that the objects are different.

Fry replies that the experiences are not similar at all. The basic difference between aesthetic and ordinary experiences resides in the quality or mode of response present in the experiences. Ordinary responses are to objects, sensations, or events, whereas the aesthetic is a response to *relations*, the sum of which constitutes significant form. There is no special aesthetic faculty or unanalyzed aesthetic state of mind in the experience of art appreciation; rather there is a specialized orientation of our consciousness toward objects, which enables us to single out this *kind* of experience as being different from ordinary experiences.[47]

2

THE CRITIQUE OF FORMALISM

Parker's Voluntaristic Critique

In this chapter I should like to consider some of the major criticisms made of Bell and Fry by voluntarists, emotionalists, and intellectualists, like the Marxists and the Thomists. I hope to show eventually that these criticisms are badly directed and rooted in the same fallacious presuppositions as are accepted by the position being attacked. I should like also to expose the essentially specious character of the dispute between contemporary formalists and their critics, especially as that dispute has been articulated by both parties to it.

One of the leading, if not the most vehement, critics of the formalist theory of Bell and Fry is DeWitt Parker. Parker's aesthetics is itself one of the more brilliant contemporary systems, and we shall return to it many times in the course of our inquiry. Our interest in it here will be confined to those aspects of his views that are relevant to his critique of Bell and Fry.

All art, Parker begins, has a threefold character: as imagination, as language, and as design.[1] The conception of art as imagination, Parker points out, arose in opposition to the classical theory of art as imitation, because the latter could not explain much of art, especially the fantastic.[2] In our period, Freud has established certain psychological laws concerning the relation between art and

imagination. Also, he has revealed the kinship between imagination and desire. All of this Parker accepts. As a product of the
imagination, art is akin to the dream.[3] The imagination, itself, is
no independent, autonomous activity, functioning in a mechanical
fashion, but is secondary and derivative, being under the control
of our desires. Desires, for Parker, may be satisfied or realized in
two ways: in what he calls the "real" way, which involves some
interaction with the environment and an appropriation from it;
or in the "imaginative" way, which is completely internal and oper-
ates mainly within the medium of the day dream or the night
dream. The imagination exists, then, to provide satisfaction of
desires.

All works of art contain this imaginative element, this imaginative satisfaction of desires. The internal dream is externalized;
that is, the dream is offered to us in some sensuous form, namely,
the medium, whether it be paint or tones or words. "A work of art
is born only when imaginative vision is wedded to sensuous
shape." [4] It is through this externalization that art becomes a
language. Now, as a language, Parker insists, art must be distinguished from the language of the practical and the scientific. There
is a difference between a cry for help, a treatise on physics, and a
sonnet. The first communicates a need in order to get something
done; the second communicates knowledge primarily for the sake
of understanding and controlling nature; but the third communicates desires in a sensuous-imaginative form in order to invite the
reader to engage in an imaginative experience of his own.

There is no language without syntax, Parker continues. Consequently, the language that we call art must have a syntax. It is
this syntax that Parker designates as the form or design of art.[5]
And he means by form the way in which a work of art is organized, the relating of the various elements. In his famous discussion
of form,[6] he enumerates certain principles of form. The first of
these is the principle of organic unity, by which Parker means that
everything in a work of art must be evaluated in terms of its being

aesthetically relevant, that is, as making or not making a contribution to the whole of the work. Theme and variation are two further principles; in every work of art, that is to say, one or more elements, be they certain lines or colors or melodies, dominate the others; and these elements are so varied as to prevent monotony. Balance among the various elements is another principle. Parker means by this the equalizing of the opposing or contrasting elements. Evolution and hierarchy are the final principles. Evolution has to do with the process of development within the work of art. In what Parker calls "dramatic" art, this development occurs by means of climaxes and denouements; and in "nondramatic" art, i.e., art in which climaxes are not stressed, by mere unfolding of the elements. Hierarchy refers to the fact that in all art not every element is equally important, but that one or a few elements control the others and count for more in our appreciation of the work.

The form of art, like the content, incorporates basic satisfactions of desire, Parker contends. In real life experiences we desire unity, variety, balance, evolution, and hierarchy, but we seldom, if ever, get them. However, in artistic activity, whether as artists or spectators, because we gain control over our projected experiences, we are in a position to satisfy this desire for form, either by creating a work of art or by beholding one. Artistic form, therefore, is rooted in the instinctual life of man. It is not, as it is for Bell and Fry, the imaginative as against the instinctual, the form as against the content, but the instinctual being manifested in *both* real life situations and the imagination.

It is important now to see how Parker applies this general aesthetics to the art of painting. All paintings possess what Parker calls musical values; these belong to the lines and colors as such, with no reference to representation. This is beauty on the level of sensuous surface.[7] Besides this factor of the musical, paintings may possess certain representational values, which are of two sorts: the values of nature, like space, light, motion, texture, and weight; and the values of life and the mind, the spiritual values. These include the religious, philosophical, social, psychological, dramatic, historical, and literary themes of human experience.

For example, all that Pater or Muther found in the face of the Mona Lisa was what I am calling a spiritual meaning, to be distinguished from the plasticity of the face or the distance in the background; or in Rembrandt's Old Woman Cutting Her Nails, the profound revelation of the inner life there is again a spiritual value, to be distinguished from the light and modeling.[8]

The greatest art is the successful integration of both kinds of representation: "That artist is the greater who can express and communicate the larger world of values; hence a painter who is able to express, without neglect of plastic values [i.e., the representational values of nature], poetic and psychographic values as well, is a greater painter than one who expresses plastic values alone." [9]

Parker's third factor in painting is the formal; that is, the unity, variety, balance, evolution, and hierarchy of art. Parker considers this to be the *sine qua non* of painting.

Among the four sources of value distinguished, there is a hierarchy. Most indispensable is the last, design. Unless a picture have design, no amount of significance in the parts can make it beautiful . . . Next in importance to design are the musical values of color and line, without either one of which, again, there can be no picture. But . . . painting must contain something more, namely . . . some at least of the plastic values, and, above all, the spatial ones . . . Then, finally, the work of art may, although it need not, possess spiritual values . . . Thus one can begin with the musical values and build up to the spiritual, but not vice versa. The most sublime of religious ideas will never make a picture, neither will the most convincing of dreams. The supreme works of art . . . contain all the four types of values.[10]

We are now ready to submit for evaluation Parker's critique

of the formalism of Bell and Fry. Most of it is summarized in two paragraphs:

> Arguing from the universality of design some students of art, called formalists, have claimed that design was the essence of art, the very thing we call beauty.
>
> Yet despite the importance of design in art, the claim of the formalist is unjustified. For the underlying impulse to art is the demand for satisfaction of wishes in the imagination; design is a necessary, not a sufficient, condition of beauty, as many a faultless but cold and meaningless work attests. Moreover, design is no independent thing, imposed as from the outside upon imaginative expression, but a perfectly natural and inevitable development of expression, when it is an end in itself.[11]

Parker's main criticism against the formalism of Bell and Fry, then, is that it has singled out one element, the form, as the essence of art, to the total neglect of the imaginative and linguistic elements, the content.

To this criticism we may reply that, in the first place, Bell and Fry (except in his last period) do recognize the aesthetic legitimacy of the linguistic dimension of art. That is to say, they emphasize, as much as Parker, the importance of the musical values of line and color. Parker's criticism may apply to some formalists like Herbart, who took as the essence of beauty the *relations* that exist among elements, but it is incorrect when employed against Bell and Fry.

Secondly, so far as the imaginative element is concerned, that is, the representational, both Bell and Fry do accept as legitimate constituents of pure art the plastic values of space, light, motion, texture, and weight. To these, of course, they add line, color, volume, and composition. Furthermore, like Parker, they insist upon the importance of *certain* of the spiritual values of art, namely, those having to do with the emotional properties of the plastic elements. An excellent example of their recognition of the legitimacy of the spiritual values is Fry's deliverances on the importance of the qualities of power and delicacy as they inhere in the lines and masses of Raphael's "Transfiguration." [12]

What Bell and Fry repudiate is the aesthetic relevance of the nonplastic spiritual values, those that are associated with the religious, philosophical, psychological, and social elements of the painting. And this rejection, I think, brings us to the heart of the real issue between Parker and Bell and Fry: Ought art to contain these nonplastic spiritual values? Bell and Fry, for reasons which we have already set forth, assert that art ought only to exhibit our vision of reality as significant form; that pure art ought to embody only the plastic-emotional character of reality; and that art ought to satisfy only one desire, the desire to see and communicate significant form. Parker, on the other hand, insists that art ought to contain *any* vision, *any* imaginative desire. Thus, the real issue between them has to do with the *range of communication* that art should possess. Ought art to embody any experience; or should it limit itself to one, our experience of reality as significant form?

Thirdly, Parker's conception of form is quite different from that of Bell and Fry. Parker's "form" is abstract and has to do with certain properties that belong to the organization of elements within the work of art.[13] Also, his form excludes line and color. Bell's and Fry's conception of form is concrete and includes as part of its meaning line, color, combinations among them and, in Fry particularly, light, space, and other plastic elements.

Parker's second criticism is that the formalists do not realize that many works of art have form but are essentially cold and meaningless. I take it that he means by this criticism that there are many works, for example, a good number of David's, which have unity, balance, variety, evolution, and hierarchy, but are lacking in qualities that make for great art.

This criticism presupposes a distinction between form and feelings, which, of course, Bell and Fry would not accept. For them, form that is cold and meaningless is a self-contradiction, since the very meaning of form is certain plastic combinations whose qualities (like delicacy or power) evoke from the spectators an intense emotional response, namely, the aesthetic emotion. Here, too, Parker's criticism is misdirected, resting upon a conception of form that is so very different from that of Bell and Fry.

Parker's second criticism leads to his third and the final one that we need consider at this stage of our inquiry. Art communicates and evokes emotions, and the formalists deny this. But, again, we must reply that this is a completely unwarranted criticism, since both Bell and Fry affirm as strongly as Parker that art communicates emotion, and that this communication evokes a similar emotion in the spectator. What Bell and Fry do deny is that art ought to communicate and evoke *any* emotion. Therefore, this issue resolves into the first: Ought art to be concerned with all emotions or only the emotion that is engendered by our apprehension of significant form?

To sum up, then. The real issue between Parker and the formalists, Bell and Fry, has to do with the range of expression in the arts. Ought an aesthetic theory to prescribe the limits of artistic communication? May art express anything?

Ducasse's Emotionalistic Critique

Parker's last criticism brings us to the conflict between emotionalism and formalism in contemporary aesthetic theory. The criticism that formalism arbitrarily limits the range of artistic expression is continued by one of the foremost contemporary representatives of the emotionalist theory, C. J. Ducasse. Ducasse's main contention about art is that it is a language. Like I. A. Richards and the positivists, Ducasse distinguishes between two basic kinds of linguistic functioning, the language of emotions and the language of factual assertions. He places art completely in the category of emotional language.[14]

Like Bell, Fry, and Parker, Ducasse accepts the distinction between the form and the content of a work of art. "In any aesthetic object it is possible to distinguish two fundamental aspects: *Form*, and *Content* (or Material). By form is meant simply *arrangement* or order; and by content or matter, whatever it happens to be that is arranged, ordered." [15] Content, for Ducasse, comprises certain dramatic, and form, the abstract, elements of a work of art. Dramatic elements are representations of people or events, and abstract elements are lines, colors, tones, and the like, with their temporal, spatial, or causal relations.[16] Both content and form have their distinct emotional character; lines and colors as such, for example, communicate emotions as surely as do representations.

We are now ready for Ducasse's objection to formalism:

> The dogma that would exalt design as alone of importance not only requires of design something it cannot really do but also acts to deprive painting, arbitrarily, of resources it does have and for which there is no substitute — namely, the resources that representation of dramatic entities provides. For . . . what can be expressed in this way cannot be expressed in any other way; and surely to apply such epithets as "illustration" or "narrative" or "literary" to paintings that avail themselves of these particular resources is not to give a reason why what they do thereby express should not be expressed. If these epithets are meant to imply that what is here done with paint could have been done better, or indeed done at all, with words, then they imply something patently false. No better example of this could be cited than Walter Pater's famous words on the "Mona Lisa." They are indeed themselves a noble example of literary art, but obviously in no way are they a substitute for the painting itself. *No art can express exactly what another art does. Not even two works of the same art can express exactly the same thing.* In the language of thought, the words of which owe their import to convention, there is such a thing as two differently worded statements that mean exactly the same thing; but in the language of feeling, which art is, there are no synonymous expressions.[17]

Ducasse's criticism, brilliant as it is, raises another fundamental issue between formalism and its opponents which has nothing particularly to do with the conflict between emotionalism and formalism. The issue, again, is what ought each of the arts to do?

The formalist or "purist," for that is what he is on this issue, like Bell and Fry, believes that the arts ought to do what they can do best and what distinguishes them from each other. The reason he rejects narrative representation, for example, in painting, is not that painting cannot as a matter of fact depict events but that he is convinced that the discipline of narration belongs intrinsically to literature, since literature can serve narration best; and, further, that painting which offers more than a rendition of significant form constitutes a violation of the *medium* of the art of painting.

Ducasse's counterclaim is that painting ought to do narration and, in fact, any kind of representation because it is not alien to the medium of painting, but belongs to it as much as line and color. Painting can and ought to represent because the *kind* of representation that it can offer cannot be done better — in fact, *it cannot be done at all* — in literature. Thus if, in their quarrel with formalism, Parker has raised the issue of the extent of communication in the arts, Ducasse has specified it by asking what are the limits of communication in each of the separate arts.

Véron's, the Neo-Thomist, and the Marxist Critiques

There is another emotionalist, Eugene Véron, who, although he preceded Bell, Fry, and Ducasse, offered a valiant objection to formalism that we should consider in our present discussion. Véron, like Ducasse, regards the essence of art as the embodiment of emotions that the artist experienced and placed in his art creation.[18] But more important than this definition is his distinction between two kinds of art, the decorative and the expressive. Decorative art is that in which form is emphasized, that is to say, in which qualities like harmony, grace, and the sensuous are stressed. Expressive art is that which embodies *profound emotions* and *great subjects*. It is, therefore, primarily intellectual and moral art. Like Parker, Véron insists upon the formal, decorative base of such art. Without the beauty of the sensuous, the expressive falls flat. But without the richness of the expressive, the decorative remains thin. The greatest works of art are combinations of the two.[19]

Véron's implied criticism of formalism, which, once more, has little to do with emotionalist aesthetic doctrines, is that formalism ignores the importance of "elevated" themes, important subjects, the whole realm of the *ideational* in art. Formalism necessarily reduces art to sensuous surface and decoration, thereby incapacitating itself to explain much that is important in artistic communication.[20]

In contemporary thought, there are two extremely powerful philosophical movements, the Neo-Thomist and the Marxist, which have, in their aesthetic reflections, reiterated the sort of criticism of formalism that Véron offered.

In the aesthetics of the leading exponent of Neo-Thomism, Jacques Maritain, there is this same insistence upon the importance of the ideational in art. There is also drawn the same distinction between the form and the content in the work of art, which we have seen to characterize all the aesthetic theories that we have discussed thus far.

For Maritain, every art object is the sensuous embodiment of a universal or a group of them. This is taken to be the fundamental content of art, and it is asserted that no adequate aesthetic theory can overlook its importance. This content is rendered within some medium where it is treated with some degree of clarity, integrity, and harmony. These latter are regarded as the formal characteristics of art.[21] Both content and form have an ontological significance but we need not be concerned with that here where our interest is in the Neo-Thomist critique of formalism.

On Maritain's theory, formalism is that doctrine which excludes from aesthetic consideration the ideational content, the presentation of universals, of the work of art, and concerns itself only with the clarity, integrity, and harmony of the work. In other words, formalism is rejected as being only half an aesthetic theory.

This criticism is not quite correct. Bell and Fry, at any rate, do recognize the aesthetic legitimacy of *some* universals in art, namely, those relating to significant form or what we may refer to as plastic structure. Space, light, color, line, mass, etc., are universals, and Bell and Fry, as formalists, certainly insist as strongly as any aesthetician upon the artistic importance of them. What Bell and Fry deny is that art, i.e., painting, ought to embody *any* universal. And, of course, this renders the conflict between the intellectualism of Neo-Thomist aesthetics and the formalism of Bell and Fry identical with that of Parker and the formalists: What is the aesthetically legitimate range of artistic expression?

The most severe critics of the formalists in our period, I think, are the Marxists, for they have tied up the theory with the art-for-art's-sake movement and the political decadence implied in that movement. In general, Marxist aesthetics concentrates upon the socio-economic origins and effects of art. When it deals with actual specific works of art, its main concern is with the political and social values contained in them. And since it is in literature that these values are most discernible, Marxist aesthetics has focused upon that art.

The Marxist theory of art is part of its general theory of culture. Every society, it is maintained, is rooted in certain economic institutions that have to do with the prevailing modes of production. These institutions are said to constitute the structure of that society.

Every society has also its customs, social beliefs, religion, philosophy, and art. These constitute its culture, which the Marxists call the superstructure of the society. The basic ideas of each society, as they are reflections of prevailing modes of production, the Marxists refer to as the ideology of that society. The fundamental thing about every ideology is that it is an articulation of the class struggle occurring in the prevailing society. In our own period, of course, the dominant ideology has been, perhaps still is, the bourgeois, in which all the values embodied in religion, social thought, philosophy, and the arts are the expressions of our capitalistic economy.

However, in each society, because of the dialectical character of the class struggle, there arises a counterideology which represents the interests of the class that is aiming to come into power. And in our period, that new ideology, with its new philosophy, social thought, and aesthetics, is that of the proletariat. Every thinker, nay, every human being, like it or not, it is contended, must choose between these two mutually exclusive ideologies. This holds for aesthetics as well.[22]

In aesthetics, the Marxists also accept the distinction between the form and the content of the work of art. The content is all the ideological values of the work, and the form is the *way* in which these values are expressed, the "style" of the work. Both the content and the form, it is affirmed, are conditioned by economic structures and, consequently, both are manifestations of the prevailing class struggle.

We may now present the Marxist criticism of formalism. Its fundamental objection is simply that aestheticians like Bell and Fry find no place for content — ideological values — in art. No work of art, the Marxists say, can be understood or evaluated without a complete analysis of the social and political ideas contained either openly or unwittingly in it. Like Véron and Maritain, the Marxists regard *what* is said in art as at least as important as (in the case of the Marxists, perhaps much more important than) *how* it is said. And any theory which does not recognize the importance of what is said or which concentrates only upon the how of a work of art, the way the formalists (supposedly) do, is inadequate; and furthermore, it reflects a completely decadent ideology, a desire to escape from the social and political struggles of our time.[23]

Summary, and Further Criticisms of Bell and Fry

In contemporary aesthetic theory there is much talk about formalism, on the one hand, and emotionalism, voluntarism, Marxism, Neo-Thomism, on the other. In these last two chapters we have attempted to elucidate this conflict; and, if our exposition has been adequate, we have seen that there are real issues involved here but that they have little to do with the omnibus labels, formalism, emotionalism, intellectualism, etc.

Instead, we have seen that the conflict between formalism and its critics resolves into certain issues that have to do with problems like the nature of representation; form and content, and the respective importance of each; the medium; and the aesthetic legitimacy of emotions, desires and ideas in art. All of these problems and issues converge on the central questions of the nature of art and its capacities as a mode of communication.

There are important problems in contemporary aesthetics and most of these are involved in the conflict between formalism and its critics; but they can be dealt with best, I think, if we specify them and unravel them one at a time. Is the form more important than the content, or vice versa? Are they coequal? Or is the distinction itself illegitimate? Is representation a contributing factor to painting? Or, perhaps, is the whole of art representational? Are ideas and emotions, of any kind, legitimate constituents of any art? Is formalism, itself, as an omnibus aesthetics, committed to an arbitrary limitation of artistic expression? These are among the specific problems that we must discuss if we are to develop an adequate philosophy of art.

Before we begin our aesthetic reconstructions, there are a few more criticisms that should be made of the views of Bell and Fry, as these views concern the nature of the art object. In the first place, a reading of their histories of various painters and schools of painting discloses a curious inconsistency between their critical practice and their aesthetic theory. In the various writings of Bell one can find many favorable observations on the nonplastic qualities of art. In *Since Cézanne*, for example, he refers quite approvingly to the ideational paganism of Bonnard, to his wit, whimsy, and fantasy. "Like Renoir, he loves life as he finds it. He, too, enjoys intensely those good, familiar things that perhaps only artists can enjoy to the full — sunshine and flowers, white tables spread beneath trees, fruits, crockery, leafage, the movements of young animals, the grace of girls and the amplitude of fat women. Also, he loves intimacy. He is profoundly French. He reminds one sometimes of Rameau and sometimes of Ravel, sometimes of Lafontaine and sometimes of Laforgue." [24] So, too, with Fry. In all of his critical works, he discusses art partly in thematic, representational terms, with no evidence of the repudiation of their aesthetic validity. Now, of course, this does not mean that Bell's and Fry's aesthetic theory is incorrect, only that they do not practice it.

A more serious criticism, I think, has to do with the entire inadequacy of their conception of significant form; for they leave it much too unanalyzed to be considered seriously as the essence of art.[25] Bell construes it as the aesthetically moving combination of line and color; Fry, as relational spatial structure. But this reveals so little about the essence of art. Significant form becomes a kind of mystical quality, to be apprehended only by intuition, and really quite an ineffable quality at that, in spite of Bell's plea as to its objectivity. For the objectivity, in the end, reduces to a subjective thing, since significant form can be discerned only by someone in a state of rapture. Such a standard cannot allow for any real dispute over the presence or lack of significant form, since there is nothing to dispute about. One either has the state or one has not. Consequently, their theory leads ultimately to an aesthetics of irrationality in which no practical critical discussion of the aesthetic merit of a particular work of art is possible. Their theory, I think it is fair to say, offers no adequate criteria for criticism. Certainly it will not do to say that nonrepresentation is the criterion in terms of which we ought to judge whether a work of art is good or has significant form, since not all nonrepresentational art is good, even on their theory. Also, their theory does not explain in any satisfactory way just *which* particular combinations of line and color are significant and deserving of our critical praise. Finally, even in plastic terms, painting is more than combinations of line and color or spatial composition. As Fry himself recognized in "An Essay in Aesthetics," plastic form also includes light, space, shade, rhythm, and mass. And one might add: texture, drawing, movement, and volume-tension.[26]

One may conclude, quite rightly, I think, from our first objection to Bell and Fry that any theory which proclaims that art is essentially significant form must offer a richer analysis of significant form than theirs; and that one test of the adequacy of any aesthetic theory is the criteria it offers in the aid of practical criticism of the various arts. In fact, ultimately, this is probably the best way to judge any aesthetic theory: if it works itself out in concrete criticisms of specific works of art.

Finally, one may object to the theory of Bell and Fry on the grounds that it does not explain *all* of the arts. Even if we grant that it applies to painting and music, it has very little to say about the novel, poetry, architecture, the dance, and the motion picture.

3

RESOLUTION: THE ORGANIC THEORY

Analysis of the Form–Content Distinction

In this chapter I should like to propose an empirical theory of art that will resolve the basic issues between formalism and its critics. A number of analyses are required. Let us begin with the analysis of a distinction that, I think, is responsible for more of the difficulties in contemporary aesthetic thought than any other — the form–content distinction.

Now, in order to understand the significance of this distinction in aesthetic (and critical) theory, it may be well to consider the various ways in which the distinction appears in ordinary, common-sense language and in technical logical analysis.

Common sense, to begin with, regards form as a synonym of shape, and content as synonymous with matter in much of its talk. We say, for example, that two pennies, one copper, the other lead, have the same form, meaning shape, and different content, meaning matter. Or we say of two pieces of silver jewelry, where one is round and the other square, that they differ in form but not in content. Or, if we are in the presence of two round tables, one of which is made of oak, the other of mahogany, we may remark that whereas they have the same shape, meaning form, they differ in their matter, meaning content.

But this is not the only way in which common sense distinguishes between form and content. It also employs form as a synonym of appearance, as when it says of a dilapidated house, for example, that its outward form or appearance is ugly.

Further, the distinction manifests itself in ordinary speech in the distinction between the "what" as against the "how" of certain complexes or states of affairs. Consider the presence of four children's playing blocks, called A, B, C, and D. These blocks may be arranged in many different ways, as BACD or ACDB, and so on. In this situation, we could say that the blocks, the "what" of the complex, are the content, and the serial order arrangement, the "how" of the complex, is the form.

The "what–how" usage, however, usually occurs in the distinction between certain elements and the organization of them. Consider the statement of the four freedoms of the Atlantic Charter. The four sentences of the total statement, complete with their meanings, we call the content, the elements, of the total statement. We further recognize that these elements, these individual sentences, the content, can be arranged or organized in different ways. That is, in one case we may write the sentence about freedom of religion above the sentence about freedom from fear; or we may reverse that order and get a new organization of elements. In these two cases the organization of, the relations between, the elements differ; but the elements — the individual sentences — remain the same. The form changes while the content is constant.

Serial order, however, is not always present in the "how–what" variety of the form–content distinction. Consider the message, "Come home!" We may write it, wire it, telephone it, yell it, or gesture it. Here the content remains the same throughout the different modes of expressing it. The form usage in this example is not rooted in "how" as serial order but "how" as the *way* in which something is said, the mode of expression, the medium.

Common sense also means by form in some of its linguistic usages class, kind, or species; and in this context it means by content the members of the class. We say, for example, that England

and America have the same kind or form of government; or that the dance and music as art forms are similar; or that the movies are a form of escape; or that Russia is a form of totalitarianism. Now, in all of these cases, England, America, the dance, music, the movies, and Russia are members of certain classes, the content of certain forms.

The final way that we shall consider in which common sense uses the form–content distinction is in its distinction between abstract pattern and the completion of the pattern. All magazines have in their pages at various times what they call "subscription forms." These are patterns, partly blank, partly filled in. In its original state, each of these has form but no content. It is a variable; we say in logic, a propositional function. When we fill it in, i.e., give values to its variables, we give a content to it; and we may then say it has both a form and a content.

Contemporary logical theory has itself contributed much toward the understanding of the form–content distinction, even as it obtains in aesthetic and critical usage. Bertrand Russell has dealt extensively with the concept of logical form and has elucidated its fundamental meaning. The best way to define form, he declares, is in terms of propositions.

> In every proposition . . . there is, besides the particular subject matter concerned, a certain *form*, a way in which the constituents of the proposition . . . are put together. If I say, "Socrates is mortal," "Jones is angry," "The sun is hot," there is something in common in these three cases, something indicated by the word "is." What is in common is the *form* of the proposition, not an actual constituent.[1]

From any of these propositions we can derive the others, by a process of substitution; and that which remains unchanged when we replace constituents and get different propositions is the form of these propositions. Form is thus the variable invariant of a number of specific propositions. And the content may be designated as the specific values of any of these propositions. The form of the above propositions is subject–predicate, which mathematical logic symbolizes by Px, where P stands for the predicate and x for the subject. From the variable function Px we can derive, by substituting subject values like "Socrates" or "Jones" or "the sun" and predicate values like "hot" or "angry" or "mortal," the propositions, "Socrates is mortal," "Jones is angry" and "The sun is hot."

Besides the variable function Px there are *relational* variable functions; e.g., aRb or $aRbc$, which are the forms of numerous dyadically and triadically relational propositions like "Socrates loves Plato" or "Mary hates John" and "John gives Joan a book." Mathematical logicians have enumerated others of these logical forms which can be abstracted from our language and actual states of affairs; these include molecular, existential, general, and completely general forms. However, detailed considerations of these belong to more technical discussions in mathematical logic and are not relevant to this aesthetic context.

We may now consider the form–content distinction in contemporary aesthetic theory. In the first place, the common-sense usage of form as shape appears in concrete discussions of the arts. Many aestheticians and artists use shape as a synonym of form. Henry Moore and Alexander Calder, for example, talk about certain natural and human forms.[2]

It is difficult to understand the meaning of content in this linguistic context. Presumably, it has both a narrow and an extended meaning. Narrowly, it refers to *what* is shaped, be it the representation of a man, a horse, or a tree. But in its more extended reference, it denotes the entire work, in which case the forms comprise only part of the total content. Consequently, on this first extended adaptation of the form–content distinction, content and form are not taken as coördinate values of the work of art, but as its genus and species.

Aestheticians (including artists and critics) also mean by form and content the "how" as against the "what" of a work of art.

And, so far as I can determine, this usage has at least three distinct variations.

(1) The what of a work of art is its theme, "what it is about," the subject, the "Idea"; and the how is the way in which the Idea or theme is expressed. Artist-critics like A. E. Housman and aestheticians like C. J. Ducasse sometimes talk this way.[3]

In this linguistic context, the content is but one element in the work of art, *the most abstract*; and the form becomes everything else: the lines, colors, even the specific representations of people and events! For example, consider two famous "Crucifixions," one by El Greco, the other by Grünewald. One could say, and quite in keeping with aesthetic usage, that the content of both pictures is similar, namely, the crucifixion, which is the theme of both paintings, "what they are about"; and that the form, which is the manner in which the crucifixion is exhibited, is very different because of the colors, the design, *and* the representations near Christ — in the El Greco, the Virgin weeping on the right of Jesus, with no one on His left; and in the Grünewald, the Virgin again on the right of Jesus, but with John the Baptist on His left, pointing his finger at Him.

The form here includes not only the specific individuals represented, but also all the emotions associated with them. Furthermore, on this view, the content may be said to be repeatable from picture to picture, so that all the "Crucifixions" that there are could be said to have the same content. Also, in this context, aesthetic formalism is the doctrine that it is *how* something is said, not *what* is said, that is all-important.[4]

(2) The what, or content, of a work of art is its terms or elements, which may include dramatic entities like people as well as colors, lines, or shapes, tones, etc., in the case of the arts other than painting; and the how, or form, is all the relations — spatial, temporal, or causal — among the elements.

This usage, I suppose, is the most generally accepted one in contemporary aesthetic analysis and corresponds pretty much to the way in which form and content are mostly used in ordinary linguistic contexts. Content is the terms; form, the organization of them.

In present aesthetic theory Ducasse, although he is diversified and even ambiguous in his usage, is the champion of this interpretation of the distinction. "By form is meant simply *arrangement* or order; and by content . . . whatever it happens to be that is arranged, ordered." [5]

Formalism, in this usage, is the view that in art only the relations are important, not the terms related. Such a theory was held by Herbart and Zimmermann.

(3) The what, or content, is the Idea or theme; and the how, or form, is the medium in which it is presented. Hanslick offers us an excellent example of this usage. He is arguing that in music there is no distinction between form and content which, he continues,

> presents a sharp contrast to poetry, painting, and sculpture, inasmuch as these arts are capable of representing the same idea and the same event in different forms. The story of William Tell supplied to Florian the subject for a historical novel, to Schiller the subject for a play, while Goethe began to treat it as an epic poem. The substance [content] is everywhere the same . . . and yet the form differs in each case.[6]

A third way in which discussions of the arts employ the distinction between form and content is similar to species (2) of the second, except that it is more specific and normative. The content of the work of art is regarded as the elements and the form as a certain kind of *successful* arrangement, i.e., as an arrangement of elements in which certain principles of balance, proportion, and harmony are realized. This usage is as old as Pythagoras; and both Plato and Aristotle sometimes construed artistic form in this way. In present aesthetics, Parker has also advanced such a doctrine.

Formalism, in this tradition, is the view that in art it is harmony, balance, and proportion that are all-important.

The final way that we shall consider in which the distinction between form and content occurs in contemporary theory leads us away from the common-sense usages to the logical one that we discussed above. Aestheticians speak of the sonata form or the sonnet form or fugal forms. What they mean by these terms are certain generic invariants of structure that can be abstracted from many different works of art in the same way in which mathematical logicians abstract invariant patterns from different propositions and facts by substituting variables for values. The musical aesthetician speaks of the classical ABA sonata form, and he means by it what Russell means by the classical subject–predicate form: a pattern that is shared by many different things in the world. The ABA sonata form is that abstract "musical propositional function" which becomes a "musical statement," so to speak, when the three variables, A, B, A, are filled in with the concrete values: exposition, development, recapitulation. When we say, therefore, that Haydn and Mozart, for example, compose in the sonata form, we mean at least that their symphonies have first movements which are alike in that they all have an exposition section, followed by a development section, in which the themes are expanded, inverted, contracted, etc., and a concluding recapitulation section in which the exposition returns to the tonic.

What is true of the meaning of sonata form obtains in the usage of sonnet form as well. Here, too, we are dealing with an abstract pattern, or series of patterns, if we distinguish between the Italian, Shakespearian, and Spenserian sonnet forms, that is, with the variable invariants of a number of different poems.

In this usage, we may say that many works of art have the same form but differ in their content; which usage is the exact opposite of that in which the content of a work of art is said to be the Idea and the form the way in which the Idea is expressed.

In the light of this discussion of the form–content distinction,

let us return to the interpretation of the distinction offered by
Bell and Fry. Bell construes artistic form as an aesthetically moving
combination of lines and colors. This is a simple enough definition;
and yet the more one examines it, the less it seems to be in accord
with any of the above usages. His conception of form is not that
of shape, mode of expression, relations, organization, or medium.
Rather, Bell means by the form of a work of art *certain elements
in certain relations*; that is, lines and colors in combinations that
excite us. Form does not include certain other elements in relation, namely, the so-called representational ones. These Bell calls
the content of the art object.

There is at least one linguistic difficulty with this conception
of the distinction between form and content. Consider once more
Cézanne's "Italian Girl." When all the representations of objects
and the girl are resolved into line and color combinations, the
picture, strictly speaking, no longer has a content, but only a
form. Now, it seems rather odd, linguistically speaking, to say that
this painting and, in fact, all great painting has form but no content. This is, I think, only one of the difficulties aestheticians get
into by using the form–content distinction altogether.[7]

In spite of this linguistic oddity, Bell's conception of form is
rather good in that he understands by it elements in relation
instead of relations versus elements. This usage at least emphasizes
the organic character of a work of art, which the mathematical
usage of relations versus elements does not.

In Bell's aesthetics, each art object has a "whatness" and a
"howness," but both of these include elements in relation, i.e.,
an *organic complex* of elements and relations. The what, or the
content, of a work of art is all the dramatically representative
elements in certain causal relations; and the how, or the form, all
the lines and colors in spatial relations. Bell's formalism, then, is
the doctrine that in painting it is the plastic elements in relations
that are all-important, and the nonplastic elements in relations
that are totally irrelevant.

Fry also distinguishes between, and even, in his third period, separates, form and content. Content includes those elements in the work of art that represent people or events and the associations attached to them, as all of these relate to each other. In Raphael's "Transfiguration," for example, Fry designates as the content all the Christian narrative elements in their causal relations to each other, the main one being that of mutual dependency.

Form (in the second period) is all the plastic elements — line, color, light, volume, etc. — as they relate spatially to compose a unity in variety; or (in the third period) it is mere spatial relations as against *any* of the elements. Thus, in his second period, Fry is a formalist in Bell's sense: It is certain elements in certain relations that count for everything in art. In his third period, he returns to the traditional mathematical formalism of Herbart: It is the arrangement, the relations, the how, not the elements, the what, that is all-important in art.

The great importance of both Bell and Fry (at least in his second period) lies in the fact that they offered a new conception of the distinction between form and content, one which comprehended the art object in more organic terms. In rejecting the mathematical approach to art — specifically, in repudiating the form–content distinction in terms of relations versus elements — and in suggesting that the form of a work of art comprises certain elements in relation, as the content includes certain other elements in relation, they brought us closer to an empirical conception of art.

Resolution of the Distinction

One of the overwhelming characteristics of contemporary aesthetic theory — and, I daresay, of past aesthetic theory as well — is its insistence upon the form–content distinction. It is, I suppose, one of the basic categories of aesthetic thought, analogous in its fundamental character to the substance–attribute distinction in metaphysical and logical thought. In our previous section we offered a rather extended sampling of the ways in which the form–content distinction has been construed in aesthetic theory. All of these usages have their historical, linguistic roots; hence they cannot be rejected in any cavalier fashion. But what we can do — and this has its parallel in contemporary metaphysics and logic in their repudiation of the substance–attribute, subject–predicate philosophy — is to recommend the rejection of all of these usages on the grounds that none of them does full justice to the nature of the art object; and, furthermore, that they lead to misdirected or specious aesthetic disputes.

I propose now to offer a new usage of form and content which is rooted in a more empirical consideration of the actual nature of works of art. This total analysis is based, in part, upon the writings of Bell, Fry, Parker, A. C. Bradley and Dewey in aesthetics and, more importantly, upon the articulated or suggested doctrines of practicing critics and artists like Cleanth Brooks, Albert Barnes, Martha Graham, Frank L. Wright, Elizabeth Selden, Henry Moore, Hanslick, Picasso and Matisse, to mention only a very few.

The hypothesis in terms of which the form–content distinction will be considered has to do with the definition of art. Every work of art, the hypothesis states, is an organic complex, presented in a sensuous medium, which complex is composed of elements, their expressive characteristics and the relations obtaining among them. I hold that this is a *real* definition of art: i.e., an enumeration of the basic properties of art.[8]

In many works of art, namely, those traditionally called representational, those which include what Ducasse refers to as "dramatic entities" or Parker "spiritual values," we must single out one element and give it a name: the "subject."

The subject is that element in a work of art that stands for, denotes, represents, means, a specific person, thing, scene, or event which exists *outside* of the work, and which is what we say the work is about. Semantically, the subject functions as a sign of specific entities — i.e., persons, events, etc.

That which the work of art is about, let us call the "referent" or "object" of the work.

Some examples will make clear our terminology. Consider, to begin with, Cézanne's "Mont Sainte-Victoire." The subject is the lines and colors that constitute certain volumes within the art object which stand for, denote, represent, mean, the actual mountain. Semantically, the subject is an iconic sign of its object, for it is like that which it means. It is to the mountain what a photograph is to the person it represents.

The object in this case is real, but it need not be. The object may be imaginary, as it probably is in Rousseau's "The Sleeping Gypsy." In cases of this sort, the object is an idea in the artist's or spectator's mind, which is being represented by the subject.

There is an intimate connection between objects and titles of works of art. In most paintings, at any rate, the title refers to the object of the work, "what it is about."

Consider, next, Milton's *Paradise Lost*. Its object or referent is the Fall of Man as it exists in the minds of the readers of the Bible or as it existed in the past, if it actually did. The subject of *Paradise Lost* is those elements in it that specify the characters and events involved in the Fall. These include God, Satan, the angels, the revolt of the angels, and so on.

It is worth noting that the subject of *Paradise Lost* is unique in the sense that Milton's God, Satan, etc., are like no one else's; whereas the object of the work may be the referent of many other works of art. Semantically, the subject, in its dimension as words, functions as symbols, i.e., as signs that have become fixed to connotations through established usage. It is only when the words conjure up images that the subject assumes an iconic significance to its readers.

In music the problem is more complex. The object or referent of the *Eroica*, for example, it is claimed, is heroism. The subject, then, is all of those sounds in the symphony that stand for heroism. However, some aestheticians have argued that music cannot have a referent, in which case, it can have no subject. They conclude from this that music (with the exception of onomatopoetic elements) has no meaning or cannot represent anything. But, as we shall see in Chapter 6, this is not a correct conclusion since elements other than subjects can mean and represent in art, including music.

Finally, the recent Koestler novel, *Arrival and Departure*, is about the problem of modern salvation, which problem exists quite independently of any work of art. The problem is specified as the conflict between the life of social action and the life of egocentric preoccupation with guilt. In the novel the subject is the hero, Peter, whose inner and outer struggles signify, in semantical terms, the externally existing conflict in modern society.

All of these works of art are similar in that their referents can provide material for many other art objects. As we would say, there are many works of art on the same Idea or theme; they refer to the same thing; they are *about* the same thing. And, as A. C. Bradley pointed out, but with a different terminology, the Idea is primarily outside of the work of art.[9] He is incorrect, however, in supposing that this is the sole existence of the theme (or Idea, referent, object). These *also* exist in the art object in the sense that the subject partakes of the same universal which is embodied in the referent. In fact, and I should regard this as central in any adequate theory of communication, the subject is capable of meaning the object to some person precisely because of the universal that is present in both.[10]

Besides the referent, what Dewey calls the "matter for" the work of art, there are the *associations* of the referent. These comprise all of those experiences that the artist had before or while creating his work of art which are relevant to it. Milton's reflections on the Fall of Man; Koestler's experiences as a Communist (which he narrates so effectively in his *Scum of the Earth*); Beethoven's reactions to democracy and heroism; and Cézanne's feelings for the mountain, Sainte-Victoire, are examples of associations. We get our knowledge of these from the letters, diaries, and autobiographies of artists or from other similar sources left by their contemporaries, or even from Freudian or sociological analyses of their art works.[11] The associations, like the referents, exist primarily outside the art object, but may also exist within, as subjects or other elements.

We come now to the *content* of a work of art. If we are to employ this concept at all, then, in order to avoid getting into the many specious disputes which traditional conceptions of content have inspired, and in order to come to grips with the essentially organic character of art, we ought to interpret the content of a work of art as *all* that is in it: all the elements, expressive characteristics and the relations that obtain among them.[12] This interpretation is in keeping with one ordinary usage of content in which we say that the content of anything is what is in it; and is much more satisfactory in its results than interpreting content as theme, subject, or elements as against relations.

On this usage, then, we can speak of our previous examples in the following way. In Cézanne's "Mont Sainte-Victoire," the content can be said to be all the lines, colors, masses, volumes, drawing, design, space — in other words, the plastic — plus the subject and the expressive characteristics, as all of these relate together. In Parker's terminology, the content of the picture is all the linguistic, plastic, and spiritual values as they organically relate to make a total artistic complex.

In *Paradise Lost*, the content includes the subject terms, the images, metaphors, attitudes, ideas, diction, versification, and their expressive characteristics, as they organically relate to each other.

In the *Eroica*, the content comprises all the tones, chords, melodies, harmonies, rhythms, perhaps the subject, their expressive characteristics, also as all of these organically relate to each other.

The content or substance[13] or subject matter[14] of or matter in[15] the work of art is the work itself, the whole thing. It is something that cannot be said in any other way. Many works may have the same theme or referent, be about the same thing, but every work has only one content. Donne, Shakespeare, Shelley, Eliot all speak *of* love, but the content of each of their poems is unique. Nowhere is the Leibnizian principle of the identity of indiscernibles more secure than in the realm of art!

Actual artistic production probably begins with the artist's experiences as they converge upon a theme or Idea. Then he selects and unifies in an imaginative way his material while embodying it in a sensuous medium. He creates an artistic content, to which he usually gives a name. But the name or title is a mere label, not to be confused with the work itself. Most spectators unfortunately regard the content of art as a springboard to the referent, and eventually, to *their* associations. Here Bell and Fry and Bradley are right: Do not respond to the referent or the associations of the referent, but to the content.

If the content of a work of art is conceived as all of its expressive elements organically related to each other, what, then, is the form? Form, I submit, ought to be construed as exactly the same thing: *the organic unification of the several expressive constituents of the work of art.* Concrete artistic form, that is, the form of an individual work of art, ought not to be regarded merely as the relations or mode of expressing an Idea or shape or proportion of the work but as all of the expressive elements in relation. Form and content are to be regarded not as coördinates in art but as constituting the same coördination of elements, characteristics, and relations. Thus, there is *no* distinction on this usage between form and content in art.

There are elements and there are relations. But there are no elements, relations, or even grouping of them that can be singled out and designated as the content or the form except in an arbitrary and vitiating way.[16]

Our proposal to eliminate the form–content distinction as applied to concrete works of art and to construe them as synonyms is no *mere* stipulation as to the way in which we wish to use terms, no *mere* recommendation to effect an alteration of our aesthetic language in an attempt to abuse the language of common sense. The positivists and the Wittgensteinians are undoubtedly correct in their assertion that much of philosophy is of this character, but it is not our intention either to stipulate usage or commit linguistic abuse. Rather, we are offering a new way of talking about art which will not give rise to unnecessary aesthetic disputes and will be more consonant with its actual organic character. An aesthetic language that does not employ terms like form and content — which, let us be the first to admit, are essential for some philosophical and ordinary modes of discourse — or, if it does use them, regards them as synonyms, so our hypothesis about the nature of art implies, is a more adequate language than those languages found in the aesthetic systems considered thus far. It is more adequate ultimately in the same sense that Russell's relational logic is more adequate in interpreting reality than the traditional Aristotelian subject–predicate logic: that is, it is a truer language because it corresponds to the facts.

Now, in the sense that art is an organic complex of elements, expressive in character, embodied in a sensuous medium, it is significant form. But to say that art is significant form is to say that it is also significant content. The two statements mean the same thing: that art may include as its constituents lines, colors, tones, words, emotions, concepts, feelings, meanings, representations, and subjects. Just as there is no artistic distinction between form and content, so there is no antithesis between form and ideas, representations and emotions. The problem, raised by Bell and Fry, of the legitimacy of these constituents remains, and it will be equivalent to asking whether or not these elements can *integrate* successfully with each other.

The analysis of form and content that we have been offering has, I think, been approximated by at least three recent or contemporary aestheticians, Parker, Barnes and Bradley.

Parker affirms the distinction between form and content in his aesthetic writings.[17] But a careful reading of his formulation of the distinction reveals, I think, a position similar to that which we have been developing. By content, Parker means certain linguistic elements, like line and color, and certain plastic and spiritual representations, all in spatial, temporal, and causal (telic) relations to each other. Parker does not, like Ducasse, for example, accept the mathematical distinction between form and content (i.e., relations versus elements) as a legitimate aesthetic category, but regards content as being constituted by certain elements in relation.

Form, for Parker, is a set of abstract properties of these elements in relation. It has to do with the unity, variety, balance, evolution, and hierarchy of these elements in relation. Consequently, Parker means by form certain second-order properties[18] of the content of art. But when we consider the concrete individual work of art, the distinction between form and content vanishes since both refer to the same thing: the linguistic and imaginative elements of art in organic relation to each other.

Barnes, in *The Art in Painting*, distinguishes between two inseparable aspects of painting, plastic form and subject matter.[19] The plastic form is the unity of the line, color, light, shadow, design, volume, and composition, whereas the subject matter includes the spiritual and dramatic values of the work of art. Nowhere, however, does Barnes refer to the subject matter as the total content to be contrasted with the total form. Rather, the subject matter is one element among others, to be contrasted with the others only because it is nonplastic in character. Now, if we rephrase Barnes, which we can do without any violation of his doctrine, his similarity to our own position, regarding art as organic and form and content as indistinguishable, becomes apparent. For Barnes, the art object is the unity of plastic and nonplastic elements in relation; and the whole object is significant form, that is, a complex of expressive, ideational, and plastic elements organically related to each other.[20]

In Bradley's "Poetry for Poetry's Sake" there is the same recognition of form and content which are taken as inseparable albeit distinguishable elements of art. The content is regarded as the *whole* poem, the form as the versification. But it is quite arbitrary and unnecessary to call versification the form of a poem. Bradley does so because he persists in thinking of form in mathematical, relational terms. Actually, however, Bradley does deny the coördinate character of form and content. The poem is really an integration of elements organically related to each other, in which one element, among others, is versification.

Meaning of the Organic in Art

Art, we have stated, is an organic complex or integration of expressive elements embodied in a sensuous medium. It is now necessary to examine the meanings of the organic and expressive in order to clarify our definition of art.

First, the nature of the organic in art. In general, at least two kinds of complex or system can be distinguished in the world, the mechanical and the organic.

Consider, as an example of a mechanical system, the *statement* of the four freedoms in the Atlantic Charter. In this "statement system" there are a number of constituents, including certain elements or terms, their characteristics, and the relations obtaining among them. The terms, i.e., the individual statements, such as "There shall be freedom of religion," are significant and understandable by themselves. Their meanings are not dependent upon each other. The relations that any one of these statements has to each of the others do not change the meaning or the nature of the other statements. Nor do the terms themselves change the nature

of the other terms. We may say, then, that the elements, characteristics, and relations of this linguistic complex are externally
constituted in the sense that no one element, characteristic, or
relation is an attribute of any of the others. The constituents, in
their nature and meaning, remain the same no matter what the
relations among them. Even the serial ordering of the four statements or their serial reordering makes absolutely no difference to
the statements themselves, so far as their meanings are concerned.
That is to say, it does not matter to the meanings of the statements if the statement about freedom of speech, for example,
comes before or after the statement about freedom from fear. Here,
then, is an example of a system in which *what* is said — namely,
the four freedoms — is distinguishable from *how* it is said.

In contrast to systems like the statement of the four freedoms,
there are complexes in which the constituents *do* make a difference
to each other because of the nature of their relations or of their
characteristics. If this is taken as the essential feature of an internally constituted complex, then we may say that an organic
system is an internally constituted one. That is to say, it is a complex in which every constituent, be it element, characteristic or
relation, plays its role not only in terms of itself, but *also* in terms
of the other constituents. Every element, every characteristic,
every relation, even that of mere serial order, makes a difference
to every other. This means that no constituent can be understood
by itself but must be seen in its relations to the others as well.

In logical terminology, we may say that an organic complex is
one in which any constituent a is an argument variable of all the
others $\hat{x}(C-a)$, that is, the class of all the constituents minus
the original one.

The central difference between a mechanical and an organic
system, then, is that in the first every constituent is externally
constituted; whereas in the second, every constituent is internally
constituted. Unlike the monists and the monadists, we do not
mean by an organic system one in which there are no relations or

in which relations can be *reduced* to predicates of terms or Wholes; but rather one in which (*a*) relations, real in the sense of being irreducible, (*b*) elements, and (*c*) their characteristics are *part* of the nature of each other.[21]

As a disciple of contemporary realism, which roots itself historically in the rejection of the doctrine of internal relations and a fortiori in the doctrine of internal constituency, I should like very much to deny the existence of organic systems and remain content with a cosmology in which all complexes are pluralities of terms externally related to each other. But aesthetic inquiry, it seems to me, demands that we recognize and accept at least one kind of internally related and internally constituted complex, namely, the work of art. To resolve a work of art into a mechanical system is tantamount to destroying its aesthetic nature.

Let us see how this distinction between mechanical and organic constituents and complexes applies to art. Consider, to begin with, a novel. Is the cover of the novel a mechanical or an organic constituent? What about the quality of the paper? Both of these, it is obvious, do not make a difference to the novel, i.e., to its characters, plot, themes, etc., hence, are mechanical elements. Change the cover, rebind the book, improve the paper, and the novel has not been affected because these are not factors in it as a work of art.

Contrast this with the frame of a picture or the quality of its surface area! The theory of framing is quite undeveloped today but everyone recognizes that the frame is one element among others, which the artist or museum director must consider when he is concerned with the picture as a work of art.[22]

So far as the quality of the surface area is concerned, that this makes a difference to all the plastic and subject elements of the painting has been recognized by artists for centuries. In contemporary art, the experimentations on wood, glass, cardboard, etc., and the attempt to derive from these materials certain expressive effects show the contributory roles these painting surfaces play. Because they do make a difference to the expressive qualities of the colors, lines, luminosity, even the subject elements, they are organic constituents.

Another way in which the organic character of constituents manifests itself in painting is in the treatment of colors. Artists distinguish between dominant colors, like red and yellow, and recessive colors, like blue and green. Red, when we look at it, has the tendency to come forward; blue, to go backward. (This is a psychological fact, characterizing the perceptual experiences of Western peoples, not necessarily a physical fact characterizing colors all by themselves.) An artist who wishes to preserve a balance within his picture would hesitate to put a large red volume on the front planes of his canvas if there were nothing on the back planes to counteract it, since the volume would tend to "spill over" the frame. Consequently, he paints his large frontal volumes in recessive, soft colors and his back volumes in dominant, loud colors.

There is nothing absolute about this specific treatment of colors, but it is certainly a characteristic of much great art. Two excellent examples are Brueghel's "Peasant Wedding Dance" and Seurat's "Sur La Grande Jatte." In both of these, the two main large front figures are in soft blues. These are related immediately in space to other figures that are in brighter colors, and this relation leads us from the one to the other parts of the canvas. Both artists recognize the organic character of color in relation to the volume of the figures. They realize, whether consciously or not is irrelevant, that the aesthetic value of the color of the large front figure volume will affect the aesthetic value of the color of the back smaller figure volumes. Hence, they visualize each color volume not only in terms of itself but also in terms of the other color volumes. The contemporary French painter, H. Matisse, has stated this organic character of color in a clear and revealing way:

> If, on a clean canvas, I put at intervals patches of blue, green, and red, with every touch that I put on, each of those previously laid on loses in importance. Say I have to paint an

interior; I see before me a wardrobe. It gives me a vivid sensation of red; I put on the canvas the particular red that satisfies me. A *relation is now established between this red and the paleness of the canvas.* When I put on besides a green, and also a yellow to represent the floor, between this green and the yellow and the color of the canvas there will be still further relations. But these different tones diminish one another. It is necessary that the different tones I use be balanced in such a way that they do not destroy one another.[23]

We find the same insistence upon the organic character of all the arts in many contemporary critics and artists. The best statement in practical criticism with which I am acquainted of this organic principle that every constituent of an artistic complex must be understood in terms of itself in relation to the other constituents is that of C. Brooks and R. P. Warren, two American exponents of the "New Criticism," instituted by I. A. Richards and T. S. Eliot in England.

A poem is not to be thought of as merely a bundle of things which are "poetic" in themselves. Nor is it to be thought of, as the "message hunters" would seem to have it, as a kind of box, decorated or not, in which a "truth" or a "fine sentiment" is hidden. We avoid such difficulties *by thinking of a poem as a piece of writing which gives us a certain effect in which, we discover, the "poetry" inheres.*

This is very different from considering a poem as a group of mechanically combined elements — meter, rime, figurative language, idea, etc. — which are put together to make a poem as bricks are put together to make a wall. The question, then, about any element in a poem is not whether it is in itself pleasing, or agreeable, or valuable, or "poetical," but whether it works with the other elements to create the effect intended by the poet. The relationship among the elements in a poem is therefore all important, and it is not a mechanical relationship but one which is far more intimate and fundamental. If we should compare

a poem to the make-up of some physical object it ought not
to be to a wall but to something organic like a plant.[24]

One may raise the question of the ontological character of
mechanical and organic complexes. Many philosophers would undoubtedly assert that the essential characteristic of these complexes,
which determines their organic or mechanical nature, lies in the
complex itself. But this is too dogmatic a view. All that one can
say, on empirical grounds, is that the kind of system we have before
us depends, in part, at least, upon our human purposes and interests. A chemist, qua chemist, would treat a painting quite differ-
ently from a critic interested in it as a work of art. To a chemist,
let us say, who is concerned with placing the picture in its historical
period of origin, the painting becomes a mechanical system, in that
he isolates certain chemical constituents of the colors on the
canvas without any concern for their relations to the other constituents. But to the critic, there can be no such isolation since his
main concern is with the nature of the constituents as they relate
to each other.

Meaning of the Expressive in Art

A work of art, according to our hypothesis, is an organic complex
of expressive constituents. What, now, do we mean by *expressive* in
this context? There has been a great deal of discussion in recent
aesthetic theory of this concept,[25] but I should like to propose
a real definition of the expressive in art without entering into the
diverse usages of the concept.

The meaning which we shall consider is that which affirms of
some particular work of art, "the colors are expressive but the general design is not," or "the melodies are deeply expressive." Our
problem is, what does the word "expressive" refer to, if anything,
in this context, which is the one basic to our general definition of
art?

My own view is that anything in art is expressive (in the above sense) if it is construed by some spectator to be a *sign*[26] of (1) a specific emotion or feeling, (2) an emotional quality, or (3) something that is a sign of an emotional quality or emotion. An example of (1) is the emotion of turbulence; of (2) the quality of the lyrical as against the dramatic in human experience; and of (3) the volume figure in Picasso's "Woman in White" that is a sign of the property of voluminousness, which is itself a sign of some emotion to all of us.

I think that this is what we mean when we assert, for example, that "the colors of this painting are expressive"; the colors are functioning as signs of emotions to us. To state that any constituent of a work of art is expressive is to say that that constituent is associated with some emotion or emotional quality by us. This is the basic meaning of the expressive as that term is applied to the art object. Also, it is in this fundamental semantical sense that we may claim of art that it embodies emotions.

As signs, the expressive in art, like all signs, has both a presentational and a representational character. Aestheticians do not question the presentational aspect of the expressive in art; that is, its immediately given sensuous character.[27] But the view that every artistic constituent, because it is expressive, is representational, is certainly a novel one and likely to create some misgivings among many aestheticians. Our thesis, however, is clear: Because every constituent in art — not only the subject — functions as a sign of human emotion, it is representative of, means, denotes,[28] either directly or indirectly, some human emotion or emotional quality.

Expressive properties of artistic elements may represent or mean in different ways. Consider, once again, Brueghel's "Peasant Wedding Dance," specifically, the color red, which is one of the leading colors in the painting. Now, (1) this red color may mean any red color; that is, it may mean its universal. In this context, the red color is iconic with all the other instances of red that there are.

(2) The color red may mean the concept "red," in which case we say that the color is a symbol of the concept. (We could equally well say that the concept is a symbol of the color red, if we were reading the word "red" in a poem instead of seeing red in a picture.)

(3) The color red may mean that which we call, but with great inexactitude, warmth, liveliness, gaiety, where these latter are certain emotional qualities of our experiences. Here the color red functions as a symbol of warmth, etc., but because of certain psychological conditioning and general social and cultural (anthropologically speaking) acceptance, it is a symbol which is rather fixed in its meaning, in the way that the word "red" is rather fixed in its meaning. Because of this intimate association between the color red and the quality of warmth in our culture, we may call red in this context a *transparent* symbol of the warm, gay, or lively.

(4) In contrast to transparent there are *opaque* symbols. The color red may mean adultery, peace, anxiety, a frog, love, hate, communism — in fact, anything at all. Iconological research, for example, might reveal that the color red in the Brueghel painting represented lechery to the artist and to his contemporaries. Now, in the sense that this red means lechery to Brueghel or anxiety to someone else or a frog to a third person who has a passion for a zoölogical *Weltanschauung*, it does not mean what most of us today call warmth or gaiety or liveliness. The association of red with gaiety is easily made by all of us who share the same conditioning, whereas the association of red with lechery, anxiety, or a frog is made only by those who understand the limited language of the artist or the spectators.

It should be obvious, of course, that the difference between a transparent and an opaque symbol is in part, at least, cultural. Perhaps the whole difference is cultural, but to say so is to commit oneself to a view that is too dogmatic. It may very well be that physiology and psychology will someday disclose the intimate con-

nection between red and the feeling of gaiety in such a way that
we could claim that some symbols are physiologically transparent
and others physiologically opaque.

(5) The seeing of the red color may be like the experiencing of
gaiety, liveliness, or warmth; hence we may say that the visual experience is iconically expressive of the experience of warmth, etc.
That is to say, a person who sees the color red may interpret his
visual experience as being like an emotional tone of some of his
other experiences which he refers to as liveliness or warmth or
gaiety, if he is conditioned to do so. To paraphrase Carroll Pratt,
red may look the way the lively feels.[29]

The color red, then, even in one picture, may represent or mean
in a variety of ways: iconically, either expressively (5) or nonexpres-
sively (1); or symbolically, either transparently (2,3) or opaquely
(4).

Consider, next, the progression of chords in the exposition section of the *Eroica*. This chordal progression is said by everyone to
be profoundly expressive. Of what? we may ask, and this is tantamount to asking, of what is it a sign? Once more, we may say that
the artistic constituent, the chordal progression, is expressive in the
sense that it is a sign of many things, all of which are associated
with emotional experiences by human beings. To some, the chordal
progression means massiveness and its attendant quality of power;
to others, Napoleon, or democracy on the march. In the sense that
it functions as a sign of massiveness and power, the progression is
a transparent symbol because we have been conditioned to associate these loud, full sounds with the massive and the powerful.
The *hearing* of the chordal progression is iconically expressive of
the powerful or the strong to contemporary Western listeners
since, as an auditory experience, it is like our experiences of the
powerful. Both the auditory and these other experiences have
the qualities of bigness, massiveness, and strength about them.
In the sense that the chordal progression is a sign of, means, repre-

sents, democracy or Napoleon on the march, it is, either as sound stimuli or our full interpretations of it, opaquely symbolic.

Subject terms are also expressive in art and, as such, are representational. In Cézanne's "Italian Girl," for example, certain of the colors and lines function as a sign of a girl. These configurative colors and lines are iconic signs in the same sense that a photograph is an icon of the person it represents. Now, a girl, all by herself, is a sign to all of us of various emotions, the specific one depending upon our psychological conditioning and growth. In the Cézanne portrait, the girl exhibits the quality of pensiveness; that is, she is a representation of a pensive person. Her pensiveness may further function as a sign of different emotions, some of which may be merely opaquely related to pensiveness. But in any case, as the subject of the painting, the pensive girl represents many things to many different observers.

To sum up: According to our hypothesis, *every* constituent in art — line, color, melody, rhythm, gesture, etc. — not merely the subject, is representational in an expressive sense. That is, every constituent means certain emotions or emotional qualities to every spectator, though, perhaps, different ones to different spectators. The traditional view, which is shared by all aestheticians who dichotomize art into its form and content, and equate content and representation, and representation and subject, and who identify form with the nonrepresentational, is completely unsound from the correct semantical point of view and must be rejected. In art, there are elements, their expressive characteristics, and the relations that these have to each other. But there are no *special* representational elements. A line, a color, a melody, a spatial mass, may mean as much, and in exactly the same way, as any other element. The whole problem of representation versus nonrepresentation and the legitimacy of representation in art, as raised by both Bell and Fry and their critics, is a specious issue and rests ultimately upon inadequate analyses of form and content, representation, and the expressive in art.

The Organic Theory and the Requisites of Aesthetic Theory

In our general critique of Bell and Fry we suggested that any adequate theory of art, especially one that is sympathetic to the aims of formalism, ought to satisfy the following requisites:

(1) It ought to provide a richer analysis of form than that presented by Bell and Fry. The organic theory, I think, succeeds in this. Artistic form is construed as a complex of various constituents, which is taken to be amenable to analysis, and empirically ascertainable and objective; which is the common referent of discussion and dispute; and, finally, which is open to educational procedures. If, on the organic theory, we ask, Does a particular work of art have significant form? we can reply by inquiring into the presence or lack of integration of the expressive constituents of the work.

(2) It ought to furnish, either explicitly or by implication, certain working criteria for intelligent criticism of the arts. These criteria and the whole general problem of the possibility of a theory of criticism will be dealt with in Chapter 9, where we discuss the nature of artistic appreciation.

(3) It ought to offer an explanation of all the arts. Here, too, the organic theory is successful. Every art object is an organic complex of its several expressive constituents. The problem is always the *specific* one of ascertaining the varying constituents; and these, of course, differ in the different arts.

(4) It ought to render intelligible certain phrases like "French painting," "Russian music," "the proletarian novel," or "the romantic drama"; which are quite meaningless in the formalism of Bell and Fry. The organic theory accepts these concepts as legitimate. Works of art may be French, Russian, proletarian, or romantic in at least two ways: (*a*) through their subjects or themes, where the *kind* of subject or theme, the class struggle, for example, or the defiant hero who stands alone against society, defines the work as proletarian or romantic; or (*b*) through any of their expressive qualities. In painting, for example, we may say — even Fry

has said it! — that much of French art is delicate, witty, precise; and these aesthetic adjectives apply to the expressive qualities of the plastic elements.

Our theory allows also of a socio-economic-philosophical interpretation of art. What we do in this case is to abstract certain constituents from different works of art and discuss them in relation to certain categories as a cohesive group.

(5) It ought not to limit in an arbitrary way the range of artistic communication. That is, no theory of art should rule out, unless it must, on the most cogent of grounds, nonplastic, spiritual values. On the contrary, the overwhelming force of the history of art requires from aesthetics a theory that explains how art is able to contain, legitimately and successfully, representations and meanings of any sort, and even different *Weltanschauungen*. Further, aesthetics ought to show, if possible, that fullness of expression and communication in art does not necessarily destroy its purity or provoke sentimental appreciation.

The organic theory, primarily because it rejects the traditional distinction between form and content, which has been basic in the repudiation of meanings, subjects, and representations in art, does not limit the range of artistic expression. Rather, it destroys the props of traditional limitations, and asks only that artistic communication be an expressively integrated one. It refuses to rule out the nonplastic spiritual values for the very simple reason that these can contribute as much to art as line and color.[30]

Furthermore, on the organic view, the purity of a work of art does not consist in the elimination or plastic dissolution of the subject but in the effective working together of *all* the elements. It is the absence of integration, as in the Shelley poem, "Death," which makes for artistic impurity.

Also, there is no reason to suppose that subjects necessarily evoke sentimental, ordinary emotions. As we shall show in Chapter 9, the proper attitude to assume toward art is the contemplative and nonsentimental one, no matter what the constituents of the particular art object may be.

(6) It ought to show that formalism is not necessarily the view that it is of no consequence what a work of art says so long as it says it well; that the what is artistically indifferent and it is only the how that counts.[31]

The organic theory, which may be construed as an *expanded* formalist theory of the art object, repudiates this version of formalism by denying the distinction between the what and the how in art (although it accepts the distinction when it is applied to mechanical systems, including art objects, when they are treated in a mathematical or quantitative, scientific fashion.) In art, we have been insisting throughout our present chapter, *how something is expressed is what is expressed*. Both the how and the what, like the form and the content, refer to the totality of the work, not to any set of separate constituents.[32]

4

THE ARTS: PAINTING

Introduction

In the next four chapters we shall attempt to illustrate and vali-
date the organic theory of art. The validation will not be complete.
Instead, our desire is to examine the arts separately in terms of
some of the various aspects of the organic theory. Thus, in this
chapter, we shall discuss painting with especial emphasis upon its
different elements, expressive characteristics, and relations. Our
main concern will be with the *intrinsic* characteristics of the various
constituents of painting, rather than with the ways in which these
constituents affect each other. In the succeeding chapter we shall
deal with poetry by examining at length one poem, Eliot's "The
Love Song of J. Alfred Prufrock." This will be followed by a chapter on music, with almost complete focus upon the problem of the
meaning of music. Finally, there will be brief treatments of the
other arts in terms of the basic concept of the medium.

Analysis of the Constituents of Painting

Painting is an organic complex of expressive constituents. These
constituents include color, line, texture, plane, volume, space, light,
shadow, subject, representation or meaning, design, drawing, com-

position, and movement. We shall now discuss all of these, beginning with the element of color.

The great importance of *color* in painting was not fully recognized in an articulate way until the modern era, in the work of the
Impressionists, but especially in Cézanne and the ensuing theory
of the structural and dynamic properties of color, that is, that colors
build and relate on the canvas.

Intuitively, of course, many of the old masters recognized the
importance of color, in seeing it as more than decoration or naturalistic detail. In Western art, since the fourteenth century, theories
of color have ranged from the view that it is only a sensuous,
decorative, ornamental element, to be applied upon, but not in
conjunction with or in relation to, the other elements, to the
modern view that its importance is equal to that of the other elements. This issue of the role of color in painting parallels the
conflict in poetic theory about the significance of metaphor, which
has ranged from the narrow view that it is mere embroidery of
theme to the all-embracing view that poetry *is* metaphor, specifically, the unfolding of metaphor.

Certainly, before the Impressionists, in Realism and Romanti-
cism, the most common view was that color is a mere decorative
device and ought to be applied upon the canvas according to certain realistic standards. For example, real grass is green; hence, the
representation of grass in a picture ought to be painted green.

The Impressionists revitalized the importance of color by making
it central in their work. They did this by resolving all the elements
of painting into color atmosphere and by returning to the practice
(used by Rubens and El Greco, among others) of mixing colors
on the canvas instead of on the palette. These two contributions
led to the new vision of Cézanne, who recognized the dynamic and
relating properties of color: that colors are more than sensuous
ornamentation but can build up a picture and even change the
qualities of the other constituents. In fact, the Cézannean vision
has so impressed some contemporary aestheticians that they have

made color all-important. Albert Barnes, for example, believes that everything in painting is color or a modification of it.[1]

The modern movement in art since Impressionism has encompassed many artists who have been classified as colorists. Henri Matisse, for example, is considered universally as primarily a colorist in painting, although this must not be taken to mean that his work is merely decorative (which is what many critics have done), for in his paintings color is employed as the fundamental building element.

No one who has experienced much of modern art accepts the naturalistic criterion of color any more either. Colors are to be chosen not because of the objects they are supposed to represent but because of their intrinsic qualities of brightness, hue, and saturation and their expressive properties. Color distortion is no longer interpreted as a form of shock treatment. No sophisticated art lover is disturbed by red horses or blue cows or yellow skies any more because we have come to understand that the naturalistic dictum, shared by Romanticists and Realists alike, is rooted in a misconception of the artistic nature of color and its potentialities to create plastic and expressive qualities in pictures.

There is much that can be said about the physics, physiology, and psychology of colors. But we shall deal with these only as they relate to the expressive, since this latter constitutes the aesthetic domain of colors. *That* colors are characterized by emotional or expressive qualities has always been recognized by aestheticians; *why* they are and what it *means* to say that they are, are still inadequately answered questions. If our analysis of the expressive in art is correct, then it means that colors are characterized by or *embody* emotive or expressive qualities, that colors function as signs of emotions to spectators, and that the seeing of the colors is sufficiently like other experiences that we may say that the visual experience is iconic with certain emotional experiences. The visual experience may itself be highly emotional but it need not be; and the contention that it always is is rooted in an emotionalist theory of artistic appreciation which is itself highly questionable, as we shall see in Chapter 9.

Let us now consider the aesthetic domain of some of the colors, beginning with red. Many people say that red is a warm or lively color in itself, that is, that one of its properties, along with its properties of hue and saturation, is warmth. On this view, to say that red is not warm or lively is to utter a self-contradiction; the warmth and liveliness of red are construed as two of its analytic properties. This is an extremely attractive view because, if it were true, we could then say that red means warmth in an iconic way. Unfortunately, there is no empirical evidence for the theory. The most we can say is that those of us — and in our Western society that probably means all of us — who have been conditioned to re-act to red find it warm, lively, gay, ringing. Consequently, for us it is a transparent symbol, in the way that the word "red" is a trans-parent symbol of the color red.

Red has been interpreted in many different ways in history, as a symbol of passion, war, holiness, truth, virtue, adultery, com-munism, etc. Some of these are more transparent than others. In our time, red as a symbol of communism may become as historically fixed a symbol as the association of red with the lively or the gay. But as for the others, they are more or less opaque interpretations. That red is a symbol of truth and virtue, for example, would be known only by a Chinese or a scholar of Oriental culture. To most Westerners, red as a symbol of truth and virtue is opaque, as is red as a symbol of adultery to the ordinary Chinese.

In so far as the aesthetic experience involves the color red, the seeing of it, and our further reactions to it, we may say that the *seeing of red*, that is, the visual experience, is more than a symbol of gaiety, liveliness, or warmth. For all of us who have been condi-tioned to interpret red as a warm color, the seeing of it is an iconic sign of other kinds of human emotional experience. To paraphrase Pratt again: red looks the way the lively feels.

What has been said of the expressive semantics of red can be applied to yellow as well. It is the brightest of colors. Probably this has something to do with its being taken as a warm, cheerful color like red. But here, too, we must be careful. Yellow is not iconic with the cheerful; the seeing of yellow may be, but not the actual color. As stimulus, it is bright but not necessarily cheerful; by association it is cheerful but it has not always been so and need not be so. In the Christian Church, it has been a symbol of dishonor; in popular symbolism it has been a symbol of jealousy, decay, and cowardice. And in the Orient, it is a symbol of faith and consequently a sacred color.

Green and blue are recessive colors rather than dominant, as red and yellow are. Because of our psychological and environmental conditioning, red and yellow, when we look at them, tend to come forward in our field of vision, and blue and green to go back. Aestheticians speak of blue and green as cool, calm, quiet colors. Semantically, they are transparent symbols of those emotional states that we refer to as serenity and tranquillity; and the seeing of them is iconic with the reposeful in human experience. That is to say, for most of us, again because of our conditioning, the seeing of green and blue is like the feeling of calmness and restfulness.

White is like red and yellow, a bright, usually joyful color, but again not intrinsically, only by cultural associations. If our comprehension of Chinese mores is correct, white, to the Chinese, is a transparent symbol of death and consequently, probably, a somber, serene color.

Gray and black, expressively, are melancholy, rather depressing, colors. We construe them as transparent symbols of the depressing and the melancholy. Here, too, we may say, the seeing of these is to us Westerners iconic with certain depressing human experiences. Picasso, in the "Guernica," has utilized in a remarkable way the expressive values of gray and black. These are the only colors in the picture, and together with the other plastic and subject elements, they make for a magnificent embodiment of the blackest kind of melancholy.

Texture is the second element in painting; it refers to the appearance of the paint surface. Paint may lie on the canvas like a thin film or a veil, as in glaze, or it may be put on thickly, as in impasto.

There is great emphasis upon texture in much of modern art. It is sometimes referred to as the "paint quality" of painting. Texture is also recognized as a structural, building, relating element. Specifically, it has to do with the *weight* of the plastic elements line, color, and volume. It is a psychological fact that we associate our visual sensations with tactile ones; in painting, when we are looking at it, we almost feel the colors, lines, and volumes. One might even say that in painting, as in sculpture or architecture, the tactile is as important as the visual.

Some paint looks, consequently feels, heavy; and this acts as an expressive iconic sign of solidity, which is itself an important structural property in painting. Klee's *"Ein Verständiger"* and Rouault's "Christ Mocked by Soldiers" constitute two excellent examples of this textural solidity. In the first, I should go so far as to say that the element of texture — the white color which is painted in a rough, heavy manner and surrounds the solitary figure like an envelope — is the controlling element, plastically speaking, keeping the colors and lines and volumes intact. In the Rouault, the chunkiness of heavily applied paint embodies a sense of power which together with the expressive humility of the Christ figure offers us a total contrast of power and humility that is one of the miracles of modern art.

In complete contrast to the Rouault and Klee, there is much contemporary painting in which the surface is thin, soft, and delicate. John Carroll, especially in his Detroit murals, has created many such attenuated textural surfaces.

Considered in its expressive dimension, softness, roughness, chunkiness or heaviness belongs to the texture as an intrinsic property. Some paint is heavy in a way that red is not warm. Heaviness, in other words, characterizes paint in the way that it characterizes an elm tree. This does not mean that heaviness either is or is not a metaphysical property of the paint or the tree, existing independently of our experiences of these entities. The Berkeley–realist controversy need not concern us here. Our contention is that *all* normal human beings will interpret the expressive, tactile, textural qualities of paint in the same way, just as they will respond to the tactile qualities of a tree in the same way, in so far as these qualities are related to lightness and heaviness. But not all people will respond to colors in the same way. Our emotional interpretations of color are primarily psychological, whereas our emotional interpretations of texture are primarily physiological. Granted the region of vagueness in the continuum of light–heavy texture, every person with a normal nervous system and normal eyesight will recognize the lightness of one texture as against the heaviness of another. And apparently that is not true of colors. One man will interpret a particular color as quiet; a second person may find that same color exciting. If this analysis is sound, it follows that textures, as they inhere in the painting, are expressively or emotionally iconic with certain features of human experience, and not merely transparent or opaque symbols.

Some paint textures are like some features of human experience. This is our thesis. The rough, heavy, chunky texture of the Rouault is iconic with the rough, heavy traits of our bodily experiences. And when we see the picture, we may say, quite correctly, that the texture, taken independently of the other elements, means, represents, or denotes power, since the rough, the heavy, and the chunky are constituents of power; and the total picture means the conflict of power (or force) and humility in human experience.

The aesthetics of *lines* has been treated in greater detail than the aesthetics of color and texture. A number of different lines have been enumerated and their expressive properties noted. First, there is the horizontal line. Consider Cézanne's "View of Auvers." Here the straight or nearly straight lines of the various planes that mark off the green and the orange meadows from the skyline, and these from the foliage, all contribute to communicate the quality of repose and quiet. They do this as line; and together with the other lines (mainly the vertical), colors (mostly cool), and subjects (quiet cottages, trees, shrubbery, meadows), they offer a total presentation of the simple, quiet dignity of nature as Cézanne conceived it.

The horizontal is the traditional line of repose. It is said to embody repose.[2] This is its expressive quality, which belongs to it in the way that warmth belongs to red and power to chunkiness of texture. But since we have seen that power is iconic with chunkiness and delicacy with attenuated lines, and that red is not iconic with warmth but a transparent symbol of it, we must modify this traditional conception of the horizontal. Is the horizontal in relation to repose like red in relation to warmth or like chunkiness in relation to power? There is not conclusive evidence on this matter[3] but because of the physiological-psychological fact that the long horizontal line is restful in a way that red is not physiologically warm or that chunkiness *is* physiologically powerful, we may say that the horizontal has as one of its intrinsic properties (i.e., a property the omission of which would render the entity self-contradictory) *that* which is like the reposeful and restful in much of human experience. It is not only the seeing of the line but also the actual line as it exists independently of the seeing of it that is iconic with the restful. In other words, the reposelike quality of a horizontal line belongs to the stimulative aspect of human experience as much as it does to the associative aspects, which is not the case with the expressive character of colors.

What has been claimed of the iconic character of the horizontal can be asserted of the vertical line, except, of course, that the expressive properties are different. The vertical embodies the expressive property of dignity, solemnity, and the uplifting — provided that these are not taken in too literal a fashion, but more as emotional tones of our experiences. The four verticals of the Cézanne "View of Auvers," for example, or the tremendous verticals of the

Gothic in architecture or in painting, are characterized by qualities that are like the aspiring, the dignified, and the uplifting in human experience. Physiologically, there seems to be this surging upward when we experience aspiration and dignity, and this same upward tendency is found in the vertical.

The undulating line, of which the master is El Greco, embodies the melodramatic, the twisted, the brooding, anguish. None of these terms will quite do, but this is a general fault of our English language, not of the undulating line. Anguish, torture, brooding, as human experiences, have about them a twisted, undulating character. We even speak of "twisted personalities." The undulating line is iconic with these experiences in the same sense that a map is iconic with the territory that it represents. The undulating line means or represents, in an iconic way, the anguish quality of much of human experience.

The jagged or swirling line, perhaps better than any of the others, discloses the expressively iconic character of some of the elements in painting. Conflict, tension, violence, turbulence all have a genuinely jagged character to them. The human personality is in a state that could be described as a $\mathcal{M}\mathcal{M}\mathcal{M}\mathcal{M}$ state. The jagged line in a picture can be taken as iconic with jagged experiences. In Van Gogh's "The Starry Night," for example, the total intensity of conflict being represented is in part due to the contribution of the jagged lines as they delineate the cypress tree, the mountains, the shrubbery, and the sky.

The curved line, the traditional "line of beauty," has had attributed to it the qualities of tenderness, prettiness, and voluptuousness. But should we ask whether these are intrinsic properties of the curved line, we shall see that they are not. Rather they are like warmth in relation to red. The curved line is no more pretty, tender, or voluptuous than any other. It is because of our association with these lines in relation to the human body (usually the female) that we interpret them to be tender, etc. But they could as easily be interpreted as the contrary of the tender or the voluptuous, for example, the flaccid or the cold, if we were conditioned to do so. At most, therefore, the curved line is a transparent symbol, not an iconic sign of the voluptuous, the tender, and the pretty.

What is intrinsic to the curved line is the quality of the mellifluous, and in so far as the tender, pretty, and voluptuous are similar to the mellifluous, it is an expressively iconic sign. There is in much of human experience a mellifluous character, a lilting, "melodic" character. The curved line, embodying as it does this mellifluousness, can be said to be iconic with the mellifluous character of human experience. Matisse's "Dancers" is an excellent example of linear rhythms which possess this mellifluous character.

Planes are series of lines that establish a depth quality in painting and thereby give it representational dimensionality. In El Greco, in much of Chinese landscape, in Seurat's "Sur La Grande Jatte," and in much of Cubist art, planes have been exploited for their ability to create these depth qualities in painting.

Volumes are aggregates of lines and colors built up into masses. Plastically, volumes are important because of this character of mass; but they are just as significant for painting in so far as they are used for subject representation. Mass, even if it is implied, representational mass, is characterized by solidity, strength, structure, and their attendant expressive properties. Masses are important in painting because they create certain axial tensions between them; and these tensions give rise to plastic mobility or movement *within* the canvas. The great "Crucifixions" of El Greco, the "Card Players" of Cézanne, and "Christmas Night," by Matthew Barnes, illustrate this property of tension between masses. Many artists, who have failed to realize this fact that masses and volumes relate to each other and must be equilibrated, have come to grief. Courbet's famous "The Young Bather" is an excellent example of a painting in which the volumes tend to spill over the frame because there is nothing to act as their counterpart and counterthrust within the picture.

The first thing that we must recognize in the analysis of the element of picture *space* is that, unlike modern non-Euclidean and non-Newtonian, *relational*, physical space, picture space is a *substance* that is to be filled in; otherwise gaps result in the picture.

Secondly, space is not subordinate to any theory of perspective. The naturalistic theory of space, which developed along with the naturalistic theory of color and drawing, each a part of a general theory of realistic, scientific imitationalism in art, is no longer defensible. Spacing need follow no scientific theory of perspective or vision. It has its own laws, which are arrived at plastically, and in different ways by different artists. Natural, common-sense space may be ignored, shortened, distorted, or given extraordinary depth; the controlling factor is the expressive intent of the artist. One of the great examples of the distortion of ordinary space and perspective is contained in El Greco's "Feast in the House of Simon." In this picture El Greco has painted a leaning tower in the background which seems to be falling into the open window where Jesus and the Apostles are eating. Plastically, the forward-leaning tower functions to keep the spectator from leaving the room because the moment he leaves through the window, the tower pulls him back. The tension between the figures in the room and the tower is plastically and expressively exact for it creates an intensely exciting totality.

Thirdly, we must not interpret so-called "empty" space as unessential to painting, for even darkened space plays its role. In Rembrandt's "Old Woman Cutting Her Nails," for example, the darkened space behind the head of the figure of the old woman is as important as any other plastic element because it gives her a certain depth and solidity without which the painting would lose much of its plastic and expressive profundity.

Space embodies many different expressive properties. In El Greco, especially in the "View of Toledo," the space possesses depth and voluminousness and their attendant iconic and symbolic expressive properties. In much of Matisse, Rousseau, Gauguin, and mural painting, space is foreshortened so that all the elements seem to be at the front of the picture. This loss of depth minimizes much of the three-dimensionality of painting and gives it a more decorative effect. In Surrealism, especially in the best work of Dali and Chirico, space is exploited in a brilliant way. Both artists have captured the infinite, unenclosed character of space, as we moderns comprehend it, and the whole expressive quality of the infinite. In fact, however we may regard their heavy insistence upon opaque symbolism in art, their exploration into the expressive potentials of infinite space has been a major contribution to modern art. One need only compare the openness and unbounded space of Dali and Chirico with the homey, enclosed space of Giotto, in which Christ, men, angels, and the earth share the same self-enclosed space, or with the somewhat enlarged structural, but nevertheless secure, space of El Greco or Cézanne. In their conception of space, together with their other plastic elements, Dali and Chirico have conveyed many of the expressive characteristics of our modern world, a world in which man feels, more and more frighteningly, his aloneness in a vast multiuniverse that reduces him to cosmic insignificance.

Light and shadow are constituents that function to create color atmosphere as in the Impressionists, or to focus the attention of the eyes upon one scene as, for example, in Rembrandt's chiaroscuro. Essentially, light and shadow are modifications of color.[4] Light has the expressive property of warmth and security; darkness, the expressive property of insecurity. Semantically, among other things, light can be said to be at most only a transparent symbol of security, whereas darkness is a transparent symbol of foreboding and insecurity.

Design is primarily a relational constituent in painting. Traditionally, design has been conceived by many aestheticians as a synonym of form, where form has meant arrangement of entities. Dewey has distinguished between two senses of design: as arrangement and as purpose.[5] That is to say, the design of a house, for example, is the *plan* of the construction as determined by the *pur-*

pose of the architect or builder. Barnes's analysis is more specific in
its application to painting. Design, he says, is to painting what plot
is to the novel, or thesis to an argument, namely, the abstract plan
of a total assemblage of elements.

It is important to distinguish abstract pattern from everything
else in painting, so long as we do not label it the form as against
the content of art. Consequently, we shall follow Barnes's usage
regarding design. And within this usage, it will be possible to say,
as Barnes does, that two distinct pictures, for example, Cézanne's
"Still Life with Gray Jug" and Titian's "Entombment," even
though their concrete elements are different, are characterized by
the same design, the same abstract pattern.[6]

Drawing is another primarily relational constituent, provided
it is taken in its largest sense. Barnes has pointed out that drawing
is more than the marking off of various color areas and the making
of boundaries of figures or objects, but is instead the *drawing out*
of all the elements. "A common mistake is that by which drawing
is considered as a matter only of line defining literal contour and
making a sharp edge or border between two adjacent objects. But
even in some of the early painters . . . drawing is a fusion of many
elements of which line is only one. When the linear motive is
dominant . . . line not only defines contours but functions as
enrichment, both by its individual expressiveness and by its relation to other lines, masses, color, etc."[7] In painting, then, the
drawing, taken in its larger sense, is the relating of line, color,
space, volume, etc., and not merely an element.

In its narrower sense, as the creation of representational figures
or objects, drawings are no longer beholden to the sciences of
physics or anatomy. Being accurate to the human figure or to
natural objects is no criterion at all. Distortion in drawing is as
defensible, on plastic-expressive grounds, as spatial and color distortion. In Matisse's "Dancers," for example, there is complete
distortion of the dancing figures but, throughout, the distortions
serve to sustain certain rhythmic effects.

Historically, and in much of modern aesthetics (Fry, for example), *composition* has been construed as the organization of
masses. As such it has been interpreted by many to be identical
with plastic form. Balance, proportion, measure, in this context,
are its synonyms. But again, for purposes of clarity, it would be better to limit the term to something more specific in painting. Barnes
has suggested, with a great deal of cogency, that it should refer
to space organization and not to the totality of form.[8] As space organization, it is to painting what staging is to the drama. It is the
arrangement of the masses in pictorial space; consequently, it is
subordinate to design, and, of course, merely a part of the total
significant form, not synonymous with it.

Sheldon Cheney, who is regarded by many academicians in art
and the history of art as a mere popularizer, but whose sensibilities,
artistic and critical, are second to none, has suggested that the essence of form in painting is *movement*. His definition of form is
too narrow and obscure but his emphasis upon plastic mobility as
one of the factors of great art is a genuine insight.[9] Cheney does
not mean by movement the depiction or imitation of natural motion in the way that the futurist, for example, fashioned it. Rather,
it is *projected* movement within the picture, directed by a path
of vision that the artist creates. Physiologically, the eye cannot see
everything at once. The artist recognizes this and creates a path
of seeing so that the eye travels naturally over the canvas. Andrea
di Giusto's "The Agony in the Garden" is a simple example of
this.

This projected movement within the canvas gives vitality and
animation to the picture. This is its expressive contribution. All
paintings embody to some degree this plastic mobility. Some paintings succeed, but more fail because there is inadequate treatment of
the thrusts and counterthrusts that contain this movement. One
manifestation of this inadequacy is called "spilling over the
frame." Courbet's "The Young Bather" is a good example. A tension or mobility is set up between the massive figure in the front

and the entire background but the background colors and masses cannot balance the main figure. The movement within the canvas, consequently, becomes plastically unequilibrated.

This is not true in Cézanne's "Card Players," where a double axis is created between the seated left-hand figure and the curtain diagonally opposite, and between the seated right-hand figure and the standing figure that is also diagonally opposite. The tension due to the passage from one figure to the next creates a plastic mobility that vitalizes the entire picture. And what characterizes the "Card Players" prevails in all of Cézanne's work, including his so-called still lifes. Actually, in great art, *there are no still lifes*, except in the trivial sense of inorganic subject representation. Every plastic element, because it relates to the others, creates tension between all the elements — certain thrusts and counterthrusts — which serves to animate the total work of art.

Movement within the canvas can be gotten in various ways. The depiction of natural movement is one way. Brueghel's "Peasant Wedding Dance" and Matisse's "Dancers" are examples. Distortion in spacing or in drawing also exhibits this movement within the canvas, as El Greco's "Feast in the House of Simon" and Orozco's "Zapatistas" testify. Lines further function in this way, as in Van Gogh's "The Starry Night," where the zigzags create a sense of violent movement. Colors, too, embody plastic mobility, especially in the play of dominants against recessives. Finally, Seurat offers us, in his "Sur La Grande Jatte," an excellent example of the use of planes to effect movement. As subject representation, the picture is almost pure stasis; but, plastically, the lines, colors, planes, and volumes, because of the way in which they relate to each other, are as mobile as the contemporary motion picture. That is to say, in all of these cases where we speak of mobility, we do not mean that the elements themselves move, but that the elements are so constituted that they force our eye to go from one to the other of these elements; and this backward and forward action on our part serves to give to the picture, unless the elements become disequilibrated because of poor handling of the relations among the elements, a tremendous sense of plastic animation.

If our analysis of the semantics of the expressive has been correct, it follows that we cannot designate certain elements as being *representational* or possessing *meaning* and certain others as being nonrepresentational and without meaning. All the elements of painting are meaningful or representational in a strict semantical sense; they are either icons, indices or symbols.

There are many dimensions of representation or meaning in painting. First, there is mere plastic representation. Lines in painting mean lines in nature. Thus, a vertical in a picture means a vertical in the "external" (nonartistic) world. In the same way, colors mean colors; shapes mean shapes; light means light, etc. All of these elements in pictures, when they have meaning in this way to spectators, are iconic signs.

Secondly, there is subject representation or meaning. All sorts of objects, events and persons can be represented in painting. And all of these, semantically, function as icons to spectators.

Thirdly, there is expressive representation or meaning. Every plastic or subject constituent in painting is expressive, that is, means, either iconically or symbolically, some aspect of human emotional experience. Red is a transparent symbol of warmth; a crooked line, an icon of turbulence; Rouault's Christ figure, an icon of humility.

The organic theory, unlike the formalism of Bell and Fry, recognizes the contributory positive character of the subject in painting. The subject is one element among others. To the question, can it be integrated successfully? there is only an affirmative reply, just as color can be integrated successfully with line. The problem is to see the *way* in which this integration occurs. And here examples are needed. Consider, then, to begin with, one of El Greco's famous "Crucifixions" (the one in the Philadelphia Museum, for instance). Here the subject is the crucified Christ, shown in a state of suffering and anguish. The expressive power of the subject is matched by the same expressive intensity in the plastic elements, especially in the twisted, undulating lines that enclose the figure of Christ. Integration here lies in the total fusion of the expressive quality of suffering.

Compare this with the "Ascension" of Giotto. Here the subject is also Christ, but in His moment of ascension, a Christ of human tenderness and love. The simply balanced design, the enclosed space, the soft pink and blue colors all embody the same qualities of simplicity and tenderness. Expressively, the whole picture exhibits those humanitarian feelings which we associate with the philosophy of Saint Francis.

In the Rouault "Christ Mocked by Soldiers," we have once again Christ as the subject. Expressively, He embodies humility, not suffering or beatitude. The soldiers, caricatured as barbarians, rough and sadistic, contrast with the representation of Christ. Plastically, the emphasis is also upon the rough and dramatically intense. Expressively, the total work of art is the conflict between the humility of Christ and the aggressive character of the other elements. Together, they comprise an integration of disparate elements. Here is Christ, embodiment of humility, in a world full of evil and hostile force.

In all of these works there is no conflict between the spatial and the spaceless, as Fry maintained and which he offered as his chief reason for the rejection of subject representation in art. The two elements fuse and coöperate as easily as color and line since both are ultimately spaceless in that their expressiveness occupies the spaceless world of psychology.

And as for Bell's argument against subject representations, that they reduce our aesthetic reactions to ordinary sentimental ones, there is no reason to suppose that this is the case for subjects any more than it is for colors or lines. In the appreciation of all of these there need not be (as we shall show in Chapter 9) any sentimental identification with the expressive or emotional qualities in the picture.

Furthermore, an acceptance of the expressive character of art calls for a serious alteration of Bell's and Fry's theory of the nature of artistic creation. The artist does more than reveal the plastic structure of nature; his creative activity consists initially in his envisioning of reality in terms of some *expressive philosophy*. Giotto, El Greco, Rouault, Cézanne, all artists, ultimately, in their creations, communicate their emotional *Weltanschauungen*. Rouault envisions the world — at least the human one — as the conflict between brute power and humility; Cézanne as a geometrical order; El Greco as intensely melodramatic (in the way that Shakespeare would); and Giotto as secure and providential.

We may go even further in our reply to Bell and Fry, and show that in some paintings subjects are of *central* importance. Certainly this is the case with Picasso's "Guernica," which Barr has called the greatest painting of the twentieth century,[10] and which I should like to name "The Picasso Altarpiece," for it is to our period what the great altarpieces of the fourteenth, fifteenth, and sixteenth centuries were to theirs.

In the "Guernica" the subject is the brutal destructiveness of Fascism. It determines all of the other constituents of the painting. The mother and her dead child, the disintegrated warrior, the dying horse, the bombed-out women, the dead cock, the bull, almost intact, surveying the whole carnage, the gray and black colors, and the utilization of Cubistic techniques combine to form a total organic offering of the violent brutality that is Fascism.

The "Guernica" is sometimes referred to as "propaganda" art. But propaganda art is, after all, only art in which subject is uppermost. And in this sense, religious art is propaganda art, too.

Sometimes propaganda art is good art; sometimes, bad. When it is good, it is so because the expressiveness of the subject is intensified (by contrast or reiteration) by the expressiveness of the other elements. When it is bad, it is because the other elements act as mere accessories of the subject and not as contributing factors.

Besides the "Guernica" there is a great deal of excellent contemporary art in which social and political themes or subjects are represented. The Mexican group, consisting of (the early) Rivera, Orozco, and Siqueiros, have provided us, especially in their murals, with the best examples of this kind of art.

In the whole of this "revolutionary" art, where the subject is the class struggle in its various manifestations and its attendant expressive qualities of violence and suffering, there is present the intensification of this violence and suffering in the treatment of the plastic elements.

Further, in the "Guernica," and in all of the new revolutionary art, the *ideational*, in the sense that the Marxists and Véron conceive it, is integrated as successfully as any of the other elements within the total work of art. Ideas, like subjects, may also contribute to a work of art.

The major problem in the whole general question of the meaning of art has to do with the meaning of abstract art. In painting, this problem has become especially acute during the last quarter of a century in the rise of so-called "abstract painting." The prevalent view regarding this art is that, because it is nonrepresentational, it is nonmeaningful. Cubism, the Nonobjectivism of Kandinsky, and the later work of Mondrian are usually specified in this connection. Let us examine briefly this interpretation of the meaning of abstract painting and try to point the way to a sounder conception.

First, Cubism. Cubism, of course, is a variegated movement and much has been written about it. The theoretical origins are ascribed to Cézanne's remark to Emile Bernard that "you must see in nature the cylinder, the sphere, and the cone." Both Picasso and Braque took seriously Cézanne's invitation to geometrize nature and, in a series of paintings beginning around 1906, exploited Cézanne's notion. Matisse coined the term, "Cubism," to serve as a derisive one, when he referred to their works as "les petits cubes."

Cubism, as we comprehend it in its historical perspective, is based upon two ideas, one plastic and the other perceptual, although the two are finally merged. The plastic idea is that all natural or imaginary objects can be broken up into planes which may then be reorganized into more expressive wholes. The perceptual idea is that we see objects not from one perspective, but from many, some of which are gotten from memory and others from anticipation. All of these, or as many as the artist can integrate successfully, according to his plastic vision, are exhibited as one simultaneous perception. Cubism, then, is the attempt to embody or communicate the way reality (or rather, parts of it) look and feel to the artist. Specifically, and here it distinguishes itself from other Post-Impressionist movements, it exhibits this expressive-perceptual experience by means of the exploitation of planes for plastic and visual reasons. This is the central theme of Cubism.

Two examples of the perceptual side of Cubism are Picasso's "Portrait of a Lady" and "Girl Before a Mirror," both of which represent the simultaneity of different perceptions of the same person. His "Guitar and Violin" and "Three Musicians" exemplify primarily the plastic side of Cubism. In the first, the subject — the guitar and violin — is dissolved into planes or, more ultimately, into lines and colors and their expressive properties. In the second, the subject is kept in view but is reorganized visually and plastically.

Now, if these four are characteristic samples of Cubism, we may generalize from them in order to point out that much of Cubism is representational even in the old-fashioned sense of having a subject, even though the subject is not the important element in the painting. What is important, from the point of view of representation, is the expressive meaning of the whole work. In the "Portrait of a Lady," the colors combine with the gestures to represent a satirical version of prettiness and the general chi-chi quality of so much of human experience. "The Three Musicians," with its variegations of colors from bright red-yellow to subdued brown-black and its subject, represents a light, slightly sentimental, jazz mood. In "Guitar and Violin," we approach pure expressiveness, that is, expressiveness that resides in the plastic alone, with little or no reliance upon the subject. In this painting the title is misleading, for it makes us anticipate the sentimental, wistful, and slightly melancholy, whereas actually the picture is somber, ascetic, very strong, and angular, broken only occasionally by soft lines. What is being represented here in our first real approach to abstract art is certain somber and ascetic qualities of human experience. This is its meaning on a combined iconic and transparently symbolic level.

There is no pure abstract art in any of the four Picasso examples. But we do find it in the "Compositions" [11] of the leading Nonobjectivist, Kandinsky, and in the later work of Mondrian. Consider, first, Kandinsky's "Light Form" (which is in the Nonobjective Museum in New York). Our first reaction to this painting, after we have looked at the colors and lines without being able to find any recognizable representations of objects, is to ask, What does it mean?

One answer, suggested by the aesthetics of Bergson and enunciated by the artist himself, is that the whole picture means cosmic order or spiritual harmony. Nature, so the claim goes, has surface meanings — the realm of everyday objects — which are at most practical, useful meanings but never metaphysically true, and inner meanings that are grasped only by artistic and philosophic intuition. These inner meanings add up to cosmic order.

There are difficulties in this interpretation, both in its ontological assertions and in its semantics; these have been enumerated by the many critics of Bergson (Russell, for example), and are applicable to Kandinsky's theory as well. The main difficulty, so far as the problem of meaning is concerned, is that the theory really tells us nothing about the meaning of a work of art since the category of cosmic order or spiritual harmony is so general and vague that anything in art, even a work whose constituents are completely different from the original Kandinsky, can be said to mean exactly what the original means.

It is because of this difficulty that other interpretations have been suggested. One such interpretation is that the picture means nothing but is an arabesque of pure line and color. It is to painting what a Bach fugue is to music, something absolute and autonomous. There is no meaning in the picture because there is no subject and hence no representation, and without representation there can be no meaning. This interpretation, plausible as it may seem, breaks down on purely semantical grounds, since meaning is not solely a function of subject representation or even of iconic significance, but of expressive representation as well.

The theory I should like to propose of the meaning of Kandinsky's "Light Form" is that it means, in a combined iconic and transparently symbolic way, certain characteristics of human experience, even though it would be hard to enumerate these characteristics in our ordinary, quite inadequate, English language. Specifically, because of the warm colors, the soft, mellifluous lines, the gentle rhythms, and the delicately charged volumes, all of which we Western observers interpret as a total sign (partly iconic, e.g., the gentle rhythms; partly transparently symbolic, e.g., the warm colors) of the lyrical in human experience, we may say that the picture means to Western observers the quality of the lyrical in human experience. If the picture means anything else to us, as it most certainly can, it functions as an opaque symbol, and must be comprehended in that capacity.

Kandinsky's so-called nonrepresentational, abstract art is meaningful in a sound semantical sense; it does function as representational art, even though it possesses no subject. And this is what is characteristic of abstract art: *It is art without subject; not art without meaning.*

What is true of Kandinsky also applies to Mondrian's abstractions, the artist's protests notwithstanding.[12] Mondrian, in a severe attempt to destroy representational art, and to reëstablish a pure

Bach-like classicism, produced a number of paintings in his later life which, for him at any rate, were totally without representation or meaning. One of these is the popular "Composition in Black, White, and Red."

The painting is a series of rigid vertical and horizontal black lines on a white background, with a red bar on the extreme bottom of the picture. Although there is configuration here, there is no subject. But there *is* meaning and representation, even without any appeal to opaque symbolic meaning. The red bar gives Mondrian's show away, for it constitutes a dramatically intense element functioning in a rather subdued complex of black and white.

There is iconic meaning in the picture in that the rigid vertical and horizontal lines mean rigid vertical and horizontal lines in nature; there is iconically expressive meaning in that the lines are like rigidity in human experience; there is transparently symbolic meaning in that the red color means — and in this context especially — something very dramatic and assertive, in contrast with the other constituents. And, taken in its totality, the painting means, in a nonopaque way, the contrast between the restrained and the animated qualities in human experience. Perhaps it is true that Mondrian is like Bach, but only because Bach could also offer passion in the midst of fugal abstractions!

No analysis of the problem of meaning in painting can be complete without some discussion of the nature of so-called "symbolic art." Now, in strict semantical terms, symbolic art would be any art in which certain constituents function as signs of certain things to artists and spectators, where there is no likeness between the signs and the things meant but instead a fixed association, the way there is between the color red and the word "red." But this is not the only way that the term has been used in discussions of art.

Consider the "symbol" of the dove in Christian art. The dove, outside the realm of art, is a bird that possesses, among its various characteristics, the qualities of whiteness and gentleness. Whiteness is a transparent symbol of purity in our Western culture; and gentleness, an iconic particular sign of the universal, gentleness. Purity and gentleness are like certain salient characteristics of the Holy Ghost. Because of this resemblance, semantically speaking, the dove becomes a "symbol" of the Holy Ghost. All of this occurs outside of art, in the realm of Christian imagery. The dove is interpreted not only as an icon of other doves or of other birds but, more importantly, as a representation of the Holy Ghost.

In Christian art, the dove has one and only one meaning, the Holy Ghost. It does not even mean dove, for when we see it represented in a painting, it is as if the Holy Ghost were being represented. Thus, the dove, in Christian art, is not a symbol, in the strictly technical semantical sense, but an icon of the Holy Ghost, being like it, although to a lesser degree, in the way that an artificial red apple in a store window is iconic with *any* of the real fruits inside the store. It is odd, I think, that what we have traditionally called a "symbol" in Christian art should turn out to be an icon instead. Of course, it is not iconic in the way that a self-portrait of Rembrandt is, but it is nevertheless, strictly and semantically speaking, an icon.

Then there is the "fish symbol," which represents Christ in Christian art. But the fish means Christ not because it resembles Him, rather because of certain ingeniously concocted philological associations that were conceived by the early Christians in their attempt to communicate certain of their meanings without divulging them to the hostile Romans. "Fish" is *ichthys* in Greek. The Greek letters comprise the first letters of the words in the phrase, "Jesus Christ, Son of God, the Saviour." This association enables the representation of a fish to function as a Christ "symbol" in Christian art. Semantically, the fish is a symbol of Christ in the way that the word "fish" is a symbol of actual fish. It is a visual sign that is fixed in its meaning by historically developed conventional usage.

There is a third kind of "symbol" in Christian art, which further complicates the whole problem. In Roger Van der Weyden's

"Adoration of the Magi," which represents the birth scene of
Jesus, there is also represented, in the form of a traditional crucifix,
located in the upper center of the picture, the death of Christ.
This is indeed a fascinating juxtaposition of elements, the simultaneous presentation of the birth and death of Christ. Here the
artist obviously is using the crucifix as an *indexical* sign. That is,
the crucifix points to the direction of the life of the Child. It is
impossible to exaggerate the dramatic impact of this combination
of elements. In its ability to intensify all of the elements of the
painting, it functions in the way that Agamemnon's act of stepping
on the purple carpet reserved only for the gods in the Aeschylus
trilogy does, to *indicate* the coming occurrence of a powerful
event with which the spectator is already familiar.

Since the disintegration of the "Christian Myth," as it is now
called, Western art has produced innumerable new myths or
"symbolisms." Contemporary art is almost lost in a vast sea of
"symbolism." The work of Klee, Chagall, Dali, Ernst, etc., etc.,
is full of conflicting, sometimes incomprehensible, "symbols"; and
the problem arises of their proper role in artistic understanding
and appreciation. In order to deal with this welter of contemporary "symbolic" art, I shall choose one example that brings into
clear focus the various difficulties inherent in this art. The example is "The Spanish Prison," by Robert Motherwell, a young
American painter. The painting consists of a number of different
series of vertical, horizontal, and curved lines converging on a
central orbit. So far as I can make out, it is a piece of abstract art,
quite like Mondrian in its complete absence of subject. But this
is what the artist says about it:

> It consists of a dialectic between the conscious (straight lines,
> designed shapes, weighed color, abstract language) and the
> unconscious (soft lines, obscured shapes, *automatism*) resolved
> into a synthesis which differs as a whole from either. The hid-
> den Spanish prisoner must represent the anxieties of modern
> life, the intense Spanish-Indian color, splendor of any life.[13]

The question now arises, what shall we make of this interpretation? First, let us examine the semantical dimensions of the "symbols."

(1) Soft lines no more resemble the unconscious than they do the conscious. If the artist were to say that they are flabby and imprecise in the way that the unconscious is, we could counter this by pointing out that the straight line, because of its piercing, sharp quality, is as much a representation of the unconscious as is the soft line.

The same consideration prevails in the relation between the conscious and the straight lines. Consequently, these "symbols" cannot be construed as iconic. Nor are they transparently symbolic, for we do not in our ordinary modes of communication interpret soft or straight lines as meaning the unconscious or the conscious. Therefore, the most we can say is that these are opaque symbols, the meanings of which are determined by the artist, who has no interest in deriving these symbol-referent associations from a larger recognizable group of meanings.

The difference between the "fish symbol" and the "soft-line symbol," however, must not be exaggerated. To be sure, the one is transparently symbolic, and the other opaquely, but Motherwell can always argue that his "symbols" may someday become as transparent in our culture as the "fish symbol" has been in Christian culture. There is, after all, no a priori reason why a soft line cannot become a culturally fixed symbol of the unconscious.

(2) The Spanish prisoner is the supposed subject of the picture. He is hidden. Hence we have a semantical situation in which the *lack* of elements comprises a symbolic sign of a Spanish prisoner! This is indeed maddening to semanticists and spectators of art alike who feel that the artist is pulling their leg. One is reminded of the revealing Taylor cartoon in *The New Yorker* of the completely empty canvas which is interpreted by the artist as the exploitation of pure, virgin space! The most we can say of this symbol, then, is that it is completely opaque.

(3) The hidden prisoner is a "symbol" of the anxieties of modern life. With this "symbol," if we accept the second, we come to our first iconic sign, since a prisoner does resemble modern anxieties, especially in his enforced pent-up character. He is a "symbol" in the way that the dove is in Christian art.

(4) The Spanish-Indian color, as a "symbol" of the splendor of life, is a transparent symbol.

Now, before returning to the general problem of the nature of "symbolic art," it may be well to deal first with a question that constantly arises when we try to evaluate this art. How legitimate are these "symbolic" elements? One reply to this question, of course, is that they are as legitimate as any other constituent of art. Advocates of modern "symbolic art" could argue that Christian art without the element of the "symbol" would be as emasculated as Christian art without the subject. Further, if Christian "symbolism" is legitimate, there is no reason to reject non-Christian "symbolism." To repudiate it would be tantamount to pure authoritarianism in the arts; an arbitrary limitation of artistic communication. It is the artist who is the final arbiter of the *extent* of his communication; and if he attributes "symbolic" elements to his work, then it behooves us as spectators to partake of his "symbolic" intentions and see the picture in his terms.

However, even if we accept this evaluation, we may still insist upon one criterion: that the symbol be integrated with the other elements and play a contributing role. Such a criterion would rule out much of "symbolic" art in which the plastic elements are so hopelessly inadequate that no amount of "symbolic" manipulation can save it.

An alternative reply would be to repudiate the "symbolism," if it be of the opaque variety. This would mean, in the case of "The Spanish Prison," that we would reject the "symbol" of the lack of elements as meaning a Spanish prisoner. We would also reject the connection between the soft lines and the unconscious and the straight lines and the conscious. In effect, our evaluation would reduce the painting to an abstract one, whose meanings would be functions of the plastic-expressive constituents of the work of art.

If we support this alternative, we shall discard all personal, arbitrary, and attributed "symbolism." We shall make art less esoteric, but we shall also make it less profound by reducing its range of expression and communication. If we do not adopt this alternative, we must be prepared to accept all sorts of "symbolism" in art, not only that which the artist supposedly finds in his work, but whatever *any* spectator supposedly finds in the work.

I know of no way of choosing between these two alternatives. Both have their advantages and disadvantages. In practice, however, perhaps the best way to deal with these "symbols" is to try to understand them as the artist conceived them and, if there are others that he did not consciously comprehend, as any of us conceives them; and then to see if they *work* with the other constituents of the work of art. If they do work, and play their contributory roles in relation to the other constituents, they are to be considered as legitimate as any of the other constituents and must be regarded as a factor in our understanding of art.

We still have before us the problem of the nature of "symbolic art." Our survey of four rather different examples of "symbolic art" has disclosed, I think, that it will not do to say that this art is one in which there are symbols in the technical semantical sense since these are signs which mean their referents only by fixed association with them, and not by being like them or by pointing to them. Traditional "symbols," that is to say, are not only semantical symbols but indices or icons as well.

Perhaps a better answer is that "symbolic art" is simply that art in which there are certain constituents — they may be subjects, themes, plastic elements, like certain colors or lines, or even the omission of elements, if we wish to give an adequate account of paintings like "The Spanish Prison" — which become fixed in their *very definite meanings* by the artist's or spectator's interpretations of these constituents. This theory provides for a generalized unity of interpretation of the "symbols" of the dove, the fish, the crucifix, soft lines, the Spanish prisoner, and the Spanish-Indian color. It also presents us with a fourth kind of meaning in art, a "symbolic" one; the other three being, it will be recalled, plastic meaning, subject meaning and expressive meaning.

5

THE ARTS: POETRY

Introduction

Poetry is also an organic complex of expressive elements. These include words, images, allusions, metrics, subjects, metaphors, and themes. In this chapter, rather than discuss these elements seriatim, as we did with the elements of painting, we shall present an aesthetic analysis of a single poem in order to examine further the claims of the organic theory.

Our poem is "The Love Song of J. Alfred Prufrock," by T. S. Eliot. It is our choice for at least two reasons. In the first place, it is a so-called "modern" poem, quite difficult to understand, "symbolic," even esoteric, according to many of its readers.

Few people in our society read poetry of this sort. In fact, few people read poetry of any sort any more. And this is not because of any general decline of interest in art as such, since more people than ever before listen to music and look at pictures. It is difficult to ascertain the causes of the decline of interest in poetry. Some critics, like Max Eastman, place the blame on the modern poet for instigating and furthering a "cult of unintelligibility." T. S. Eliot, they contend, is such a poet; and his "Prufrock," an example of unintelligibility. Consequently, one thing we shall try to do in our examination of "Prufrock" is to evaluate this criticism of modern poetry.

Secondly, so far as I know, there is no extended, detailed analysis of the poem; and since, in the opinion of many critics, it is one of the great poems of the twentieth century, it may not be amiss to offer such an analysis, regardless of the aesthetic conclusions we draw from it.

In our analysis or *reading* of the poem, we shall exclude a number of things. First, we shall not be concerned with the poem as a biographical datum relating to the poet's life. The aesthetic analysis will be carried through without any attempt to derive from it any evidence regarding Eliot's attitudes during the period in which he wrote the poem. Furthermore, we shall raise no questions of orthodoxy concerning the implied religious views of the poem. Neither shall we read the poem in a political or sociological way, inquiring into the conservatism or liberalism of the attitudes toward the upper and lower classes that are implied in the poem. Nor shall we read it philosophically, in an attempt to deal with the truth or falsity of the ultimate claims put forward by Eliot. Finally, we shall not even be concerned with the poem in a "critical" way, that is, in the sense either of placing it in the totality of Eliot's work or of relating and comparing it to the totality of the work of Eliot's contemporaries. All of these are legitimate enterprises, but they are not the same thing as an aesthetic reading (although they may grow out of it), since their primary emphasis is not upon the analysis of the various constituents of the poem as they relate to each other in an organic way. Our analysis, therefore, will be a reading in which the poem will be regarded as a self-contained system in the sense that it can be understood with no reference to biographical, religious, philosophical or social concerns.

A "Reading" of Eliot's "The Love Song of J. Alfred Prufrock"

We come, then, to the poem itself. The title, to begin with, is a rather curious one. It is paradoxical in that it juxtaposes the lyrical and the pompous, thereby initiating a kind of tension or challenge: Is this ultimately an ironic poem or one in which the contrary attitudes are reconciled? Is this a true love song? In the end we shall see that it is; that it is a kind of wooing to salvation.

The poem begins as a soliloquy or monologue in which Prufrock is meditating upon his experiences. It starts, moreover, in the middle of his soliloquy, abruptly, as the word "then" reveals. The whole first line, "Let us go then, you and I," is a kind of invitation to the dance, for Prufrock is speaking to us. We are the "you." This raises immediately the questions, *why* go with him, and *where?* Already we are tied to Prufrock.

The next few lines, but especially the simile of the second and third lines, "When the evening is spread out against the sky / Like a patient etherised upon a table"; build up, in a descriptively dramatic way, the local environment surrounding Prufrock, and relate it to his general mood and character. A vacuous, nonconvivial and dank atmosphere and locale are created. The simile itself refers to the semiconscious, half-dead, half-alive, limbo quality of Prufrock's character and environment. It is an image which thus ties up a number of things even at the very beginning of the poem: Prufrock's state, the local environment, i.e., the actual heavy character of the evening, and some sort of all-embracing negative value quality. The next few lines, mainly through their adjectives, reinforce this limbo-like quality: "half-deserted," "muttering," "restless" are all qualifications of the local environment, which relate to the etherized character of the evening and of Prufrock. The streets are neither deserted nor full; the retreats are neither silent nor noisy; the nights offer neither sleep nor wakefulness. Everything is like the etherized patient, half-alive, half-dead.

The "Streets that follow like a tedious argument / Of insidious intent" are like Prufrock and ourselves, the you and I: wandering aimlessly. Our wanderings, however, do not lead nowhere but rather to "an overwhelming question." And yet we do not ask,

"What is it?" Instead we "make our visit." That is, we do not raise the question of the meaning and purpose of our experiences, but we think of something else.

Not raising the question at this juncture functions not only to reveal Prufrock's and our own indecisiveness, but in a technically dramatic way, to keep the poem going. To answer the question now would be to end the poem!

The next two lines, "In the room the women come and go / Talking of Michelangelo," are transitional in nature, but they also constitute an integral part of any soliloquy, in that the latter is an association of ideas.[1] We are introduced to another facet of Prufrock's experiences which conveys, in a satirical way, his impression of the women he knows from the many soirées he has attended with them.

The next stanza reinforces this general mood, emphasizing the sultry, heavy, semiconscious character of Prufrock's reality. It has another function, too, which occurs in the first line, "The yellow fog that rubs its back upon the window-panes." This line is slightly varied in the next stanza and is tied up with the notion of time, which becomes the basic idea of the third stanza; thus, through the first line of the second stanza, all three stanzas are brought together.

Time is an important concept in "Prufrock." There are recognized two kinds of time, real and false. False time comprises those experiences that get nowhere, like the aimless streets. This is the time of the third stanza, a time that allows of everything but actually nothing since all the events turn back on themselves. This is the time that includes all the etherized experiences like preparing a face to meet the faces that we meet; creating and murdering; and all of our indecisions, visions, and revisions.

The contrast between murder and creation is interesting here. In the realm of limbo, which embraces our purposeless experiences, these are one and the same, since both are vacuous and insignificant.

"To prepare a face to meet the faces that you meet" has also a deeper significance than merely living falsely. It suggests the wearing of a mask, a death mask, such as would characterize the faces of those who would ordinarily be taken to be alive, but who are not because they fulfill no function or purpose in their lives. The image of a prepared face, thus, relates directly to the image of the etherized patient, and each image enhances the dramatic value of the other.

The third stanza is not entirely negative. In fact one must not interpret it in terms of the negative as against the positive, for this is too sharp a dichotomy. The poem as a whole is not the conflict between the true and the false, the alive and the dead. Eliot rejects this dualism and asserts rather an *immanence* theory in which the real or true is already present in the false, and the significant already part of the insignificant, waiting to be perceived by all of us. Just as the streets *do* lead to an overwhelming question, so the insignificant in human experience does embody as one of its dimensions the significant.[2]

And real time, which is time that encompasses significant experiences, those that have purpose and direction, is immanent in false time, the time that returns unto itself. This is the meaning of the lines, "And time for all the works and days of hands / That lift and drop a question on your plate." All experiences, from creation to murder (death), contain as their ultimate dimension the overwhelming question.

Prufrock turns next to the events of the soirée. The fourth stanza begins with the challenge of real time. "And indeed there will be time / To wonder, 'Do I dare?' and, 'Do I dare?' " Time includes the asking of big questions, especially, do I dare to raise the overwhelming question itself — to rise from the etherized table?

But real time is rejected by Prufrock and he sinks back into false time to reflect upon his acquaintances of the soirée. His first reflection is of their thoughts about his hair growing thin. Prufrock wonders if he ought to *dare* (to disturb their universe) while they wonder about his *hair*. The most profound as against the most trivial — this is the difference between these kinds of questions. The people who come and go, talking of Michelangelo, are those who think of Prufrock only as outer appearance, as a prepared face. They perceive him as one etherized patient sees another. Their observations of him, as disclosed by Prufrock's meditations, reveal his own awareness of his specifically prepared face and outer appearance, with its conventional, impeccable character: "My morning coat, my collar mounting firmly to the chin / My necktie rich and modest, but asserted by a simple pin."

Shall Prufrock remove his mask, rise from the etherized table, disturb their universe? No, instead he (and we, too) will make our visit, that is, sustain our trivialities.

The next four stanzas describe Prufrock's sessions with the women of the soirée. He has shared many experiences with them; ". . . evenings, mornings, afternoons, / I have measured out my life with coffee spoons." His life with them, as he sees it, has been ultimately a series of driblets of experiences, each dissolved into nothingness, like the sugar of the coffee spoons placed inside the cup.

These are the women whose voices are "dying with a dying fall." Voices are ordinarily signs of life, but not their voices. Theirs are articulations of the semiconscious, the half-alive, half-dead, the voices of those who are in limbo, who can say nothing because they do nothing.

"So how should I presume?" Can he ask the overwhelming question of them, these people who can perceive only the death mask, whose main concern would be in converting his question into a sadistically oriented epigram? "The eyes that fix you in a formulated phrase, / And when I am formulated, sprawling on a pin, / When I am pinned and wriggling on the wall, / Then how should I begin . . . ?" The simple tiepin of Prufrock becomes the pin that sticks him to the wall. How ridiculous it would be to disturb them, "To spit out all the butt-ends of my days and ways," the driblets that are his life.

There are also the sexual experiences that prevent his asking the question: "Is it perfume from a dress / That makes me so digress?" Are not these experiences real, purposeful, creative? Can Prufrock say to his women that he has seen the spiritual poverty "Of lonely men in shirtsleeves, leaning out of windows?" Can he introduce a questioning element in their lives?

Then, in the midst of these meditations, Prufrock offers his evaluation and rejection of this way of life, in the first positive assertion of the poem: "I should have been a pair of ragged claws / Scuttling across the floors of silent seas." As a crab in the sea, at least he would be alive and with purpose; a creature with a role to play, even if only a creature on one of the lowest levels of biological existence.

But Prufrock retreats quickly and returns to the soirée — where everything is peaceful. Or is it? "It malingers." It is a false peace, pregnant with turbulence (and the overwhelming question). Shall Prufrock try again, "to force the moment to its crisis?" Shall he tell them that he has seen the Truth? But again they will treat him with ridicule; even look upon him in the way that Salome, at the court (soirée) of Herod, laughed at the decapitated head of John the Baptist, except that the Salomes of Prufrock's soirées will laugh harder because Prufrock's head is slightly bald!

Once more fear and indecision stop him. "I am no prophet — and here's no great matter." False time sucks into its vacuum the moment of his greatness. Prufrock sees himself at the occurrence of his death being greeted by the figure of Death, who regards him as a human driblet. "And I have seen the eternal Footman hold my coat, and snicker."

Prufrock tries again to resolve his indecisiveness, to capture the Significant. Should he squeeze "the universe into a ball / To roll it toward some overwhelming question, / To say: 'I am Lazarus, come from the dead, / Come back to tell you all, I shall tell you all.' " Again the answer is no; there will be no raising of the question.

The next stanza further complicates Prufrock's problem, for it introduces a note of genuine doubt of the totally insignificant character of the soirée existence. His meditations and evaluations become nebulous, shadowy and abstract, "as if a magic lantern threw the nerves in patterns on a screen." There are certain moments of real beauty in this limbo-life: "The sunsets and the dooryards and the sprinkled streets, / . . . The novels . . . the teacups . . . the skirts that trail along the floor — / And this, and so much more." It is these reflections that make an easy decision so difficult.

In this stanza the poem rises to great heights by bringing in this complexity of attitudes toward human experience. A lesser poet than Eliot would have been satisfied with painting the limbo-life in total black; but not Eliot, who employs other, less somber, and even lyrical colors.

The next stanza is the resolution of Prufrock's conflict. Hamlet's problem was to be or not to be. But this is not Prufrock's. His problem is rather whether to raise the question (of being or not being) or not to raise the question. Shall he rise from the table or remain there as the etherized patient? Shall he cease his aimless wanderings and reach the overwhelming question? Shall he transcend cyclical, hence nonexistent, time and enter into the flow of real time?

Unlike Hamlet, who finally answered his question, Prufrock does not. This is his decision: Not to raise the question, to remain in limbo.

> No! I am not Prince Hamlet, nor was meant to be;
> Am an attendant lord, one that will do
> To swell a progress, start a scene or two,
> Advise the prince; no doubt, an easy tool,
> Deferential, glad to be of use,
> Politic, cautious, and meticulous;

> Full of high sentence, but a bit obtuse;
> At times, indeed, almost ridiculous —
> Almost, at times, the Fool.

Prufrock, then, does not question the universe, but raises little (driblet) questions, which serve to augment his trivial drama of life. Hamlet, in this stanza and context, becomes both the total play and the hero of the play; and Prufrock sees himself not as the hero but as a Rosencrantz or Guildenstern, who are like the formulated phrases wriggling on the wall; or he even sees himself as the Fool who amuses the court in the manner in which he now amuses the soirée crowd.

The meditations continue. Prufrock imagines himself as becoming more meticulous, more superficial, more prepared in his outer face, more masked, more trivial. "I grow old . . . I grow old . . . / I shall wear the bottoms of my trousers rolled. / Shall I part my hair behind? Do I dare to eat a peach? / I shall wear white flannel trousers, and walk upon the beach." No longer does Prufrock dare disturb the universe; but now he does not even dare to indulge in the slightest gaucherie.

All of this depiction of trivia is followed by a series of crescendo-like assertions, beginning with: "I have heard the mermaids singing, each to each." Who are the mermaids? In the first place, they are of the sea; and when we tie this up with the crab and the last line of the poem, they can be construed as symbols of that which is alive, active, and purposeful. Further, they are feminine, hence to be compared with the desiccated women of the soirée. Prufrock conceives them in all their brilliant, vibrant beauty:

> I have seen them riding seaward on the waves
> Combing the white hair of the waves blown back
> When the wind blows the water white and black.

But they will not sing to him, he realizes. That is, he recognizes that it is not his decision to follow that which is directed to the life of action and purpose.

The final stanza is the most difficult in the poem:

> We have lingered in the chambers of the sea
> By sea-girls wreathed with seaweed red and brown
> Till human voices wake us, and we drown.

One may interpret this stanza as follows: All of us, who are like Prufrock, have remained indecisive ("lingered") in the midst of the possibilities of salvation ("sea-girls"); and we will continue in our indecisiveness, our limbo existence, our etherized state, until the voices of the soirée crowd make us die. On this reading, the poem ends in complete pessimism, and all hope of salvation is dissolved into the waters of death.

But such a reading, plausible as it may seem, simply does not do justice to the stanza and to the rest of the poem. It leaves out and distorts too much; it allows too many of the tensions of the whole poem to remain unresolved. Consequently, a more inclusive reading is called for:

We etherized patients, we who exist in a state of doing nothing, have been near the sources of salvation, that is, the life of significance; we will remain in our etherized state until voices that are *truly* alive — voices like that of Lazarus or of the mermaids singing — wake us and we cease our state of mere physical existence, which is a kind of spiritual nonbeing, and enter into real life.

In justification of this interpretation, consider the following: Lingering in the chambers of the sea is organically tied to the questions that are dropped on our plate and the streets that lead to an overwhelming question. The possibilities of salvation, of transcending limbo, have been close at hand; we have lingered in them, next to the mermaids with all of their beauty and purpose. Further, there is the meaning of the human voices that wake us. Our first thought is that these are the voices of the women of the soirée. But this cannot be so, since their voices are *dying* voices, not efficacious at all. The voices of the soirée women can neither say nor do anything; therefore, they cannot wake us, for to wake is to make alive. "Human," it must be seen, is used with paradoxical intent. The really human voices, the poem is saying, do not belong to those who are in limbo, on the etherized table, but to those that play a creative role, like John the Baptist, Lazarus, and the mermaids. Finally, on this reading, "we drown" means that we cast off our limbo existence, in a kind of baptismal way, and enter into the life of significance and salvation. Such a reading, I think, is much richer than the first, and brings together the many strands of the poem.

Further Analysis of the Poem

This concludes our detailed reading of the poem. This reading is the *sine qua non* of an aesthetic analysis. The question now arises, are these extended interpretations part of the poem or a substitute for it? They are not the latter since the poem certainly includes the written sentences and their meanings, which cannot be said in any other way. But these interpretations are part of the poem's *total* communication; they comprise the depth meanings[3] of the poem, that is, all of those meanings that are suggested by the printed meanings. For example, the poem says "I have measured out my life with coffee spoons"; but this implies *within* the poem, "My life has been trivial," which is not part of the written material, but is nevertheless part of the poem. It will not do to claim, as Cleanth Brooks has done, that these are mere scaffoldings which lead us to the poem but are never within it.[4] A poem is always much richer than its *printed* meanings.

Let us continue our aesthetic analysis of the poem. Ultimately, of course, this poem, or any poem, is constituted of words, or rather word sounds. There is much that can be said about the aesthetics of word sounds. Aestheticians have recognized that these word sounds can have specific meanings. But it happens that many words are ambiguous, that is, have a number of specific meanings. Science tries to reduce this ambiguity, poetry to exploit it. Poetry is based upon ambiguity, or — a better term — plurisignation,[5] since simile and metaphor grow out of it. "Coffee spoon," for example, means a measuring instrument, quite small in relation to a tablespoon. Also, it means something that holds only driblets. Both of these connotations are exploited by Eliot in "Prufrock."

Word sounds function in an expressive way in poetry. Consider the expressive quality of Eliot's language in "Prufrock." "Deserted streets," "etherised patient," "muttering retreats," "cheap hotels," "sawdust restaurants," "yellow fog," "pools," "drains," "soot," "butt-ends," are all hard-bitten, brittle, everyday, "unpoetic" word sounds. Yet in relation to the realistic tone of the poem, they are poetic; and they comprise one constituent which relates to the others that make up the poem.

With words and their meanings, Eliot builds up the other elements of his poem. The first of these are the images. Consider the image of the women coming and going, talking of Michelangelo. It is a description of the desiccated women of the soirée; and it relates to the image of the etherized patient, which image is the controlling one of the poem. The image of Prufrock, as he describes himself, unruffled in his outer appearance but deeply troubled inwardly, is also related to the other elements of the poem. So, too, with the image of the mermaids, in all their vibrancy and power, which functions as a contrast to the essentially lifeless and insignificant character of the soirée women.

Certain contrasts are developed in the poem which are also organically contributing elements. The tedious argument as against the overwhelming question; the dare versus the hair; the cakes and ices contrasting with the forcing of the moment to its crisis; and the walking on the beach in opposition to the hearing of the mermaids — each of these is intrinsically expressive but, considered in its relations to the other elements, it takes on certain *intensifying qualities* that enhance it and, consequently, the entire poem.

The paradoxes are also organic elements. There is the paradox of a time in which there are indecisions, revisions, and decisions which a minute will reverse, that is, of a time that is really static. Also there is the paradox of an existence in which murder and creation are ultimately identical. A third paradox concerns the women of the soirée whose voices are dying in contrast to the voices of the mermaids that can wake us.

Then there is the element of drama in the poem. The whole technique of the association of ideas is intrinsically dramatic. "Shall I raise the question?" "I shall." "No, I shall not." Climaxes and anticlimaxes, denouement, and final resolution, with its epilogue.

There are also allusions in the poem: to John the Baptist, to Death, to Lazarus, to Hamlet, to Rosencrantz and Guildenstern. All of these play their roles in relation to the other constituents, including Prufrock's character and the fact that he would know these allusions readily, being a person of education. For the comprehension of these allusions we need no private, opaquely symbolic key. General education discloses their meanings in the way that it reveals the meaning of the coffee spoon to any intelligent reader in the Western world.

This brings us to the "symbols" of the poem. Both the etherized patient and the prepared face symbolize the life that is really limbo, the state of being that is mere mechanism, without meaning or purpose; a life that is really spiritual death. Both symbolize what we may call the world of *psychic surface*. Semantically, both are more transparent than opaque symbols. That is to say, a careful reading *of the poem* discloses the symbolic meaning of etherized patient and prepared face. One does not need an external set of references to unravel their meanings.

The coffee spoons, of course, symbolize the ephemeral, trivial, transient character of limbo experiences. The dying voices symbolize the state of being which is a kind of nothingness. The women coming and going symbolize the same world of psychic surface.

Prufrock, himself, is a symbol of the conflict between the life of meaning and significance and the life of mere mechanism. *Hamlet*, as a play, symbolizes the realm of total experience, the drama of life as Prufrock sees it. Hamlet, the individual hero, symbolizes the ultimate conflict of coming to a decision, except that his is more on a purely physical level than on the psychological one. The crab is a symbol of real life even on the lowest sort of level; Lazarus, a symbol of real life even in physical death; so, too, with John the Baptist; and the mermaids are a symbol of real life even in myth. That is, even as mythical creatures, they are more real than the inhabitants of limbo. Finally, the last act of drowning is a symbol of the giving up of the physical and insignificantly psychical life for salvation; or, more specifically, it symbolizes the giving up of a life that is really a kind of death in the sense of being nothingness for a death (the casting off of the purposeless existence) which is the first stage of true life or salvation.

This brings us to metaphor. No poem illustrates better than this one the modern view, suggested by Cleanth Brooks, that a poem is not a theme embroidered by metaphor, but the *unfolding of metaphor*.[6] The whole of "Prufrock," we may say, is the unfolding of a tremendous double metaphor: life and death, on a conventional level, in which they have no meaning or significance, are like etherized patients, endless streets, static time, and dying voices; and life and death, on their true level, in which they are directed toward salvation, are like the crab, Lazarus, John the Baptist, and the mermaids singing.

The idea or referent of the poem is the briefest, most abstract condensation of the metaphor: There are two kinds of life and two kinds of death; one, the conventional, is sterile and vacuous; the other, the religious, is fertile, truly human, significant.

This theme or Idea is *in* the poem, as a depth meaning; but it would be wrong to say with Housman that the poem is this theme embroidered by metaphor. The poem *is* the metaphor.

This theme also exists outside of the poem as the theme of

many different poems. In fact, it is one of Eliot's favorite themes, as his other poems show.

What, finally, is the subject of the poem? It is that element which epitomizes the Idea or theme, which represents it, semantically speaking. And, of course, it is Prufrock himself who is the subject for he is the epitome of the conflict between the two ways of life and death.

To sum up: Every word, image, contrast, paradox, allusion, symbol, etc., is what it is because of its intrinsic character plus its contextual character. The etherized patient, for example, has his own meaning in the poem, independently of the other elements; but in relation to the endless streets, Lazarus, the women talking of Michelangelo, and so on, it takes on characteristics that enlarge, modify and intensify its poetic nature.

6

THE ARTS: MUSIC

Introduction

Music is also the organic integration of constituents. These constituents are, fundamentally, the tone and the lack of tone, or silence. There may be some dispute about silence being an element of the art of music; but compositions like Beethoven's last quartet, especially the slow movement, are inexplicable without bringing in this element. Silence in music may be compared to empty space in painting.

By means of tones and pure silence, the elements of the chord, harmony, melody, and rhythm are created. Further, because music is an interpretative art, functioning through certain instruments, these instruments must be taken as constituting one element among others. And all of these elements are characterized by certain expressive properties.

In this chapter I shall deal with these elements only briefly, since there are many excellent discussions of them in contemporary treatises on music. Instead I wish to concentrate upon the basic question of musical aesthetics today: Does music mean anything?

Remarks on the Elements of Music and Their Expressive Qualities

Tones differ among themselves in pitch, color, intensity, quality, and length. These properties are to tones what hue, saturation, and brilliance are to color in painting. A succession of tones, involving certain rhythmic and pitch factors, produces melody, one of the basic constituents of music. Melody is tonal organization, not a mere succession of tones. It is a kind of advancing pitch curve, in which there is present rhythmic organization.

Harmony is often regarded as tone simultaneity and contrasted with melody, which is tone progression. But this definition will not do. It is chords that constitute tone simultaneity, not harmony which, like melody, involves succession of horizontal advance. Harmony, it is more accurate to say, is a succession of chords.

Rhythm, in music, has to do with the grouping of certain tones according to accent and stress. All activity, in nature or in music, involves periodic grouping, at least so far as human response to this activity is concerned; and no flow or progression is a continuum, rhythmically speaking, but is broken up into groupings by human response. The recurrence of accent and stress upon one or another of the elements in the groupings constitutes rhythm.

In the realm of instruments, there is the percussion group, the wind, string, and brass groups, and the human voice. Now, each of these elements has its own expressive quality. Even a single tone, because of its specific pitch, its loudness or softness, its brilliance or dullness, has an expressive quality.

Melodies most certainly have their attendant expressive qualities. One need only compare a typical melody of Mozart's, characterized by its restraint and serenity, with one of Tchaikovsky's, with its turbulent, overpassioned character, to comprehend the expressive dimension of melody.

The restlessness of the dissonant as against the relative stability of the consonant; the hollow, flat character of a fifth or the rich, lively character of a major third; and the power of a chordal progression such as we find in the exposition of the *Eroica*, exemplify the expressive qualities of chords and harmony.

In the realm of instruments, Western listeners have a rather uniform characterization of the oboe, for example, as embodying

the expressiveness of the pastoral; or of the piccolo as being somewhat shrill and tangy in quality; or of the cello as having a certain
smooth, velvety quality; or, finally, of the bassoon as being a little
rough in its expressive appeal.

Finally, rhythm also possesses certain expressive qualities, which
are specified by the names we apply to the different rhythmic oc-
currences in music as they relate to tempo: the largo (slow) or
the adagio (lingering) as against the allegro (animated) or presto
(vivacious), for example.

The Problem of the Meaning of Music

Traditionally, the question, "Does music mean anything?" has
been identified with the question, "Is music a language?" Both
affirmative and negative answers to these questions, it is important
to note, have been based upon the same assumptions as to the
nature of a language and the meaning of meaning. Musical aestheticians who have argued that music does not mean anything
have done so primarily because they have seen in music no similarity to ordinary languages like French or German or English.
Their opponents have countered their arguments by pointing out
that music can function like ordinary languages if certain conven-
tions, like program notes, are adopted. But in neither of these two
groups has there been any systematic analysis of either the nature
of a language or the meaning of meaning. Nor has there been any
pronounced recognition that without such analyses the problem
of the meaning of music is insoluble.

In order to unravel the traditional answers to our problem and,
if we can, to secure a sounder one for ourselves, let us begin by
inquiring into the nature of language.

There is at the present time not as much unanimity about the
nature of language as would be desirable; but most semioticians
agree that language is in its essence a system of signs that functions
as the basic instrument for communication. Whatever else lan-

guage may be, one of its salient characteristics is its ability to make communication possible.

Some semioticians regard the essence of communication to be the *issuing forth of propositions*. That is, language is taken to be communication in which propositions are affirmed (or denied). On this view, music would be accepted as a language if it could be used to assert or deny some *proposition* or other.

But this seems to be an unnecessarily narrow view, for there are modes of communication in which nothing is asserted (or denied); that is, no *claim* is made; rather, something is exhibited or presented. A map, for example, asserts (or denies) nothing, but it may communicate something to someone. Consequently, we must distinguish between at least two modes of communication: one in which something *means* something else to someone and the other in which a proposition is *asserted* (or denied) by someone to someone else. The first involves only meaning; the second, meaning and assertion.

Our general problem can now be stated: Is music a language in the sense of meaning anything, not in the sense of asserting anything? To answer this question we need first a criterion of meaning. Our criterion will be that which is advocated by almost all contemporary semioticians: Something x means something else y to an interpreter a if x stands for, represents, designates or denotes y to a. Therefore, music may be said to have meaning if it represents, stands for, designates, or denotes something to someone.

Historically, there have been two answers to this problem of the meaning of music, the "autonomous" and the "heteronomous." The advocates of the autonomous point of view claim that music means nothing (with the trivial exception of onomatopoetic sounds) because it does not have the capacity as a medium of communication to stand for, represent, or designate anything else. For music to have meaning, it must be a language; to be a language requires a *vocabulary* that can refer to specific things. The essence of a language lies in its words with their fixed connotations and denotations. Musical tones are not like words, therefore, music is not a language, and consequently cannot mean anything.

The essence of music, the positive side of this autonomous view maintains, is pure meaningless sounds — "arabesques of sounds," as they are sometimes called.

The heteronomous view is that music is a language of some sort and does mean something to hearers of it. There are many varieties within this group. The most extreme heteronomists are the proponents of the "programmatic" theory of the meaning of music, which has been the dominant theory since Wagner. For these aestheticians, music is a language and has meaning like any ordinary language. It can mean specific ideas, emotions, events, characters, inner psychological struggles, etc. They do not affirm that music *must* have meaning in this way, only that it can if the composer supplies his listeners with the set of specific references which are to be associated with his musical sounds. Like their "autonomous" opponents, they recognize the place of nonmeaningful music in the long history of music. They would agree that much of Mozart or Haydn, for example, is meaningless in character because the composers furnished no specific program.

It is understandable that the most severe critique of this version of the heteronomous approach has come from the autonomists, or from aestheticians who are identified with them, like Gurney and Hanslick. In the main, their refutation is based upon their claim that music is not capable of meaning specific things because it has no fixed vocabulary. They further point out that any specific interpretation which is made of the sounds is purely arbitrary in the sense that there is no causal nexus or necessary connection between the sounds and the interpretation; and there is no way of deciding which among conflicting interpretations of the sounds is the correct one.[1] Semantically, the point that the critics of the programmatic school are suggesting is that it is indeed a strange language which does not offer a *common communication* but which allows for as many interpretations as there are users of it.

A modified heteronomous view has been advanced by the eminent psychologist, Max Schoen, in his recent book, *The Understanding of Music*. He writes:

> In language even a single word has a specific reference to an object or act which is the meaning of that word. When the word is abstract it at once calls up a concrete image . . . There is never such a hard and fast line of connotations in music. A single note or a melodic phrase does not stand for any one thing, act, feeling, or passion, and can therefore mean any one of a thousand things and experiences, limited only by the hearer's wealth of imagery. Within itself and by itself, then, music has the power to produce every illusion, passion, and sensuous event in the range of human experience, and even to insinuate itself into the higher mental processes.[2]

The essence of Schoen's argument is that because musical sounds mean no one definite thing, they can mean anything, definite or indefinite, specific or generic. But in one sense, to say that *x* means nothing, therefore everything, is self-contradictory and absurd. However, what Schoen means, I think, is that since musical sounds (with onomatopoetic exceptions) are noniconic, they can function, semantically, as symbols of anything to different listeners.

This version of heteronomy is more plausible than the others. Meaning, it implies, is a relation not between sounds and things, but between sounds, *associations*, and things. To have meaning is not necessarily to be like something, but to be associated with it. The composer and the listener attach references to musical sounds; and these references constitute the meaning of music. This theory, which identifies the meaning of music with symbolic sign functioning rather than iconic significance, has been offered by Carroll Pratt.[3]

The basic difficulty with this view is similar to that which Hanslick found in the programmatic version of heteronomy, the extreme relativism of music as a language. In ordinary language, the symbols are more or less fixed in their meanings. But in music, even if we allow the sounds to function as symbols, they are not fixed at all. The word "red" means red in one poem and in another, and in hundreds of them. But four related tones may mean, in a semantically symbolic way, fate in one symphony, love in another, and perhaps cruelty in a third.

One might reply to this that musical meanings resemble the opaque symbols of painting. Straight lines mean consciousness in one painting, the dignity of man in a second, and the egocentricity of a bird in a third. If we accept this symbolic process in painting, why not in music?

So far as I can see, there is no ostensible argument against this reply, but some of its implications, I should think, would be semantically embarrassing to its advocates. Music, on this view, is a *completely* opaque language. That is, every reference depends upon someone's external associations with the sounds. And all the meanings of a certain composition are personal, arbitrary, capricious, and different with different listeners. This is a curious phenomenon, that a language should consist of nothing but opaque symbols; that there should be recognized no icons, indices, or transparent symbols.

The essential or at any rate the distinguishing feature of language is its capacity to function for communication. Communication means *common* understanding; this is part of its definition. But the theory that we are now considering seems to violate this very feature of language. With nothing but purely personal, arbitrary, and capricious symbols and references, there can be no common understanding, only a welter of wild, imaginative flights into the realm of associations.

One must conclude, therefore, that this version of heteronomy reduces to self-contradiction because it involves the incompatible notions that music is a language and yet does not function in communication.

Another variant of the heteronomy school is the theory of Scho-

penhauer, which has also been championed in our period by Pratt
(who, I think, is really maintaining two views of the meaning of
music). Their contention is that music means nothing concrete
— no *specific* event, emotion, or struggle — but rather the activity
of the will. The ceaseless activity of musical sounds, with their
rises and falls, means the strivings, the ups and downs, the advances and recessions of the human will.[4] Music is thus an iconic
language which has but one referent, the fluctuations of human
volition.

This heteronomous theory, it is true, does avoid the pitfalls of
the preceding ones. But it is too narrow in its formulation. There
is no reason why music cannot represent more than pure volition,
why its constituents cannot refer to many more specific attributes
of human experience than the will. To have shown that it can do
so is the contribution of Hanslick.

Everyone considers Hanslick to be one of the staunchest advocates of the autonomy doctrine. He is the inventor of its famous
slogan: "The essence of music is *sound and motion*."[5] He is in
the Herbartian tradition of German aesthetics, and a disciple of
Herbart's pupil, Zimmermann. Furthermore, his attacks on the
extreme heteronomists, especially the emotionalists, who claimed
that music is a language of the emotions, all tend to support this
interpretation of his point of view.

And yet I must insist that his book, *The Beautiful in Music*,
is not an argument for autonomy at all but an attempt to establish
a limited but sound heteronomous theory.

Hanslick's basic thesis is that music means, is a language of,
certain *diversified features* of human experience. Musical sounds,
functioning as the stimuli of our auditory experiences, have certain
physical properties: strength, motion, ratio, and rhythm. By means
of these, other properties are created: intensity waxing and waning;
motion hastening and lingering; and progression. And through
these, music obtains certain expressive qualities which we may call
the graceful, the violent, the vigorous, or the elegant.[6]

All of these expressive qualities, Hanslick maintains, characterize the musical sounds as stimuli, and exist quite independently of the listener's associations with them. They are intrinsic, not extrinsic, characteristics of music. Our aesthetic adjectives, like graceful, for example, refer to our stimuli, not to our reactions or associational interpretations of them. To say, then, that the opening theme of the "Adagio" movement of Mozart's *Quintet in D Minor* is wistfully sad is like saying, for Hanslick, that the red in some painting or other is luscious.

In my opinion, Hanslick's theory is closer to the truth about the meaning of music than any of the others we have considered. To be sure, there are semantical difficulties in it. For example, one does not know how to interpret these intrinsic aesthetic qualities that Hanslick finds in the musical stimuli. Are they iconic with the graceful, etc., in human experience or only associated with these features of human experience in the way that transparent symbols are? But his fundamental claim is sound, so far as it goes. Human beings have many experiences, each with its physiological and psychological dimension. Music, even on an iconic level, can mean these aspects of human experience. The purely rhythmic motion of music, for example, represents to all listeners with normal nervous systems the rhythmic motion of our bodily experiences as well as the waxing and waning character of our psychic emotional life in an iconic way. Music is a language, and in so far as it means or represents certain kinetic, kinaesthetic, and emotional characteristics of human experience, it is a purely iconic language. This is the basic thesis of Hanslick and the soundest compromise between the autonomous and heteronomous positions in musical aesthetics.

Considered independently of its historical development, we may say that the whole problem of autonomy versus heteronomy is not one that has ever been formulated correctly by musical aestheticians. Both schools have accepted the same assumptions about language, meaning, and representation in the way that both

Bell and Fry and their critics accepted the same basic assumptions about the form–content distinction in their discussions about painting. If our whole treatment of the problem of meaning in painting is a correct one, it follows that the distinction between the representational and the nonrepresentational, or the meaningful and the nonmeaningful, is an illegitimate one, so far as art is concerned. The constituents of music, like the constituents of painting, are expressive in character, which means that they function as signs, that is, as vehicles of meaning, to the listeners of music. The question is not whether music means anything but what does it mean? And this is tantamount to asking what are the different ways that the constituents of music can function as signs. We have already seen in our third chapter that even one constituent, the progression of chords in the exposition of the *Eroica*, can be said to have a number of meanings.

All of the constituents of music may mean different things to different listeners. Some of the elements, like presto rhythms, for example, are probably iconic, since they are like certain of our vivacious experiences. But this same constituent may also function as an opaque symbol. For example, it may be designated by the composer to mean, let us say, the Russian army on the march.

Other constituents, like dissonance, are taken as meaning, among other things, the qualities of restlessness and instability in human experience. Some musical aestheticians see in this semantical relation an iconic one. But this is difficult to support. Rather, the relation between dissonance and instability is similar to the relation between red and the lively, in that dissonance is a transparent symbol of the unstable or restless. Many of us Western listeners, mainly because of our musical history, do interpret dissonance as a sign of the restless; but Orientals or even future Western listeners may find it as restful and stable as a consonance. Consequently, we cannot assert dogmatically that either consonance or dissonance is more than a transparent symbol of the stable or unstable in human experience.

What is true of the relation between dissonance and restlessness obtains in the relation between certain sounds and other
expressive qualities. To say, for example, that the second movement of the Mozart Concerto for Piano and Orchestra in C
Minor is heavenly in its serenity is not to utter gibberish, but to
say that the sounds, paced as they are, pitched as they are, harmo-
nized as they are — that is, as melody — are transparent symbols
of the serene in human experience, and that the extremely lingering and ethereal quality of the sounds gives them their (transparently symbolic) heavenly character.

The difficulty is not to recognize the transparently symbolic
referents of music but to be able to characterize them when we
do recognize them. And this is a difficulty that points to the
woefully inadequate language that we use when we try to name
or describe the communicating signs of music. That is, we must
say in English what is being presented (not asserted, necessarily)
in music. But the qualities that can be referred to through music
simply cannot be named successfully in English or any other
ordinary language. We say a Mozartian melody means serenity,
but so do some of Beethoven's. There is a difference in the kind
of serenity that is being communicated in a transparently symbolic
way, but we cannot specify it adequately in English. However,
we should not conclude from this inability of ordinary languages
to name the qualities that music refers to, as some have done,
that music does not mean anything because we cannot say what
it means. We ought rather to say that music means many qualities
of our experiences, some of which we can name, in a feeble sort
of way, by the use of such terms as serenity, melancholy, joyful-
ness, gracefulness, etc.[7]

To sum up: The organic theory regards music as a language
or system of signs which communicates or means certain features
of our experiences. Some of these signs are like these features,
some are associated with them in culturally rather fixed ways,
whereas others are merely associated with them in esoteric and

personal ways. Unlike the autonomy view, the organic theory finds in musical sounds both icons and transparent symbols such that we may correctly say that music *has* a vocabulary, that is, certain signs with fixed connotations and denotations. It is true, as Susanne Langer has pointed out, that the tones of music cannot be construed as words.[8] But one need not argue that they are like words in order to attribute to music a vocabulary. The vocabulary of music does not consist in its tones but in groupings of them in certain rhythmic and harmonic ways that allow them to function as transparent symbols. Further, as transparent symbols, the vocabulary of music consists primarily of terms that can mean specified but not particular aspects of experience, that is, serenity or turbulence, for example, but not the serenity or turbulence of a particular person on a particular day in a particular situation.

Unlike the view of the programmatic school and Schoen, the organic theory does not identify the language of music with purely opaque symbols. Finally, it rejects the view of Schopenhauer that music means only the fluctuations of the will by showing that music can mean more specified features of human activity than the will.

7

THE ARTS: THE MEDIUM

The Doctrine of the Purity of the Medium

The problem of the meaning of music brings us to the whole question of the nature and importance of the medium in art. In music, autonomists and some heteronomists alike claim that music is able to do some things and not others; that it is limited by the capacities of the medium of tone sounds; that it ought not to attempt what it is not able to do, namely, to narrate or denote specific things.

This total principle allows of generalization for all the arts. Each art, it is contended, has a specific function, which gives it its uniqueness; and this function is determined by the nature of the medium. This generalized principle, ancient in the history of aesthetics, received its classic formulation in the *Laocoön* of Lessing. In the aesthetics of modern art, especially since 1850, and this holds for all the arts, it would be difficult to find a principle more universally accepted by "modernists" and more influential upon creation than this one.

The medium has become a category of primary importance in contemporary aesthetics and one can find a great deal of discussion of its significance in the writings and reflections of modern artists and critics. It would be difficult to reduce these discussions

to any total unanimity but on one point there is universal agree-
ment, at least on the part of those who consider themselves
"moderns." Painting, drama, motion pictures, music, architecture,
sculpture, dance, and literature all have their special capacities
and limitations. This is the central doctrine of these advocates
of "modern art." The artist in his creative activity is inextricably
tied to his medium. He thinks and feels and produces in terms
of it. It is, as Bosanquet wrote in reply to Croce, the body of his
aesthetic creation.[1] Each medium, whether it be water color or
fresco in painting, the human body in the dance, the camera
in the motion picture, or stone in sculpture, etc., possesses its
own expressive potentials. These should be realized as fully as
possible. No medium should be made to do what it really cannot
do or what others can do better. The medium must be kept pure.
In sum: this is a new kind of formalism in aesthetic theory, one
which the Germans, with excellence of exactitude, have called a
"Purism" founded upon *Materialgerechtigkeit* — doing justice to
the nature of the material.

Purism and Painting

Consider the medium and the doctrine of purism in relation to
the art of painting. The medium, it is pointed out, is in part a
two-dimensional surface area. This surface may be made of a
number of different materials or substances, among them canvas,
wood, plaster, paper, glass. All of these surfaces have their own expressive possibilities which are to be explored and exploited in
order to realize their intrinsic uniquenesses as surface areas. One
should not try to do with glass what can be done better with
plaster, for example, the purist claims, for this leads to a con-
fusion of media and a consequent artistic failure.

Besides the two-dimensional surface area, the medium in painting includes the paint itself. And here one distinguishes between
water color, gouache, tempera, oil, etc. Each of these has its

own expressive capacities and limitations, and these should be realized, without any attempt to do with one medium what can be done better with another. For example, the purist holds that the artist who is striving for luminosity ought not to work with water colors but rather with oils, which lend themselves naturally to the creation of the expressive quality of luminosity, whereas water colors do not.

Besides these purisms within the art of painting, there is a larger purism about the whole of the art. Painting, it is held, is essentially a medium in which certain plastic qualities can be exhibited. It can explore the expressive potentials of color, line, space, volume tension, and the like. Further, it can do this better than any other art. This is its uniqueness which is derived from its essence as an art of painting. Although it can embody narrative or psychological matters, it ought not to do so since literature can do this better. It ought to limit itself to what it can do best, plastic expression, not plastic-subject expression. From Cézanne to Picasso, this principle, however we may ultimately regard it, has been one of the inspirations of modern painting.

Purism and Architecture

In architecture we find the same insistence upon the preservation of the integrity of the medium. In fact, in no other art has the call of the medium been so loudly sounded. Modern architecture is, in part, a revolt against the lack of integrity that characterized much of nineteenth- and twentieth-century architecture. The main irritation has been the unfunctional use of the materials of architecture. Modern architects see in marble palaces that function as banks or railroad stations, in colonial mansions or French chateaux that turn out to be gas stations, in Gothic churches that are public libraries, and in mausoleums that serve as homes, complete dishonesty and escapism.

Architecture is essentially buildings. These are structures of materials organized in accordance with some plan or purpose. Materials are sources of expressiveness. Ferroconcrete, steel, wood, brick, stone, and glass have their own physical and expressive potentialities. Their possible utilization in buildings is a challenge to the architect to bring these potentialities to fruition — to make steel look like steel, wood like wood, or glass like glass. Whatever their differences, and they are profound, every "modernist" in creative architecture today accepts this basic principle. Architecture must incorporate the qualities of the medium. As J. J. P. Oud writes: "A new architecture will offer us the definite values of artificial materials, surfaces polished and finished, the scintillation of steel and the brilliance of paint, the transparent openness of large windows of plate glass." [2]

One must not, of course, make the whole of architecture a function of the medium. The kind of building we have depends not only upon our use of materials but also upon our general purposes and desires that establish the plan or use of the building. "Form follows function," Louis Sullivan affirmed; and he meant, among other things, that the building and its materials are determined by the purpose of the building.

Homes, banks, churches, schools, theaters, and libraries are to be conceived and built in terms of a philosophy of man in relation to his environment. It is because of *this* principle and not because of the principle of the integrity of the medium that there is so much disagreement in modern architecture, even among the advocates of "modernism." All creative moderns in architecture since Sullivan agree that materials are sacred and that the building is a realization of material in relation to use; their disagreement is on the nature of man and the general meaning of human experience.

In so far as there is polarity in the aesthetics of modern architecture, one can discern as the two extremes concerning this purposive aspect the so-called functionalists and the organicists. The functionalists, led by Le Corbusier, who conceive of man as essentially in conflict with the raw materials of nature and who extol the transformations of these raw materials into highly contrived, artificial environments, wish to make of man an ordered being and, consequently, interpret his central architectural structure, the home, as "a machine for living in." [3]

The organicists, led by F. L. Wright, regard man as an outgrowth of nature, as a creature who is continuous with, not in opposition to, nature, as being organically tied to her. They wish to create an architecture that is the unfolding of man's immediate environment in relation to his needs, his dreams, his fantasies, in short, his complete self. The function of architecture is not to rationalize or to order the life of man but to realize his total personality. For Le Corbusier it is man who must adjust to the demands of architecture, whereas for Wright it is architecture that must become the organic expansion of man. It is, once again, the old conflict between the classic and the romantic.

But let us repeat: Throughout this conflict, both of these architects, their followers, and those great figures, like Gropius and Mies von der Rohe, who represent neither extreme, are in complete accord on the basic principle that the architect create with a sense of the integrity of his medium and its materials.

Purism and Sculpture

Modern sculpture is a further example of the importance of the medium in art. The contemporary sculptor Henry Moore has stated most clearly the intimate relation between creative sculpture and the medium:

> Every material has its own individual qualities. It is only when the sculptor works direct, when there is an active relationship with his material, that the material can take its part in the shaping of an idea. Stone, for example, is hard and concentrated and should not be falsified to look like soft flesh — it

should not be forced beyond its constructive build to a point of weakness. It should keep its hard tense stoniness.[4]

In Moore's own work, there is remarkable preoccupation with the intrinsic physical and expressive qualities of wood, stone, bronze, copper, and marble. With some few exceptions, his work is the full exploitation of the plastic qualities of these materials and their attendant expressive effects. Literary values and psychological pose, so important in realistic and romantic sculpture, and even in the work of Rodin and Maillol, two early moderns, are completely rejected. The function of sculpture is to exhibit the spatiality, mass, colors, texture, and tension of basic materials, irrespective of the subject elements. This is the basic conviction not only of Moore but also of Brancusi, Archipenko, Zadkine, Lachaise, and Lehmbruck, all of whom are among the creative forces of modern sculpture.

Purism and Drama

In the drama we encounter much difficulty in trying to understand its peculiar medium. There is little unanimity in the aesthetics of the drama. One theory interprets the medium as psychic action and development; another, as essentially theater or staging.

It is curious that in the drama there is no one in the modern period whose role is analogous to Cézanne's or even a Pissarro's in painting! Dramatic theory and writing are still in the main a function of Aristotelian habits of thought. It is the case that technological inventions, especially lighting, have led to revolutionary theories of the drama but, with certain exceptions, in German Expressionistic drama, for instance, these have never been realized. Those who do maintain that drama is more than psychic action with staging serving as an accessory, but *total staging*, which includes, in an integrated manner, acting, lighting, directing, psychic and physical action, are either unrecognized or else crushed by a host of hostile theatrical enterprises. One need only survey the American theatrical scene during the last decade to realize the total artistic as well as aesthetic decadence of the drama. Not only has there been no experimentalism with non-Aristotelian modes but the plays of the traditional stamp have been of an inordinately undistinguished character. I do not think it would be an exaggeration to say that the drama is at present the most conservative of the arts, and especially in its aesthetic, theoretical development.

Purism and the Motion Picture

The motion picture, like the drama, is an ill-defined art today. But part of the explanation is the relatively shifting and experimental character of the motion picture as compared with the drama.

The problem of the nature of the medium of the motion picture is extremely difficult, mainly because there has been so little discussion of it in the writings on the motion picture. Eisenstein has advanced a theory to the effect that the motion picture is essentially *montage*, that is, the simultaneous presentation of different areas of action.[5] But this seems too narrow a view and cannot even explain his own recent productions, *Alexander Nevsky* and *Ivan the Terrible*.

E. Panofsky has come closer to the truth, I think, in his claim that the art of the motion picture "can be defined as *dynamisation of space* and, accordingly, *spatialization of time*." [6] Although there is little clarification of these categories in Panofsky's discussion, one can gather from his examples that he considers the essence of the motion picture to consist in its *fluidity*; this view breaks down old distinctions of time and space.

It is in line with Panofsky's thinking that I should like to suggest, by way of hypothesis, that the medium of the motion picture is essentially the external projection on a screen of the visual and physical mobility that is afforded by the camera and its film. This is the uniqueness of the motion picture: that it can show physical, fluid action of all sorts with a speed that no other art can achieve.

Some practicing theorists of the motion picture, especially Maya Deren and Jean Cocteau, have suggested that its medium, its physical, visual mobility, is self-sufficient in that the total art of the motion picture ought to be the realization of this mobility. This thesis may be disputed. In Deren's work, the exploitation of mobility becomes interesting only when it assumes certain rhythmic effects; and when this occurs, the picture becomes an imitation of the dance, and no longer an unique art, which is what Deren wishes it to be. In Cocteau, especially in his *The Blood of a Poet*, the medium is used mainly as a way of stopping time (the beginning and the end of the picture, the falling of the tower, can be interpreted only as the *same* event) and encompassing the montage of the unconscious. In the work of both, the purity of the medium is violated by an overload of Freudian symbolism. Symbolism, of course, is not bad in itself, but it is certainly not an intrinsic part of physical or visual mobility. It may be integrated with this mobility but when it is, the medium becomes *one* element among others in the total motion picture.

No one, so far as I know, has succeeded in creating an "absolute film," that is, one in which only its uniqueness is expressively realized. Perhaps someone will achieve it, but thus far, at any rate, the medium remains an *ancillary* art, playing a role in the motion picture analogous to that of acting or lighting in opera.

To what is the medium ancillary? To dramatic action, I think: to story, plot, character. As one looks at our motion pictures, good and bad, this generalization seems to obtain. In preparation for the writing of this chapter, I saw a number of motion pictures in New York during the 1946–47 season. There were many splendid ones, mostly foreign. In fact, one could assert quite truly that the only good drama in New York during the year was to be found in the small movie houses that show foreign films.

Noel Coward's *Brief Encounter* was accepted universally as an excellent motion picture. It is essentially a dramatized short story concerning a married woman and a married man who fall in love, quite by accident, and who together realize, with a fine sense of maturity, the hopeless character of their love. The whole plot and character development is a kind of poetry of middle age and the middle class. Coward, the producer of the picture as well as its author, employs both music and camera in the picture not as ends in themselves but *always* as a means of focusing upon and intensifying every scene and dramatic situation. The railroad scenes are especially noteworthy in the way in which the camera augments the drama by calling attention to the pathetic transiency of the relationship of the lovers. Physical mobility throughout is rendered subordinate to the psychic development of the characters.

Most of the pictures were similar to *Brief Encounter* in their utilization of the medium as one element among others and not even as the most important one. This was the case even with the above-mentioned Eisenstein motion pictures. Unlike the earlier *The Ten Days That Shook the World*, where Eisenstein works completely with montage — "ideological montage," he calls it — in which ideas are communicated by means of various series of flashes that comprise different political meanings, his *Alexander Nevsky* and *Ivan the Terrible* emphasize individual psychological action or dramatic scenes, in which both montage and mobility are secondary considerations.

Besides these pictures there were a number of brilliant ones that were no more than transplanted (i.e., filmed) stage dramas. Both *Open City* and *The Well-Digger's Daughter*, two of the finest pictures of the year, are really conceived in terms of the stage. They are tightly knit and well enclosed in their action, with almost complete emphasis upon dialogue and psychic conflict. They reach their climaxes not through any physical mobility but in certain physically *static* scenes. This is especially true of *Open City*, in which the picture reaches its artistic height in the scene in which Fascist torturers, underground leader, and priest participate. The Fascists are slowly torturing the underground leader to death. The partisan priest is called upon to watch this brutal execution. The Fascist leader sneers at the priest that this is the price of silence and insurrection; to which the priest replies with a thunderous curse upon the Fascist followed by his painful recognition that he cannot act in such a manner as a servant of God. This whole torment of the Christian who wishes also to become a full human animal, who realizes the desperate character of man as the beast, occurs with no important physical action or mobility. But in its power as psychic, dramatic action, it is superb. Both of these motion pictures, then, as well as the others already mentioned and many more that could be mentioned, point up a curious and striking paradox of the contemporary motion picture. As an art, it seems to realize its greatest achievements when it concentrates upon dramatic elements and employs the medium only as a means of intensifying these elements.

Purism and the Dance

Finally, in the modern dance there has been similar recognition of the central role of the medium. As is the case in modern architecture, the modern dance arose as a protest against a long period of imitationalism and ornamentalism. The classical ballet, with its adherence to a rigid code of regulations and its hiding of the intrinsic qualities of the body, which it accomplished mainly through the tarlatan skirt and the emphasis upon the decorative skills of the dancer's feet, was the chief irritant.

Isadora Duncan was the first exponent of the modern dance. Her overwhelming desire was to liberate the human body from the trammels of the traditional ballet. Her work proclaimed the body

as a powerful source of expressive communication. But, paradoxically enough, her revolutionary aims led only to a neoclassi-
cism founded upon Greek ideals.

The real revolution began in 1914 with two other dancers,
Mary Wigman and Rudolf von Laban. With absolute conviction,
they affirmed the ability of the human body, either alone or in
groups, to serve as the total medium and source of expressiveness
of the dance. They conceived the dance in completely abstract
terms of spatial shape and line, temporal rhythms and mass.[7]
Story, character development, psychological narration, even music
(at first), were rejected as inimical to the dance as pure art. For
gesture, they substituted dynamic body movement; for the hiding
or disguising of the body, they offered the exhibition of the quality
of weight; and in place of the long melodic lines of the classical
ballet, they insisted upon massive, broken chords. With keen
understanding, they conceived of the dance as the abstract interpretation of the salient qualities of the tempo of modern life.
Strength, gravity, nervousness, tautness, movement, dynamism,
were all explored and communicated. "The dance dared once more
to be of the present, of the workaday world, of the earth. The
earth was no longer a thing to flee from, to be touched on tiptoe
only, but 'the earth from whence we came' was newly found." [8]

Following Wigman and von Laban, there have been many
brilliant dancers, all of whom have shared the basic conviction
of the self-sufficient, all-inclusive character of the bodily medium
of the dance. Martha Graham has been one of these.

Today Martha Graham is generally regarded as the greatest
living "modern" dancer. And yet, speaking only for myself, I
find in her recent work a tendency to abandon her early purism in
favor of symbolism, narration, décor, and lately, poetic recitation,
as dance accompaniments. All of these she now accepts as legitimate constituents of the dance. Especially in her "Letter to the
World," "Dark Meadow" and "Night Journey," there is a rejection of the basic abstractionist ideal of the modern dance. For

good or for bad, Martha Graham and in fact most of the "moderns," at least those who are dancing in America, have repudiated the aesthetics of purism and have returned to an enlarged conception of the dance.

Evaluation and Rejection of Purism

This concludes our brief survey of the role of the medium in modern art. Our initial purpose has been to comprehend the nature of the medium and the actual artistic success the aesthetics of purism has attained. And, if one is objective about the matter, one must admit the enormous success of the doctrine of purism in actual artistic production. In painting, sculpture, music, the dance, and architecture there has been great devotion in creation to the purist ideal in the modern period. It is only in the arts of the motion picture and literature that the purist aesthetics has met with only limited success or no success at all.

But now let us turn to an evaluation of the theory. The fundamental issue that is raised by purism is a normative one: what ought and what ought not each of the arts to do? Purists say that the arts ought to do what they can do best, what renders them unique, what grows out of the nature of their different media. Thus, purists reject narration and psychological representation in painting because they identify these with literature, and consequently regard their inclusion in painting as a violation of the medium of painting. They reject poetic recitation in the dance because the dance, they are convinced, should communicate only the values of body movements and not poetic meanings. And they repudiate program music because they interpret it as an infringement upon the art of literature.

The question now arises, *why* should the arts specify the limits of their communication in this way? Why ought each art to do *only* what it can do best; what renders it unique; what constitutes the realization of the potentialities of the medium?

In the whole of the discussions concerning the medium and the attempt to render art a function of it, there is to be found no reply to this question. There is much conviction that purism is an absolute in aesthetics but no real philosophical justification of it as an aesthetic principle.

Although there is no systematic justification of purism, there are excellent arguments against it. Ducasse's is the best of these objections. Purism, he maintains, is committed to an erroneous doctrine of artistic language in that it holds that what is said in one medium can be said in another. This is not true because the languages of the different media are not intertranslatable. That is to say, the narration in a painting is a different *kind* of narration from the narration in a literary work. One cannot say in one medium what can be said better in another. Rather one cannot say it at all in another medium for it becomes quite a new thing.[9]

I should like to offer another criticism, which has been implied already in previous chapters, that simply points out that purism is as *arbitrary* a general aesthetic doctrine as the specific view that painting should exclude subject representation. A fundamental objection to the purist aesthetics is that it limits the range of artistic communication *unnecessarily* by demanding that each art do only what it can do best and what renders it different from the other arts. The important thing in art is not that the medium be kept pure but that the constituents of art work together successfully. In place of purism, that is to say, we offer the organic theory. There is nothing categorically artistically bad about the mixture of the various media. If subjects can be successfully integrated with plastic elements in painting, and we have seen how this is accomplished mainly through the integration of expressive qualities, there is no reason to rule out any kind of artistic fusions. If the expressive qualities of poetic recitation and meanings can be successfully related to music (and surely no one can doubt that this has been done, in the *Bach B Minor Mass*, to give only one example of which there are many),[10] then by

all means, let us encourage these unions. It is expansion, not con-
traction, that should be the aesthetic ideal. There are objections
to mixed media but these should not be rooted in their supposed
"hybrid" character; rather they reduce to the same objection that
applies to unmixed media, namely, lack of integration among the
constituents. Martha Graham's "Letter to the World," for example, is intrinsically bad not because it is a mixture of poetry
and dance but because the dance, no longer regarded as the
primary thing, becomes completely subordinate to the poetry
and, in effect, functions as a mimicking of its meanings.

8

ART, LANGUAGE AND TRUTH

The "Emotive–Referential" Dispute: Literature and Truth Claims

In contemporary aesthetic inquiry there is a good deal of discussion about the linguistic character of art. Morris, Langer, Cassirer, Richards, Burke, Blackmur, Panofsky, Ducasse, Freud, and others have dealt extensively with this aspect of art. Parker has pointed out that, historically speaking, this is a rather new approach. Two other basic interpretations of art preceded this linguistic one, the dominant view of our era. First was the doctrine that art is essentially imitation, either of the universal features of reality, including human experience, or of the beautiful in nature. This doctrine, whose hegemony lasted some two thousand years and which was known as classicism, was unable to explain much of art, especially fantastic art; consequently, it was succeeded by the romantic theory, according to which art is essentially imagination. Further probings into the nature of art, especially in the last one hundred years or so, disclosed the social and communicative character of art, and led eventually to the contemporary view that art is essentially a language.[1]

The organic theory concurs with this prevalent conception of art. Because it stresses the expressive dimension of art, that is, the fact that all of its constituents may function as icons, indices, or symbols to spectators, it accepts the thesis that art is a language.

But to affirm that art is a language immediately provokes the query, what *kind* of language? The most imposing, perhaps even the most accepted, view today is that art is an *emotive* language. Ducasse and I. A. Richards are among the champions of this view. Ducasse writes: *"Art is essentially a form of language — namely, the language of feeling, mood, sentiment, and emotional attitude. It is thus to be distinguished from the language of assertion."* [2]

However, it is Richards who has offered the details of the emotive theory. According to him (and C. K. Ogden), at least in *The Meaning of Meaning,* which constitutes the prolegomenon to Richards' later work, language has many functions. It symbolizes thought, expresses attitudes of the speaker, evokes attitudes in the listener, and promotes certain effects. But these can be sharply divided into two main functions, the symbolic and the emotive. Symbolic language, or the symbolic use of words, is the statement, recording, support, and communication of thought, whereas emotive language, or the emotive use of words, is the evocation, expression, or excitation of feelings and attitudes.

To illustrate: Suppose I say, "This painting is the work of Picasso." My statement is informative, referential, and true or false, depending upon whether or not the painting *is* Picasso's. But if I say, "This painting is excellent," then, according to Richards, I am not really saying anything *about* the painting; instead I am articulating or expressing my feelings of approval toward it, perhaps even in the hope of evoking similar feelings in my listeners.

This distinction between the emotive and the symbolic (referential) uses of language Richards regards as basic to the distinction between art, especially literature, which is his main problem, and science. To understand the emotive use of language and to use it exclusively is the function of art. Art ought to abandon its quest for knowledge and truth, for it is not necessary to know *what* things are in order to express our feelings toward them. [3]

In its semantical dimension, the emotive theory of Ducasse and Richards is the view that art, as a system of signs, does not embody propositions or referential assertions, that is, *truth claims*, but serves only as the expression or excitation of feelings, emotions and attitudes. Carnap has supplemented this view, which is essentially positivistic, by affirming the kinship of artistic (also metaphysical and ethical) language and certain body gestures. I laugh, I cry, I yell, or I stamp my feet. My laughing, crying, yelling, or stamping my feet expresses my feelings and attitudes. Linguistically, when I perform in these ways, I communicate something to my audience; and I may even inspire them to similar body activity. But I do not say anything; I state no fact; I make no claim. What I do is not true or false, but an expression of feeling. So too with art; it is also a form of emotional gesture, a kind of stamping of one's feet or clapping of one's hands, but ever so nicely! Thus, the language of art, from literature to music, is closer to body gestures than it is to the language of science or empirical statements.[4]

This theory raises an extremely important question, one which is central to the contemporary doctrine that art is a language. Is art merely an emotive language or is it referential and assertive as well? *Can art embody truth claims?*

Among contemporary aestheticians who have been engaging in debate on this issue, T. M. Greene has offered the most extensive defense of the doctrine that art does embody truth claims, and he maintains that all of the arts, not only literature, embody "propositional truth." His theory has been discussed in two recent books, by B. C. Heyl and by John Hospers. Both of these critics, I think, have succeeded in exposing the inadequacies of Greene's position, so that there would be no point here in entering into *their* particular dispute, especially if one, like myself, does not accept the premises of either side of the dispute.[5] Instead, we shall present a different solution.

Hospers, in his critique of Greene, comments: "Professor Greene might have sought a way out which in fact he does not, namely, to say that works of art are *implied* assertions (or else that they imply assertions)." [6]

This "way out" has already been indicated by DeWitt Parker, in his formulation of the concept of "depth meaning."

> Many poems and some works of plastic art possess what I like to call "depth meanings" — meanings of universal scope underneath relatively concrete meanings or ideas. Thus in the following line of one of Frost's little poems
> Nothing gold can stay
> the word "gold" has its usual surface meaning, but underneath that is its depth meaning, precious; so in addition to saying that nothing golden can endure, the poet is saying that nothing valuable can abide — a more universal statement. [7]

In my opinion, the introduction of Parker's concept of depth meaning offers us a new way of analyzing the problem of truth in art. I do not think that it solves the whole problem for us but it does seem to solve at least part of it, and in the following way. Let us, for the moment, grant the positivistic thesis that literature (with the trivial exception of those statements in it that are about historical figures and places, etc.) is primarily emotive. Still, it does not follow that none of it is also referential. For if we employ Parker's concept of depth meaning, we may assert that literature is emotive on one linguistic dimension, the surface meanings, and referential on the other, the depth meanings. We can then point out that the emotive theory possesses an initial credibility only because it neglects the entire realm of depth meanings in literature by confining itself to the meanings presented immediately through the *printed* page.

As an example of a work in literature that embodies certain truth claims through the presence of depth meanings, I will choose the recent American novel, *Native Son*, by Richard Wright. [8] The novel deals with a young Negro, Bigger Thomas, who is without faith in his poverty-stricken, frustrated life. His feelings and attitudes toward life are inchoate except that he deeply resents his status as a Negro. His tragedy begins when he accepts a charity job as a chauffeur given him by one of the millionaire landlords of Chicago's South Side slums, where Bigger lives. The millionaire has a daughter, Mary Dalton, who is having her fling with Communism. Naturally, she becomes interested in Bigger and desires to get a glimpse into his way of life. She and her boy friend trick him into acting as their guide to the Negro dives of the South Side.

During the course of the evening, Mary gets drunk and, after persuading her boy friend to leave her alone with Bigger on her way home, she makes advances to him. Bigger is not interested, knowing well the penalty that would be meted out to him if he accepted her invitation. Instead he takes her home and carries her into her bedroom, trying to keep her quiet and put her to sleep. Mary's mother, who is blind, hears the noises of her daughter and enters the room. Bigger, terrified at her presence, is forced to put a pillow over Mary's head, to stop her mumbling. Mrs. Dalton finally leaves and Bigger removes the pillow, only to discover that Mary has suffocated. Desperate, Bigger decides to burn his victim rather than try to explain what happened. The rest of the story concerns the discovery of Bigger's guilt, his escape and second murder, then his arrest, trial, and finally his execution.

So much for the story. As a story it is all that an emotionalist could wish for: it is exciting and beautifully written, at a kind of white heat that keeps up with the plot. The question now arises, are there any truth claims in the novel? The answer, according to our hypothesis, depends upon the presence and nature of the depth meanings.

The first thing we notice as we read the novel is that it is not about an isolated Negro but about all Negroes and group minorities in America. Bigger Thomas, the subject of the novel, in the course of his experiences, epitomizes and embodies the truth claim that individual freedom is still an abortive ideal in America, since our social injustices cancel out individual development.

As contemporary novels go, however, this is a rather trivial thematic truth claim, and one might be led to infer from it that even if some novels do contain truth claims through their depth meanings, they are trivial and consequently aesthetically insignificant.

But a careful reading of Wright's novel will, I believe, reveal another depth meaning and truth claim that is far from trivial; in fact, it is so poignant that it saves the work from being merely another proletarian novel. It is to be found in the final pages of the novel where Bigger, having been sentenced to die, is talking with his lawyer, Mr. Max. Mr. Max is trying to soothe Bigger. He tells him that he will not die in vain, that he will be remembered as another martyr of exploitation. But all of this means nothing to Bigger, who is preoccupied with his own fate and his own life's meaning. The last paragraphs are especially significant:

"Mr. Max, you go home. I'm all right . . . Sounds funny, Mr. Max, but when I think about what you say I kind of feel what I wanted. It makes me feel I was kind of right . . ." Max opened his mouth to say something and Bigger drowned out his voice. "I ain't trying to forgive nobody and I ain't asking for nobody to forgive me. I ain't going to cry. They wouldn't let me live and I killed. Maybe it ain't fair to kill and I reckon I really didn't want to kill. But when I think of why all the killing was, I begin to feel what I wanted, what I am . . ."

Bigger saw Max back away from him with compressed lips. But he felt he had to make Max understand how he saw things now.

"I didn't want to kill!" Bigger shouted. "But what I killed for, I *am!* It must've been pretty deep in me to make me kill! I must have felt it awful hard to murder . . ."

Max lifted his hand to touch Bigger, but did not.

"No; no; no . . . Bigger, not that . . ." Max pleaded despairingly.

"What I killed for must've been good!" Bigger's voice was
full of frenzied anguish. "It must have been good! When
a man kills, it's for something . . . I didn't know I was really
alive in this world until I felt things hard enough to kill for
'em . . . It's the truth, Mr. Max. I can say it now, 'cause I'm
going to die. I know what I'm saying real good and I know how
it sounds. But I am all right when I look at it that way . . ."

Max's eyes were full of terror. Several times his body moved
nervously, as if he were about to go to Bigger, but he stood
still.

"I'm all right, Mr. Max. Just go and tell Ma I was all right
and not to worry none, see? Tell her I was all right and wasn't
crying none . . ."

Max's eyes were wet. Slowly, he extended his hand. Bigger
shook it.

"Good-bye, Bigger," he said quietly.

"Good-bye, Mr. Max." [9]

This scene, especially as it is read in its relations to the rest of
the novel, contains a depth meaning that is a profound truth claim
concerning the present state of man. Through Bigger, and in this
speech, especially, Wright is *claiming* that the only freedom left to
man is the freedom to destroy, first others and finally oneself. No
other novelist or poet has articulated this idea, so far as I know.
Nor even has any contemporary sociologist or philosopher. Here,
then, is an example where the artist not only asserts something
important (which is true or false) but is the only intellectual to
have done so.

It is only when one comes to discern this depth meaning that
the novel takes on its basic significance. Until it becomes clear that
Bigger is more than a symbol of exploitation and represents *all*
men who struggle to realize themselves in a world full of evil, the
novel remains a mere adequate proletarian one. But it is this meaning that gives the novel its universality. The symbol of Bigger,
the killer of white women, who is modern man in his own tortured
self-destructiveness, vivifies the whole work and makes of each

scene, especially the courtroom scene, something much deeper than it could possibly be when the novel is analyzed in terms of the other depth meanings alone. The novel rises above the truth claim concerning the exploitation of minorities in America to signify what Wright regards as the tragedy of modern man, that he can attain autonomy only by destruction and eventual self-destruction.

It is important to point out that the truth claims of literature are not always true. Like the truth claims of science, they may be false, too. Consequently, when we say that *Native Son* contains truth claims, we do not mean to be asserting that it contains a number of *truths*. It may very well be that the depth meanings of *Native Son* are all false. But so far as our problem is concerned, that would make no difference at all. The important thing is that much of literature contains truth claims, hence is as linguistically referential as science.

In fact, I find it incredible that aestheticians who read contemporary fiction should support the emotive theory of the language of art. A survey of our own American realistic fiction, especially the novels of Dos Passos, Hemingway, Faulkner, Steinbeck, and Farrell, cannot but reveal the presence of truth claims in the depth meanings of their work. The Farrell trilogy, *Studs Lonigan*, for example, contains as its basic depth meaning and truth claim the judgment that American life, dominated by bourgeois values, is vacuous and spiritually sick to the core.

What does it mean to say that a work of literature contains a depth meaning? That is to say, what is the logical status of a depth meaning and artistic truth claim? This is a large question, but at least part of the answer, I believe, is the following.

In *some* works of literature, where there are these depth meanings which do function as truth claims, there appear black marks on paper. These marks serve as signs of concepts or ideas of one sort or another to readers; and these ideas, in syntactical juxtaposition to each other, comprise the sentences and meanings of the work. But these are its surface or printed meanings, and they are, logically speaking, what we may call, according to the terminology of Russell's theory of logical types, "first-order" meanings. And if we grant the positivist his thesis that art is initially an emotive language, we may refer to these as emotive first-order meanings.

Now, besides these meanings, these works contain certain depth meanings which, logically speaking, are "second-order" in character. These meanings may be propositional in nature and function as truth claims. They are contained in the work of art even though they do not appear in print. To assert that they are contained in the work is to say that they are *implied* by the first-order meanings, where by implication we do not mean Russell's material or Lewis's strict implication, since neither of these conceives correctly our nonmathematical, ordinary sense of implication. Part of what is meant by implication in the sense in which we are using it has been formulated best by G. E. Moore when he writes, for example, "There seems to me to be nothing mysterious about this sense of 'imply,' in which if you assert that you went to the pictures last Tuesday, you *imply*, though you don't *assert*, that you believe or know that you did." [10] Thus, when we say that a literary work, such as *Native Son*, contains a second-order truth claim, what is meant is that some of the printed meanings imply the truth claim even though it is not expressed in the sense of appearing in print. Truth claims are second-order, then, because they depend upon and cannot exist without the printed first-order meanings. They are logical functions of the first-order meanings in the way that "Napoleon had all the characteristics of a great general" would be a second-order logical function of the first-order sentences, "Napoleon had courage," "Napoleon had cunning," "Napoleon had loyalty," etc., were these latter sentences to appear in a book on the printed page and the former not to appear in print at all but still be part of the total book.

Alfred Ayer, who supports the positivist position in its general orientation, has challenged its interpretation of the language of art. He denies that the language of art is emotive. In literature, even in poetry, the sentences are to be construed as linguistically referential in character. But, with the trivial exception of references to historical events, persons, etc., they are all false.[11]

This is an improvement upon the positivist theory of art, I think; but it, too, is incorrect, since not *all* the truth claims or referential statements of literature *are* false. There is more reason to believe that some of them (for example, that race prejudice in America thwarts individual growth) are true than there is for believing that all of them are false.

The emotive theory aside, the situation regarding the language of literature in relation to truth claims seems to me to include at least three different categories. First — and let us use examples from poetry throughout for the sake of simplicity, although let it be understood that the same analysis is applicable to drama, the novel, and the short story — there are many poems that contain truth claims as surface sentences, and not necessarily as depth meanings. Longfellow's "A Psalm of Life" contains the following lines:

> Life is real! Life is earnest!
>   And the grave is not its goal;
> Dust thou art, to dust returnest,
>   Was not spoken of the soul.

> Not enjoyment, and not sorrow,
>   Is our destined end or way;
> But to act, that each tomorrow
>   Find us farther than today.

Whatever we may think of this specimen, and it *is* pretty bad, we cannot deny that it makes a number of truth claims about the nature of life directly through the printed sentences of the poem. So does this example from Shakespeare:

> Blow, blow, thou winter wind!
> Thou art not so unkind
> As man's ingratitude.

Or this one:

> Let me not to the marriage of true minds
> Admit impediments. Love is not love
> Which alters when it alteration finds,
> Or bends with the remover to remove:
> O, no! it is an ever-fixèd mark
> That looks on tempests and is never shaken.

In both of these the poet is actually stating something that purports to be as much a revelation of certain aspects of reality (namely, the world of human experience) as any statement in science. In neither of these examples is it even necessary to paraphrase the claim since it is made so clearly; and in each case, if we wish to do so, or if we regard it as aesthetically relevant to do so, we may raise the question of the actual truth or falsity of the claim.

Poetry affords us many, many examples of printed truth claims. It is futile to deny it and I think the reason distinguished readers of poetry like Richards have denied it is that they did not want the truth claims of poetry to enter into our evaluation of the poetry. But we must keep our problems separate. Our immediate problem is whether or not poetry is able to embody truth claims. The examples given show that some poems, good and bad, do embody these claims, and within the surface-printed sentences. In no way does it follow from the presence of these truth claims that they constitute the most important element in poetry; or that they are the whole of any poetic communication; or even that they are important or aesthetically relevant at all. All of these are quite different considerations. In fact, there are at least four different questions to keep straight, and we are at present dealing only with the first. These questions are: (1) does some or all art embody truth claims? (2) ought any art to embody truth claims? (3) does the presence of truth claims make a difference to our appreciation of those works that have them? (4) ought the presence of truth claims to make a difference in our appreciation of those works that contain them? If critics and aestheticians had kept these questions distinct, we might have avoided a great deal of unnecessary debate during the last twenty-five years.

We shall discuss the last three questions in our next chapter. Let us now continue with the first and the enumeration of the categories of the language of poetry. Poetry can embody truth claims within the printed sentences; this is the first category. It can also embody truth claims as depth meanings. The truth claim of "Prufrock," namely, that there are two kinds of life and two kinds of death, is never stated as a printed sentence anywhere in the entire poem; yet it is part of the total poem as surely as the connotative overtones of coffee spoons are within the poem, even though they are never printed either.

Another example of a poem that contains a truth claim presented as a depth meaning is Yeats's "A Deep-Sworn Vow":

> Others because you did not keep
> That deep-sworn vow have been friends of mine;
> Yet always when I look death in the face,
> When I clamber to the heights of sleep,
> Or when I grow excited with wine,
> Suddenly I meet your face.

This is an extremely poignant communication, full of passion and paradox. Among its constituents is the depth meaning, not printed but present nevertheless, that one cannot erase the memory of true love; this constituent functions as a truth claim about the content of human experience.

One could with no difficulty at all list hundreds of examples of poetic communications in which depth meanings embody truth claims that serve as artistic commentaries on human experience by the poet. I conclude, therefore, that the emotive theory is simply false in its assertion that no art contains referential meanings.

The only element of truth in the emotive theory, at least so far as literature is concerned, lies in the third of our classifications. There are many poems in which there are no printed or implied truth claims, but instead articulations of wishes or commands or expressions of attitudes.

In Longfellow's "A Psalm of Life," we have the following combination of a wish and a command:

> In the world's broad field of battle,
>   In the bivouac of Life,
> Be not like dumb, driven cattle!
>   Be a hero in the strife!
>
> Trust no Future, howe'er pleasant!
>   Let the dead Past bury its dead!
> Act, — act in the living Present!
>   Heart within, and God o'erhead!

In Elizabeth Barrett Browning's "How Do I Love Thee," we have a pure expression of an attitude — of love — toward some object — the beloved:

> How do I love thee? Let me count the ways.
> I love thee to the depth and breadth and height
> My soul can reach, when feeling out of sight
> For the ends of Being and ideal Grace.
> I love thee to the level of everyday's
> Most quiet need, by sun and candle-light.
> I love thee freely, as men strive for Right;
> I love thee purely, as they turn from Praise.
> I love thee with the passion put to use
> In my old griefs, and with my childhood's faith.
> I love thee with a love I seemed to lose
> With my lost saints, — I love thee with the breath,
> Smiles, tears, of all my life! — and, if God choose,
> I shall but love thee better after death.

Finally, consider E. E. Cummings's "Portrait," in which the poet expresses his cavalier, flippant attitude toward death, and in which there is no truth claim stated or implied:

Buffalo Bill's
defunct
          who used to
          ride a watersmooth-silver
                              stallion
and break onetwothreefourfive pigeonsjustlikethat
                                        Jesus

he was a handsome man
                    and what i want to know is
how do you like your blueeyed boy
Mister Death*

Painting and Truth Claims

So much for the emotive theory and the problem of artistic truth
as it applies to literature. What can we say of painting and
truth? Can paintings make truth claims?

Erwin Panofsky, one of the leading exponents of the iconological
approach to painting, has written about painting in such a way as
to leave no doubt that he believes it does contain certain truth
claims or propositional assertions about the world. In his famous
essay, "*Et in Arcadia Ego*," which is a model of the sort of analysis
he engages in as an iconologist, Panofsky is concerned with the
Death theme in Watteau and Poussin. Here are a number of quotations from this essay:

(1) [He says of Poussin's painting, "*Et in Arcadia Ego*":]
The transformation of a mere *memento mori* into the revelation
of a metaphysical principle which connects the present and the
future with the past and overthrows the limits of individuality,
means that 'Life' is conceived as transitory yet blessed with in-
destructible beauty and felicity; on the other hand, 'Death' is
seen as a preserver as well as a destroyer. From this emerges the
magnificent conception of a cyclical succession which sub-

ordinates the existence of individuals to the inexorable laws of cosmic principles, both natural and moral, endowing every stage of this existence, however transitory, with a substantial value of its own.[12]

(2) [In summary of Poussin's art:] Thus Poussin's conception of life as a condition free though fatebound, dignified though pathetic, imperishable though variable, transpires even in a composition which seems to be nothing but the offshoot of a rather conventional allegorical tradition.[13]

(3) Watteau's *Fêtes Champêtres*, too, may be called allegories of transience; however, they neither visualize the annihilation of the past, nor the persistence of ideal forms outlasting the destruction of matter. They depict the fading away of reality as such. Existence itself seems to be subject to transience; past, present, and future fuse into a phantasmagoric realm in which the border-line between illusion and reality, dream and wakefulness, nature and art, mirth and melancholy, love and loneliness, life and the continuous process of dying, are thoroughly obliterated.[14]

It is clear, I think, from the above quotations, that Panofsky believes that paintings embody not only single truth claims but even systems of them as they become basic *Weltanschauungen*. It may be that Panofsky is too grandiloquent in his reflections upon the truth claims of paintings; but there seems to be some sense in which these truth claims can be made in painting. The problem for aesthetics, which curiously enough is similar to Kant's problem of justifying science, is to show *how* these truth claims are possible.

In order to do this, I am convinced, we must give up the positivistic version of the distinction between emotive and referential language. Perhaps the whole distinction should be repudiated, but I should not like to commit myself on this point.

There are certain kinds of activity that the positivists have traditionally classified as *pure* emoting but that upon analysis can be seen to embody referential propositional assertions about the world

that are true or false in the way in which ordinary empirical judgments are. Consider as an example the Christian ritualistic act of
kneeling in prayer. Now, according to the positivist view, this act
is pure emoting, the expression of feelings and attitudes, and an
act which, linguistically, may enter into communication, but only
in the sense of inducing similar feelings and attitudes (or perhaps
even opposing ones) in the spectators around the worshiper. And,
most importantly, the positivist maintains, there is nothing in the
act that asserts anything or constitutes a truth claim.

That kneeling in prayer is the expression of a feeling or attitude,
or that it can induce others to act, need not be denied; but that
it is pure emoting, completely nonassertive and nonreferential in
character can be denied. Kneeling in prayer in a Christian ritualistic
context includes also a referential propositional assertion or truth
claim about the world. Specifically, the act itself includes, as *one*
of its constituents, the assertion or claim that *there is a God Who
is worthy of human respect.* Instead of affirming the proposition,
"That God exists and is worthy of our respect," in ordinary verbal
ways (i.e., in English, French, German, etc.), the worshiper gestures it as part of his total act of kneeling in prayer. His action is
the medium of conveying the asserted proposition; and the assertional part of the action may be construed as a truth claim about
the existence and nature of God. It will not do to say that the
whole action is true or false, just as one cannot say that the usual
method of speaking, which is after all an act, too, is true or false.
It is only one aspect of the act, namely, the asserted proposition,
spoken or gestured as the case may be, that is true or false.[15]

I should like to propose that in paintings where there are
truth claims they are presented in ways that resemble the truth
claims offered in certain ritualistic acts like kneeling in prayer in
a Christian society. Painting can make certain truth claims mainly
through its constituents of the symbol, the subject, or both working in relation to the plastic expressive elements.

Consider, to begin with, one of Hobbema's landscapes in which, it is said, there is being asserted that nature is the conflict between the old and the new. Is this a valid conception of the capacities of painting? I think that it is. In Hobbema, it is the subject and its traditional transparently symbolic associations that embody the truth claim. The subject of the landscape is usually the representation of old, decaying trees being contrasted with the representation of young, powerful-looking, new trees. We interpret this subject as a sign of certain objects and concepts; these concepts have certain traditionally associated meanings; these meanings comprise the assertional propositional claim that nature is the struggle between the old and the new, the decaying and the living.

In the "Resurrection," by Piero della Francesca, there is present, as one of the constituents, the truth claim that man is in ignorance and darkness whereas God is in Truth and Light. Without raising any question about the whole problem of verifying such a claim, which would constitute a problem even in the prose statement of such a claim, we may say that the picture contains this truth claim through the very simple device of flooding the representations of Christ and the sky with tremendous light, and leaving the representation of man on the earth in relative shadow and darkness. All of these elements, with their transparently symbolic associations, add up to the assertional truth claim.

In the "Guernica," by Picasso, there is being asserted, among other things, that the victory of Fascism is the brutal destruction of everything. The painting asserts this through the bull, who symbolizes Fascism and who is relatively intact, and the other subjects — the soldier, the horse, the women, the children, and the houses — which are torn to pieces. All of these elements serve as a collective sign of the assertional proposition or truth claim regarding the nature of Fascism. One need only look at the painting to see that the artist is not wondering about the destructive character of Fascism, or denying it, or wishing it, or supposing it, but *asserting it*. The whole force of the painting leaves no doubt about the assertional character of the proposition, "That Fascism means the brutal destruction of everything."

Finally, one may say of Picasso's "Man with an All-Day Sucker" that it contains as one of its elements the truth claim that Fascism is the return to the infantile. This claim is made through the representation of a brutal-looking soldier (who is a transparent symbol of the Fascist), who is holding a sucker in the shape of a spear. The fact that the adult soldier is holding the weapon enables us to interpret the picture as claiming that Fascism is the return to the infantile, that is, the stage in which we lick all-day suckers.

Music and Truth Claims

So much for the arts of literature and painting as they relate to the problem of referential language or truth claims. Our primary aim has been to offer a refutation of the extravagant views of the emotive theory. We have no desire to demonstrate that all art embodies truth claims; in fact, in our discussion of poetry, we presented certain examples of poetry in which no truth claims were made. Stated in its positive form, our thesis has been that in some of the arts, especially in literature and painting, among the many elements there are to be found, either directly or indirectly, either stated or gestured, certain asserted propositions which are true or false. The extent of these truth claims in the arts is still an open question, and an invitation to further aesthetic analysis. The whole problem of truth claims in music, for example, needs a tremendous overhauling along the lines we have suggested or perhaps along other lines made possible by the continuing growth of the discipline of semiotic. The present writer, unfortunately, has doubts about the linguistic capacities of music. That music is a language in the sense of a system of signs that has meaning to listeners, we have already shown; but that music is a language in the sense of a system of signs that contains propositions in the ways that literature or painting do, we do not feel ready to accept. The position of J. W. N. Sullivan, in his book, *Beethoven: His Spiritual Development*, to the effect that music can embody a philosophy and that Beethoven's music does, while it is attractive and one would like to believe it, is open to serious criticisms of the sort mentioned already in our previous discussions of extreme heteronomy in music. The most I am prepared to say, and this very tentatively, is that some music does contain *musical analogues* of assertions or truth claims. Consider, for example, Beethoven's last quartet, Opus 135. Many critics, even the composer himself, find in it the assertion that life is good or that affirmation of life is the answer to doubt. Perhaps this is too much to find in the music, but what one does find is the sequence of *musical* doubt and affirmation. The fourth and final movement begins slowly and is characterized in this beginning section by irresolution and hesitation within the musical sounds; this is followed by an allegro section in which all the musical doubt and irresolution give way to musical materials that are completely affirmative in their expressive character. Now, if we accept musical hesitation and affirmation as transparent symbols, we may say that this fourth movement embodies the contrast between doubt and affirmation, in which the latter comes after the former, as a kind of *reply* to it. But this is a musical reply, and the whole movement is at most an analogue of the claim that in life affirmation is the answer to doubt.

9

THE APPRECIATION OF ART

Introduction

In our previous chapters our primary concern has been the nature of the art object in the aesthetic experience. We may now turn to the examination of artistic appreciation, which constitutes another central problem in aesthetic inquiry.

We shall not attempt to deal with all of the many theories of art appreciation. Instead we shall discuss a few characteristic ones in order to discern their different emphases or exaggerations, and also to justify, finally, the view that art appreciation ought to be a form of contemplation.

Throughout our discussion we shall employ the concepts of descriptive and normative, as applied to appreciation. By a descriptive theory we shall mean one that describes the way or ways in which people as spectators *do* respond to works of art; and by a normative theory, one that tells us the way in which spectators *ought* to respond to works of art. Some of the views that we shall examine do not draw this distinction and consequently remain confused mixtures of the descriptive and normative approaches to artistic appreciation.

Make-Believe and the Problem of "Poetic Belief"

Let us begin our analysis with the doctrine that the appreciation of art is a form of make-believe. This is a descriptive theory, although its advocates do not declare themselves on this matter. The theory has been shared by play theorists like Lange and Groos and voluntarists like Parker.

The play theory, which purports to be a psychological one, has stressed the kinship of art appreciation and ordinary play in respect to a number of characteristics. Both are pleasurable activities, nonpractical, conscious, voluntary; they are also the satisfactions of basic biological needs. Furthermore — and this is its central doctrine — all artistic activity is a species of the genus illusion games or play. Two sorts of games or play are recognized, illusion and nonillusion. Artistic activity is akin to illusion play; it is "an enhanced and refined illusion play adapted to the need of the adult." [1] The essence of artistic activity and illusion play is the presence of conscious self-deception or make-believe. Illusion games, like impersonations, cops and robbers, playing with dolls, and the sailing of toy boats, involve players who imagine themselves to be that which they know they are not. It is *as if* they were what they are not. All artistic activity, including appreciation, involves this attitude of make-believe and the acceptance of the imaginative and the fictional as if they were true or real.

Parker has also placed great emphasis upon this as-if character in art appreciation. It is not for him the whole of appreciation but it is central since artistic activity is basically imaginative and the essence of the imaginative is this make-believe character.[2]

In our appreciation of art, then, according to this theory, our cognitive attitude is one of make-believe and not of belief or disbelief.

Let us now evaluate this theory as it applies to our appreciation of an art, namely, literature, where these attitudes of belief and disbelief do seem to have some bearing. Specifically, let us return to "Prufrock."

Now, our normal attitude, that is, our usual cognitive response to "Prufrock," I suppose, is something like this. We distinguish between the characters, events, and themes. We do not believe that the character, Prufrock, is real or was real or that the things he did were actual events. But we do not make believe about them either. Rather we "suspend our disbelief" (Coleridge). That is to say, we regard it as irrelevant to our appreciation that these things were or are actual. Our usual attitude, then, is disbelief and the willing suspension of it. But this is not equivalent to make-believe.

Further, we *do* believe that, although Prufrock is not real, there are people like him; that he is iconically representative of them; that he is like the "you and I" of "Prufrock." We do believe that some people, including ourselves perhaps, have had experiences similar to Prufrock's — of questioning, vacillating, doubting, and self-chastising. It is important to us in our appreciation that we believe that Prufrock's experiences are like ours in many ways.

So far as the theme of "Prufrock" is concerned, our normal attitude is to accept or reject it. We have a tendency to take themes as either true or false, depending upon our nonartistic convictions in these matters. And we are influenced by our acceptance or rejection in our appreciation. Normally, then, belief and disbelief, not make-believe, are the dominant cognitive attitudes in poetic appreciation.

This usual, normal attitude has been challenged by the make-believe theory but more seriously, I think, by the "New Criticism" represented by Richards, Eliot, and Cleanth Brooks.

Eliot has remarked that Richards "deserves the credit of having done the pioneer work in the problem of Belief in the enjoyment of poetry." [3] In *The Meaning of Meaning,* as we have seen, Richards construes the language of poetry as emotive. As such, it does not contain referential statements, assertions, or truth claims. And without these, the cognitive attitudes of belief, disbelief, or make-believe are simply inappropriate since there is nothing — no statement — to believe or disbelieve or about which to make believe (that is, accept as if it were true). The appreciation of poetry involves none of these cognitive attitudes.

Poetry, Richards holds, contains the articulation of emotional attitudes. This is its great contribution. In all of his later writings Richards argues that poetry functions to organize our attitudes and value judgments, and that this organization of attitudes can be appreciated without any cognitive acceptance, rejection, or make-believe. In *Practical Criticism, Principles of Literary Criticism* and *Science and Poetry*, a new conception of poetry is offered, the essence of which is rooted in the repudiation of the "revelation" theory of poetry. A poem, it is stated, is not a truth claim or theme embroidered by metrics and metaphor. "It is never what a poem *says* which matters, but what it *is*." [4] And what a poem *is*, is the emotive articulation of the organization of attitudes and experiences. Poetry, when it is comprehended in this manner, it is affirmed, should not be read with any concern for belief, disbelief, or make-believe. These attitudes should never arise, for they are not the proper ones to have toward poetry.

> The question of belief or disbelief never arises when we are reading well. If unfortunately it does arise, either through the poet's fault or our own, we have for the moment ceased to be readers and have become astronomers, theologians, or moralists . . . persons engaged in a quite different type of activity.[5]

The appreciation of poetry, then, is reading well, which is understanding the total poem, what it *is*, that is, comprehending the working out of all its various constituents.

Eliot, unlike Richards, has vacillated on this problem of "poetic belief." In his first discussion of the problem, contained in the appendix to his essay "Dante," he writes:

> We must assume that the reader can obtain the full "literary"

or (if you will) "aesthetic" enjoyment without sharing the beliefs of the author. *If* there is "literature," *if* there is "poetry," then it must be possible to have full literary or poetic appreciation without sharing the beliefs of the poet . . .

I deny, in short, that the reader must share the beliefs of the poet in order to enjoy the poetry fully.

If you deny the theory that full poetic appreciation is possible without belief in what the poet believed, you deny the existence of "poetry" as well as "criticism"; and if you push this denial to its conclusion, you will be forced to admit that there is very little poetry that you can appreciate, and that your appreciation of it will be a function of your philosophy or theology or something else . . .

Actually, one probably has more pleasure in the poetry when one shares the beliefs of the poet. On the other hand there is a distinct pleasure in enjoying poetry as poetry when one does *not* share the beliefs, analogous to the pleasure of "mastering" other men's philosophical systems. It would appear that "literary appreciation" is an abstraction, and pure poetry a phantom; and that both in creation and enjoyment much always enters which is, from the point of view of "Art," irrelevant.[6]

In his essay "Shelley and Keats," however, Eliot shifts his position. It is Shelley's "ideas" that disturb him because he finds them adolescent and repellent. "Some of Shelley's views I positively dislike, and that hampers my enjoyment of the poems in which they occur; and others seem to me so puerile that I cannot enjoy the poems in which they occur." [7]

Toward the end of this essay, Eliot tries to resolve the inconsistency between the "Dante" view and this one:

When the doctrine, theory, belief, or "view of life" presented in a poem is one which the mind of the reader can accept as coherent, mature, and founded on the facts of experience, it interposes no obstacle to the reader's enjoyment, whether it be one that he accept or deny, approve or deprecate. When it is one which the reader rejects as childish or feeble, it may, for a reader of well-developed mind, set up an almost complete check.[8]

Eliot's view, then, is a form of the "ripeness-is-all" doctrine. That is to say, his is the view that it ought not to be of any concern to the reader what the thematic material of a poem is so long as it is developed in a mature, honest, and true way. This version of the problem has been given its latest formulation by Cleanth Brooks, in his brilliant book, *The Well Wrought Urn*.

The whole problem of poetic truth and belief, Brooks insists, arises in the acceptance of the "heresy of paraphrase," that is, the doctrine that what a poem communicates is something much less than the total poem. This heresy is rooted in the aesthetics that distinguishes between form and content as the how and the what of a poem, in the formulation of a poem as a statement embroidered by metaphor, and in the rejection of the organic theory of art.

No statement, Brooks continues, can be abstracted from a poem and be said to be what the poem is communicating. The poem is communicating *all* that it is. If we consider any poem and try to state what it communicates, we come to see that qualifications and reservations occur until we gradually perceive that the entire communication is the *total* poem in all of its complexity.

A poem is a "pattern of resolved stresses," a drama or an action instead of a statement, that is, a complex of attitudes which is unfolded through paradox, wit, and irony.[9]

The reader is not asked to accept the ideas of the poem but to apprehend them. This is what Richards should have meant by reading well, Brooks asserts. In reading well, we ought to ignore our convictions about the world in order to appreciate the unfolding in poetic, dramatic terms of the poet's version of the complexity of human experience.

Eliot's difficulty with Shelley can also be rephrased; it is not that Eliot disagrees with Shelley's ideas, Brooks points out, but that he objects to Shelley's not coming to complex terms with them.[10] Eliot should have said that Shelley is an immature poet because he simplifies attitudes.

Poetry, to sum up Brooks's position, does not state ideas but tests them: "A poem . . . is to be judged, not by the truth or falsity as such, of the idea which it incorporates, but rather by its character as drama — by its coherence, sensitivity, depth, richness, and tough-mindedness." [11]

The attempt to solve the problem of poetic belief by Brooks is a noble effort, but it has not succeeded. For, in the first place, even if we grant that a poem is a total communication, we must still recognize that the truth claim is *one* constituent of the poem. It will not do to say with Brooks that the claim or statement exists only *outside* of the poem as part of its "scaffolding," since, as we have seen in our discussion of the "Prufrock" theme and in our analysis of the depth meanings of *Native Son*, for example, the claim is part of the total poem as a work of art, existing *within* it.

If the claim or theme is an integral constituent of the poem, the problem of belief inevitably arises as the problem of our proper attitude toward this one constituent. That is to say, we must always ask, what ought our attitude to be toward the truth claims of poetry?

This objection applies to Richards, too. It is not what a poem says but what it is that matters, Richards states. But this assumes that what a poem *is* is completely unrelated to what it *says*, and this is an unwarranted assumption since, to repeat, part of what a poem is, is what it says, where "says" is synonymous with "statement" or "truth claim."

Secondly — and I should like to stress this criticism rather than the first — suppose we agree with Brooks that a poem is a complexity of attitudes; yet we may still ask why what he, following Richards, calls the inclusive rendering of this complexity is better than the exclusive? Why, for example, is Donne better than Shelley, for Brooks? The answer is quite clear. Brooks prefers the inclusive, the nonsimplification of attitudes, because he *believes* it to be a *truer* conception of human experience than the exclusive or sentimental simplification of attitudes. He prefers Donne to Shelley because he believes that Donne has come to grips with his material in a maturer, richer, more profound, and less sentimental way than Shelley, because he believes that Donne's philosophy of human experience, with its understanding of the many complexities of experience, is much more in accord with the facts of the human scene than is the philosophy of Shelley. In a word: Brooks prefers Donne to Shelley because he *believes* that Donne's total poetic communication is truer than Shelley's.

The real contribution of the "New Criticism," then, has not been the solution of the problem of poetic belief but rather the formulation of it in relation to a more organic conception of poetry than that provided by the previous "revelation" theories. It has not been able to show that the problem arises only when we accept the heresy of paraphrase since, as we have tried to show in our critique of Brooks, it also arises when we conceive of poetry as an organic complex of constituents.

A new analysis is needed. Let us begin with the fundamental contribution of the "New Criticism," that a poem is an organic complex of constituents, including the theme. Toward these constituents, but especially the theme, when it functions as a truth claim, there are at least four cognitive attitudes that one can assume: indifference or unconcern, make-believe, acceptance or belief, and rejection or disbelief.

The attitude of indifference is implied by the aesthetics of Richards. Throughout his writings, Richards recognizes that it is possible to interpret poetry as embodying truth claims, but he warns against it because he thinks that such an interpretation leads to the nonaesthetic scientific, moralistic, or philosophical readings of poetry. Consequently, his thesis that poetry is an emotive language could be construed as a recommendation that we regard it as such. I do not think Richards is at all clear whether poetry cannot be referential (embody truth claims) or ought not to be so.

We have already shown that poetry can be referential. Let us now consider whether it ought to be so. Richards suggests that poetry ought not to make truth claims because our appreciation will be perverted from an aesthetic to a nonaesthetic one. But if this is his fear, we can assuage it by offering a counterrecommendation that will prevent any such aesthetic perversion: we ought not to allow the truth or falsity of any poetic claim to enter into our appreciation of the poem if we wish to understand poetry on its own terms and not treat it as science or philosophy.

There is a subtler reason, however, than this avowed one, which Richards has never stated, that has inspired his twin doctrines that poetry ought not to make truth claims and that true aesthetic appreciation ought to be indifferent to them if certain poems do include them. This reason is, I think, the underlying assumption of Richards's whole aesthetic: truth claims ought to be the province of science and not of poetry (or art), since science is able to make them in a much better way than poetry. It is because Richards believes this and accepts it as his fundamental premise that he argues that poetry ought not to make truth claims or that true appreciation of poetry ought not to be concerned with truth claims when they are present.

It is this ultimate assumption that can be challenged because it is false. Art, especially literature, is capable of embodying many truth claims about the world, mainly about the complexities and nuances of human experiences, which the sciences do not make or have not made. Literature, with its capacity for communicating the succulent character of man's emotional *Existenz*, can say certain things about the nature of man that the sciences, which are after all concerned with the formulation of causal generalizations, are not interested in saying. No psychologist, for example, has made the claims about human motivation in the richly concrete and complex way that a Proust or a Dostoevski has made them. Even

Freud recognized this. Nor has any social philosopher exposed the sicknesses of American society in the encompassing way that our American realistic novelists have done.

It is true that science can say certain things about the world. It can tell us about the facts. It can give us knowledge. But literature can also say certain things about the world, mainly the human world. It, too, can offer us information but, as Plato pointed out long ago, it can give us more, a reconstruction and an evaluation of the facts; which leads us from knowledge to wisdom. Wisdom, that is, the evaluation of the human scene, is more than emotive; it involves also certain truth claims about the nature of life and experience. There is none of this wisdom in science. There used to be some in philosophy but not any more. It is only in the arts, and especially literature, that we can find it today.

Some of the arts embody truth claims. It is as arbitrary of Richards to recommend that we ignore these, which his attitude of indifference calls for, as it is of Fry to recommend that we disregard the element of color in painting. Whatever other requisites a theory of appreciation must satisfy, it must be a theory that comes to terms with the total character of the art object. The truth claims of poetry demand that we take up some attitude toward them. Indifference, in Richards's sense of ignoring them, simply will not do.

This brings us to the cognitive attitude of make-believe. We have already seen that this is a false theory when it is regarded descriptively as an empirical generalization. Normatively, the theory is the recommendation that we treat the truth claims of poetry as if they were true, even though we know they are false.

The difficulty with this recommendation is that it assumes that all poetic assertions are really false, that poetry contains only falsehoods and refers only to unrealities, which the reader accepts as if they were true or real for the sake of the aesthetic experience. But this is not always the case since much of poetry does embody true truth claims or, at any rate, certain truth claims which some readers accept as true and not as if they were true. The make-believe theory has no explanation of the attitude of these readers nor do its advocates try in any way to justify their recommendation to these readers.

We come, then, to the third attitude, that of disbelief, which is practiced by two distinct groups of readers. According to the first, we do and ought to appreciate a poem less the more we disbelieve the theme or claim that it embodies. Extremists of this view assert that we ought to reject the entire poem if we disbelieve the fundamental claim of the poem. Thus, in the case of "Prufrock," this group would say, if we do not believe that there are two kinds of life, etc., then we ought to reject the whole poem as a work of art. Readers of the "nugget" or "revelation" variety, and in the case of "Prufrock" these would consist mainly of atheists, might be members of this sort.

To this group we may say by way of critique that even though people do respond to poetry in this manner, they ought not to do so because they are responding to only one element of the poem, the theme, to the neglect of all the others. In effect, they are converting poetry completely into scientific statement. The supporters of the "revelation" theory, whatever faith they live by, because they evaluate poetry either primarily or completely in terms of its truth claims, are unconsciously concerned with only one thing, to destroy poetry as quickly as possible and to reduce it to that which they can evaluate as they do scientific statements, *strictly* on the basis of its truth or falsity.

There is a more sophisticated, normative version of disbelief. Here we reject the claim and refuse to accept it as if it were true; but we suspend our disbelief, not in the sense of being indifferent or of ignoring the claim, but rather in the sense of regarding it with tolerance as an alternative world view or philosophical hypothesis.

Our appreciation, if we adopt this attitude, is of a false claim, or one that we consider to be false, as it relates to the other constituents of the poem. Reading well, on this view, means apprehending the working out of all the constituents in their functional relationships while disbelieving one of them, the theme; but refusing to allow the disbelief to make any difference to our appreciation on the grounds that in art counterclaims (those that we reject) are as legitimate as accepted claims. This attitude, in sum, is akin to Eliot's "mastering of other men's systems."

Finally, there is the cognitive attitude of belief. This also has a naïve and a mature version. The naïve reader who supports the attitude of belief — for example, the Anglican who reads "Prufrock" and evaluates it favorably because he takes the religious doctrines to be orthodox — offers the same sort of argument and suffers from the same sort of inadequacies as his fellow disbelievers. The mature believer, on the other hand, is the reader who believes the basic thematic claim but refuses to allow his belief to enter into his evaluation of the poem. The attitude of mature belief recommends that we apprehend the theme as one element in a work of art and comprehend its working out in relation to the other elements. Believe in truth claims, it prescribes, for we cannot help but do so, but do not allow belief to control appreciation since truth claims are not the central factor of art.

If we follow this recommendation, we will reply to the query, what difference ought mature belief or disbelief to make in our appreciation of poetry and art? that either ought to make *no* difference. The two attitudes are equal. The true appreciator — *the well-wrought reader* — ought to treat rejected albeit tolerated themes or truth claims as favorably as he does those he accepts.

In appreciation we cannot help but believe or disbelieve; but, if we desire to distinguish between our attitudes toward science and art, we ought not to allow our cognitive attitude to enter into appreciation. Science (or philosophy) does not treat what it rejects as tolerantly as what it accepts; and when it does, we say it is assuming an aesthetic attitude, that is, not allowing its beliefs to enter into its evaluations.

How can we justify our recommendation? We can do so negatively, by pointing out that its repudiation entails the giving up of art and the conversion of it into something quite different, and positively, by appealing to the liberating function of the aesthetic experience as the one activity in which human beings can come to apprehend all of the many possibilities for human experience. Reading well, whether it involves reading what we accept or what we reject, is reading with an eye for these possibilities and the liberating effects they offer to us.

Voluntarism: Freud's Theory

The next theory of art appreciation that we shall examine is voluntarism. The basic thesis of voluntarism, which is a descriptive and not a normative one, is that the appreciation of art is essentially the satisfaction of our desires. The two outstanding representatives of this view are Freud and Parker.

Freud, whose great contributions to psychology no longer require either apology or exposition, wrote a number of books and essays on artistic activity, among them *Leonardo da Vinci: A Psychosexual Study of an Infantile Reminiscence.* Unfortunately, Freud was interested here more in the confirmation of his psychoanalytic theories than in the exploration of the artistic process. Paradoxically, however, he did offer certain systematic reflections upon art in his technical treatises on psychoanalysis, especially in Chapter 23 of *A General Introduction to Psycho-Analysis.*[12]

The whole of artistic activity or the aesthetic experience, Freud maintains, is rooted in the unconscious of man. The creation of art is the satisfaction of sexual desires that the artist cannot satisfy or realize in normal ways. The art object is the embodiment of the artist's satisfactions. And the appreciation of art is the satisfaction of the frustrated sexual desires of the spectator. Like the artist, the spectator obtains an imaginative fulfillment of his infantile, unconscious, frustrated sexual desires through his appreciation of the art object.

In Freud, desire is the basic category. It is sexual in character. The normal person is the one who satisfies it in ordinary hetero-sexual ways. The neurotic is the one who does not. He represses his desires and eventually, if he does not obtain satisfaction, be-comes seriously ill. Before reaching this stage of complete neurosis, however, there is a period in which he can achieve certain substi-tute satisfactions in daydreams and fantasies.

The artist, unable to obtain ordinary sexual satisfactions, is driven to fantasy and the road to neurosis. But, unlike the usual neurotic, he creates something quite tangible out of his frustra-tions, namely, an art object. It is this that saves him, because the art object brings him the real-life satisfactions of approval and suc-cess (ego satisfactions). The artist pours his infantile, unsatisfied desires into his tangible, sensuous, public dream fantasy, his art work. Other human beings attend to it and afford the artist real-life satisfactions. The artist's ego has been enhanced and he is saved from neurosis.

It is no easy matter to get others to listen to one's dreams and fantasies. In fact, one ordinarily has to pay an enormous amount to get a psychoanalyst to listen to one's dreams or fantasies, even if one is an artist. Is it not strange, then, that the same analyst will also pay an artist — slightly less, to be sure! — to relate to him his dreams when the analyst visits the theater or concert hall or buys a book or picture?

Freud's explanation of this is rather complex. In order to be pal-atable, the artist must transform his dreams and fantasies, with all of their infantile repulsiveness, into something that the public can accept. The transformation is similar to the transformation of the artist's or our night dreams, which is effected by the mech-anism of the "censor." The artist's fantasies are stripped of their private egocentricities. The forbidden is concealed and the re-pulsive is tempered. This is the first step in the transformation.

Then the artist employs certain aesthetic principles, "laws of beauty," Freud calls them, like design, color, or style, in building up his work of art. Throughout this process the artist is creating an object which, when it is offered to his audiences, will satisfy their narcissistic desire to control some aspect of reality. In creating a work of art, the artist creates a new image of reality the apprehension of which produces the decidedly pleasurable experience of omnipotence that all of us desire as part of our unsatisfied, infantile needs.

Like almost everyone else, Freud distinguishes between the form and the content of a work of art. The content is always the embodiment of sexual desires and satisfactions; the form, the way in which these are presented and covered up. Form is a mere accessory and must not be overemphasized for it is the cause only of the "forepleasure," not the real pleasure, of the aesthetic experience which remains the attendant of the imaginative satisfaction of unconscious desires.

The subordinate character of the laws of beauty and the central importance of the sexual in art is exemplified best in Freud's theory of wit. Consider some joke. The manner in which it is embellished, that which we usually refer to as the cleverness of the joke, is never more than the "aesthetic threshold" which functions to lead us to the real pleasure, the satisfaction of our infantile, aggressive hostility. We need this embellishment in order to enable us to cover up these infantile tendencies and to enjoy them, without being consciously aware of what we are really doing. All of us can enjoy a seduction story provided we are able to say that it is the cleverness that we admire when we are really deriving our satisfaction from the presentation of the sexual material. Also, for Freud, when we resent or reject the "raw" joke, what we are really objecting to is not the satisfactions we got from hearing it, but the fact that we are being caught in the act of an unadorned sexual satisfaction.

To sum up: The artist transforms his infantile dreams and fantasies into acceptable works of art by creating narcissistically satisfying images of reality in which certain aesthetic principles adorn his articulated sexual desires. The spectator, in his appreciation, obtains satisfactions of his own frustrated sexual desires but in ways that are completely acceptable to the moral demands of his superego.

Many criticisms have been made of the Freudian aesthetics. It has been rejected on psychological as well as normative grounds. Parker, who borrows heavily from Freud, has severely criticized Freud's limited psychology of the artistic process. Artistic activity, Parker claims, is satisfaction of desires, but not only of frustrated desires. It is also the satisfaction of the overabundance of desires. Secondly, it is not confined to the satisfaction of sexual but of all desires.

The Freudians, of course, repudiate these charges. All desires are fundamentally sexual, they reply; and all overabundance of desire is discharge of basic sexual desire or the attempt to compensate for previous frustration.

It is difficult indeed to decide this dispute either way. On introspective grounds, it seems that Parker is right and that Freud's views are exaggerated. The Freudians can always reply, however, that if we search deeply enough, with the aid of a psychoanalyst, we will come to see that all desires *are* sexual and that all artistic activity *is* the result of frustration and not the overabundance of desire. In arguing this way, however, the Freudians transform their views from empirical statements which are confirmable or confutable according to the facts to mere stipulatory definitions that can *never* be confuted since any evidence that is offered as confuting is evaluated as confirming instead by interpreting it in terms of the further probing of the unconscious. By not offering any criteria whereby we could distinguish a sexual from a nonsexual desire, they really conceive their statement that all desires are sexual as a tautological one and no longer as an empirical one at all.

The second objection is that it is too romantic an aesthetic theory in its conception of the artist as a person quite apart from ordinary beings, for it separates him too much from his fellow craftsmen. Many great artists, among them the anonymous builders of the medieval cathedrals, were as nonneurotic in their lives as our contemporary carpenters and house painters, who are after all the successors of the medieval craftsmen. Historically, the artist as sculptor has much more in common with the modern craftsman as carpenter than he has with the frustrated Bohemian that Freud regards as the typical artist. Roger Fry has made this criticism of Freud most pointedly. To be sure, Fry admits, there are artists who are Bohemian neurotics but they are mostly second-raters. The great artists, or at least many of them, are those who have withdrawn from the dream and have created an art "which is preeminently *objective* and *disinterested*, and which therefore proceeds in the opposite direction from the other kind of art [the wish-fulfillment kind]." [13]

The most important objection that has been leveled against the Freudian aesthetics is that it cannot explain the difference between good and bad art since it has no concern at all with critical matters. Its interest is completely in the genesis and effects of artistic activity. This criticism is relevant to the problem of appreciation in that no aesthetics can be considered adequate that does not furnish at least some criteria for the practical criticism of works of art. Thus far the Freudian aesthetics has shown no interest in the formulation of these criteria.

Voluntarism: Parker's Theory

Parker agrees with Freud that artistic activity is akin to the dream, and that the dream itself is dominated by desire. The imagination, Parker claims, is also dominated by desire. The imagination exists for a purpose, to satisfy desires. Parker recognizes two ways of satisfying desires, the real way, which is characterized by the appropriation of some object from the environment on the part of the person seeking real satisfaction, and the imaginative way, in which desires are satisfied wholly within the person seeking satisfaction, with no relation to the environment. The second mode of satisfaction is as genuine as the first since it makes us content.

Thus, Parker's theory of artistic activity as imaginative satisfaction has two parts that bring together the play theory and the Freudian. Art induces us to make believe; and make-believe (imagining) satisfies our desires. So far as appreciation is concerned, the spectator of the work of art satisfies all sorts of desires, sexual and nonsexual, conscious and unconscious; and these desires are satisfied in the imaginative mode of experience.

Parker's severest critic is Ducasse, who tries to refute him on factual, not normative, grounds.[14] Parker is incorrect in thinking that there are two ways of satisfying desires, the imaginative and the real. There is but one way, Ducasse insists — getting what you want. This getting may either occur or it may be imagined to occur. We must therefore distinguish carefully between satisfying a desire in the imagination, that is, in a make-believe experience; and the imaginative satisfaction of a desire, that is, making believe that a desire is satisfied. Making believe that a desire is satisfied is no satisfaction, Ducasse asserts; and, consequently, Parker's theory, which depends on the experience of make-believe as being a genuine satisfaction, is false.

Unfortunately, Parker has never replied to this objection in print, so it is difficult to know how he would answer it. The issue is, of course, a factual one and solvable only by an appeal to the facts of psychology. Now, if we examine the findings of psychology, incomplete as they are, but as they are derived from the auto-biographies and biographies of artists and the reports of our and other people's experiences with art, it does seem that Parker is correct in maintaining that, at least in a great many cases, the imaginative satisfaction of desire, that is, the experience of making believe a desire is satisfied, is a genuine satisfaction. It does seem to be true that many people, including spectators of art, get a real satisfaction from making believe that some desire or other is being satisfied.

The real quarrel with Parker, at least so far as I am concerned, is not on this issue but rather has to do with his doctrine that the imaginative satisfaction of desire is somehow a *substitute* satisfaction of a specific desire. In both Freud and Parker, there is this tacit assumption that there are various modes of satisfying the same desire. Consider our desire for fame. Both Freud and Parker claim that if one cannot obtain satisfaction of this desire in the usual manner of winning public approval, then one can satisfy that same desire through a make-believe experience, either in the dream, in fantasy, or in art.

I think that this empirical hypothesis can be seriously disputed. It is true that this imaginative experience does involve satisfactions of *some* sort, or we would not seek it; but it does not satisfy our specific desire for public approval. That is to say, it is not a substitute satisfaction of our desire for fame, but rather a genuine satisfaction of a different desire, rooted in our psychological being.

There are substitute satisfactions, but I wonder if these do not characterize our youth and adolescence, those periods when we are willing to tolerate substitutes because we feel, with our vision toward the future, that the real satisfaction will come? But no youth really feels, I am almost certain, that these substitutes are anything more than substitutes.

As we grow older and become more mature, we begin to lose faith in substitutes altogether. In fact, I wonder if when, as adults, we are presented with a substitute, it does not tend to intensify our original desire and aggravate our feelings of attendant frustration rather than to satisfy it? A mature person who wishes fame and success and who indulges himself in make-believe experiences in which he takes it as if he were a great man, will satisfy some desire — perhaps the mere desire for reverie — but I doubt whether he will satisfy his desire to be a great man. In fact, if he continues in his make-believe experience, he will probably become terribly frustrated, irritated, and eventually quite disgusted with himself. His total experience may even act as an incentive to do something with himself so that he can realize his desire for fame.

The basic truth, then, of the voluntaristic theory of artistic activity, including appreciation, is not that in our experience with art we satisfy desires we cannot satisfy in other ways, but that we satisfy desires, for example, the desire for imaginative experiences, in real ways. The aesthetic experience, in other words, is not a form of sublimation. It is as real and direct a form of satisfaction of desire as our satisfying our sexual desire in the experience of sexual intercourse.

Emotionalism: Tolstoy's Theory

We come now to the emotionalist theory of appreciation. This is, I suppose, the most widely accepted theory today. One of its most influential advocates is Tolstoy, whose views we shall now examine.

Tolstoy is a complete emotionalist in aesthetic theory. According to him, the whole of the aesthetic experience from the artist to the spectator is emotional indulgence. More specifically, the aesthetic experience is evocatively emotional in character in that the artist communicates his emotions to the spectator in the attempt to induce him to share in his emotions. Tolstoy's theory is epitomized by two statements in his essay, *What Is Art?*

> To evoke in oneself a feeling one has once experienced and having evoked it in oneself then by means of movements, lines, colours, sounds, or forms expressed in words, so to transmit that feeling that others experience the same feeling — this is the activity of art.
> Art is a human activity consisting in this, that one man consciously by means of certain external signs, hands on to others

feelings he has lived through, and that others are infected by these feelings and also experience them.[15]

Without the actual transmission of feelings from the artist to the spectator, the aesthetic experience is aborted. Artistic communication means actual emotional participation on the part of the spectator. To appreciate art is to partake of the emotions embodied in the art object by the artist.

Because of the emotional character of the aesthetic experience, Tolstoy regards artistic activity, especially the appreciation of art, as a means of uniting human beings in their spiritual progress. The artist, like a benevolent virus, infects his audiences — enhances their sensibilities, we would say today; and, if this infectiousness is of the right sort, his art becomes an instrument for civilizing us.

The right sort of infectiousness for Tolstoy is the religious-humanitarian. Tolstoy recognizes two criteria for great art: the formal, which is infectiousness and by virtue of which we can say that the greater the infectiousness, the greater the work of art; and the material, which constitutes the humanitarian feelings. The more humanitarian the feelings, the greater the art because the more it can civilize its spectators.[16]

Tolstoy is thus the great antagonist of the Kantian aesthetics. Like the contemporary instrumentalists, he insists upon the practical, moral, and active character of art appreciation. Contemplation, disinterestedness, and detachment are denied altogether.

It has been frequently pointed out that Tolstoy is his best critic. With unrelenting consistency and candor, he reduces his theory to absurdity by repudiating almost the entirety of historically accepted great art. In place of the great novels of the nineteenth century, for example, he puts inanely sentimental stories; and the whole of Beethoven is rejected in favor of some heartfelt peasant song that was sung to his daughter on her wedding day.[17]

There are other, perhaps equally serious, objections to Tolstoy's theory. Consider, first, his doctrine that artistic activity is a form of communication which involves the transmission of feelings in such a manner that they are evoked in the spectators. Without actual indulgence in what is communicated, there is no communication.

This doctrine is false; and to see that it is, let us examine first ordinary, nonartistic communication. A speaker is said to communicate to a listener if the latter understands him, not necessarily if he believes him. Belief is to ordinary communication what emotional indulgence is to artistic communication, an added factor but not an essential one. One can appreciate the emotions communicated without indulging in them just as one can understand the nonartistic thoughts and ideas communicated without believing them. The view that artistic communication entails participation in the emotions communicated is as false as the doctrine that ordinary communication entails the acceptance of the assertions being communicated.

Secondly, the whole theory of evocation of emotions or indulgence as the true mode of appreciation may be challenged. To appreciate art, Tolstoy and so many others in the modern world insist, is to be moved by it through an actual participation in the same emotions that are embodied in the art object. But, as Fry pointed out in rejecting this version of the emotionalist aesthetics, to be moved in this manner is to lose one's capacity to see the whole of the work of art.[18] For the spectator who indulges in the emotions offered him by the artist, the appreciation of any sort of complexity in art is psychologically impossible. To share fully in Othello's jealousy, for example, makes it impossible for anyone to share in the other emotions of the play, some of which are devastatingly critical of jealousy. In so far as Tolstoy's theory is descriptive on this point, then, it is false, since not all people do appreciate art by indulging in the emotions presented in the work of art; and in so far as the theory is normative, its recommendation that we indulge in the emotions of the work of art in order to appreciate it ought to be rejected on the grounds that in the appreciation of complex works of art, that is, works in which tremendous ranges of emotions are presented, it would be psychologically impossible to indulge in them, even if such a procedure were worthwhile. We have said before that the ultimate criterion of any adequate aesthetics, including the theory of appreciation, is that it encompass the totality of the art object. Any theory that recommends that we appreciate only certain aspects of the work of art is by virtue of that recommendation inadequate.

Finally, one may take issue with Tolstoy's normative doctrine that art ought to communicate only humanitarian feelings. It is important to understand why Tolstoy makes such a proposal. He does so partly, I think, because of his theory of appreciation as evocation of emotions. Like Plato, Tolstoy regards man as a "thinking reed," blowing every which way with every new idea or emotion, and in need of protection from the bad ones. Both of these aestheticians are convinced that art should contain no evil because the presentation of it leads inexorably, they think, to the promotion of it.

On Tolstoy's view, the communication of a great deal of human experience is ruled out. The whole realm of the *demonic* (the sadistic, immoral, unconventional, sordid, etc.) is rejected and art is thereby limited in its range of expression.

If for no other reason than this one, of the limitations imposed on art, we ought to repudiate Tolstoy's aesthetics. The best way to do this and to preserve the validity of the demonic in artistic communication is to reject Tolstoy's recommendation that we indulge in the emotions contained in the art object. By offering a nonindulgent theory of appreciation, for example, a contemplative one, we shall impose no limitations upon the kinds of emotions and values the artist can communicate; and we shall make possible our total appreciation of them.

Emotionalism: Hirn's Theory

Another relatively contemporary emotionalist theory, which derives from Aristotle's doctrine of catharsis, is that of Hirn. For
him, artistic creation and appreciation function as purgations of
emotions which result in the attainment of serenity. Art becomes
the reliever, the assuagement of the psychic life of man.

Artistic creation begins in the intense emotional experiences of
the artist. Seeking relief, the artist creates a work of art; and because, in the process of creation, he externalizes his emotional
pressures, he rids himself of them. He puts them in a box, so to
speak, where he can look at them objectively and calmly. Creation
is thus like looking fear in the face and curing ourselves of it
through that act.

In fact, Hirn refers to art creation as a cure.[19] Goethe, for example, at one stage of his life, was terribly depressed. Seeking relief,
he wrote *The Sorrows of Werther*, in which he objectified his
feelings. This process of purgation, in which the artist clarified as
well as objectified his feelings, offered Goethe a sense of inner
tranquillity and thereby cured him of his emotional afflictions.

The role of the spectator for Hirn is similar to that of the cre-
ator. He, too, is troubled by emotional pressures of one sort or
another. Among the various modes of relief is the artistic one in
which the spectator allows the work of art to infect him with the
emotions embodied within it. But instead of indulging directly in
these emotions, the spectator employs the infection as a means of
getting rid of them. Like the artist, he looks at them in all of their
objectivity and clarity; and this act of seeing them as existing independently of himself in an external art object brings him peace
and serenity. He, too, is calmed and cured.

Hirn's is an interesting but quite limited theory. It is completely
descriptive and, as such, can be criticized wholly on psychological
grounds. Its chief difficulty is its extreme rationalism. Hirn's basic
psychological belief is that we assuage the pressures of the emo-

tional life by displacing and objectifying them, that we cure ourselves by looking at our problems. But this is too simple. Consider,
for example, the emotion of fear, as it characterizes a child entering a dark room, let us say. Can the child be cured by letting him
enter the room and see for himself that there is nothing in it to
fear? Older psychologists reasoned so, but, if our contemporary
views are correct, it is not the looking of fear in the face that
cures him but the fact that the child is accompanied by the parent
(or someone else close to him) who he sees is without fear when
they enter the room and with whom he identifies. The child is
cured, if he is, because of the fact that someone else whom he
adores and depends upon has faced up to the situation without
fear. It is difficult to explain just what the psychology of cure is as
it pertains to our emotional life, but, whatever the explanation
may be, Hirn's theory is much too outmoded in its rationalism.

His theory of artistic creation and appreciation is also inadè-
quate. It is true, I suppose, that some, perhaps a great deal, of
artistic activity does involve assuagement of our emotions (although this does not occur generally through any process of dis-
placement); but there is a tremendous amount of art activity that
is not characterized by this sort of release at all. Hirn's theory is
too romantic, too *Sturm und Drang*.

The basic insight of Hirn's aesthetics, as it applies to appreciation, is that in our appreciation of art we do not usually regard
the object of our appreciation as a real-life situation and consequently do not react to it with turbulent emotions. Artistic appreciation does involve assuagement but it is owing to the fact that
we are engaging in a contemplative experience, and not to any
purgation that we may be undergoing.

Contemplation: Ducasse's Theory

There are more variants of the emotionalist doctrine of appreciation, the most famous being that of empathy. But they are all

essentially descriptive in their import, and each of them can be shown to be inadequate on psychological grounds. There is sufficient evidence to refute the various claims that appreciation is indulgence in the presented emotions, or purgation of emotions, or even the projection of emotions (empathy) into an inanimate object which thereby becomes a work of art.[20] Some supporting evidence can be found for each of these theories but as much contrary evidence is available, as the conflicting theories themselves show. In fact, all descriptive theories of appreciation are characterized by their inadequacy. There is some limited truth in the play theory, the voluntarist theory, and the emotionalist theory, if we construe these as generalizations about the ways in which people do respond to works of art; but none of them can be said to be an established scientific theory in the sense of a hypothesis for which there is a good deal of supporting evidence and *no* contrary evidence. One might conclude from this unhappy situation that there is no acceptable theory of art appreciation at the present time and that there will be none until we obtain more psychological data on the whole subject of appreciation.

Some aestheticians, however, consider such a conclusion unwarranted because it is derived partly at least from an unacceptable premise, namely, that the problem of appreciation is essentially a descriptive one. It seems to them that this is not the case and that the problem is primarily a normative one of how we ought to respond to art.

The most articulate normative theory in contemporary aesthetics is that of contemplation. Among its advocates are Ducasse, Bullough, Bell, and Fry. Ducasse begins his discussion of the problem of appreciation with the normative question, what is the proper attitude to take toward the art object? In order to answer this, Ducasse insists, we must first of all understand the nature of the art object and then make our theory of appreciation a function of it. The art object is the embodiment of emotions in a sensuous medium. The proper attitude to have toward it is one that will not misuse it; and the only attitude that does not misuse the art object is contemplation. Every other attitude, Ducasse states, does not constitute a response to the essential properties of the art object.[21] Artistic appreciation as contemplation is

> a "listening" for the feeling impact — for the emotional reverberations — of the object attended to. Aesthetic response to a color, for example, does not consist in recognizing or classifying it, or in interpreting it as a sign of something or other, but in savoring it — just as an ordinary person simply savors the aroma of a cigar or the bouquet of a wine . . .[22]

> It is the exact analogue, in the language of feeling, of what in the language of thought is called reading — that is, of the attempt to extract from somebody else's words the ideas, opinions, or information he expressed in them.[23]

The contemplation of art, then, is the savoring of it. Ducasse enumerates certain hindrances to this form of contemplation. Among these are those elements in a work of art that make savoring psychologically difficult or impossible. The inclusion of the disgusting, the lustful, the sordid, etc., is a hindrance because our reactions to these qualities become so strong as to destroy the possibility of savoring. Ugliness or what we have called the realm of the demonic discourage aesthetic contemplation since they lead to action, not contemplation; therefore art should not present them.[24]

However one might evaluate the contemplative theory, it is quite obvious, I think, that Ducasse's is not a true example of it. For, in the first place, it is not the case that savoring in the appreciation of art is analogous to reading of nonartistic prose. Savoring, which is a kind of mild indulgence, is akin to preliminary belief, not to mere reading, since when one reads, one need not believe, not even a little bit. One need only comprehend to read properly. Thus, savoring is to preliminary belief as true artistic contemplation is to reading as comprehension.

Secondly, Ducasse interprets contemplation as a mild form of emotional indulgence or infection. This rules out any artistic communication that tends to destroy this mild form, which, of course, constitutes a limitation upon the range of communication that the artist may seek. What Ducasse rejects in the doctrine of formalism, namely, that it arbitrarily limits the range of expression in the arts (to nondramatic entities), he avows in his own theory by imposing limits on the kinds of value the arts may communicate.

Why should not the artist present the loathsome, the disgusting, the lustful? This is the crucial question. An adequate theory of appreciation (as well as creation) must not rule out the ugly or the demonic. Instead it must justify the right of the artist to present them if he so desires. To deny this principle of the autonomy of artistic expression is to destroy the intrinsic character of art and to render it subordinate to something else, like a specific morality or convention. An aesthetics that is really concerned with preserving the integrity of art must allow the arts to express any values they wish: the brutal, sadistic, and ugly as well as the pleasant and lovely. And any theory of appreciation which reduces to an emotionalist-indulgence view, whether it be Plato's, Tolstoy's, or Ducasse's so-called contemplative one, is inadequate precisely because it cannot allow for this fullness of artistic expression.

Contemplation: Bullough's Theory

Bullough's is a more adequate theory of contemplation. His views on appreciation are a mixture of the descriptive and the normative. Like Bell and Fry, he believes that human beings are characterized by a bipolarity of action and detachment. Our ordinary attitude toward our environment is one of concern. Whatever we experience we react to in a partial manner and with a sense of responsibility for action. Sometimes, however, we truncate these usual reactions and instead perceive our environment with objectivity, that is, as not being causally efficacious upon us, as not being able to do anything to us physically or emotionally. Whenever this attitude of detachment occurs, we have attained what Bullough calls "psychical distance." [25]

In the presence of art, it is this attitude of psychic distance that prevails. Only he whom we would call a "yokel" ever treats art as a real-life situation. Everyone else is able to distinguish art from life and to view the former with some detachment. Even Tolstoy's ideal spectator, in the midst of his indulgences, views the work of art with some psychic distance, although it may be only the recognition that the object is not a real-life situation but a work of art. It is because of the presence of psychic distance, Bullough concludes, that our appreciation is primarily a disinterested, nonpractical, nonmoral, detached, contemplative experience.

Bullough takes as his central problem the relation of psychic distance to emotional indulgence. He recognizes what he regards as a psychological fact, that our appreciation of art depends in part upon our participation in the emotions presented, which fact seems to conflict with that of psychic distance. This "antinomy," as Bullough calls it, can be resolved by means of a norm which he recommends as basic to an adequate theory of appreciation and which will as a matter of fact, so he thinks, harmonize our indulgence in and our detachment from the emotions in the work of art: indulgence in the emotions of the work of art is legitimate and ought to be engaged in up to the point that psychic distance tends to disappear.

Consider this fact, Bullough proposes. All people are jealous to some extent. Because of this, *Othello* appeals to us, since we identify with the emotion of jealousy as it is embodied in the play. Now, an inordinately jealous person, Bullough insists, cannot appreciate *Othello* because he loses his psychic distance and overindulges in the play, which becomes almost his own life situation. He cannot experience it with any detachment. But most of us do not overindulge in this manner. Rather we combine indulgence and psychic distance; and if we follow the Bullough maxim, we shall never experience any incompatibility between them. Our aesthetic maturity will be that of a person who, so to speak, has learned to keep his (psychic) distance.

There are difficulties in Bullough's theory, too. In the first place, his conception of contemplation is too narrow. Contemplation of the arts involves more than detachment or psychic distance; and if we are to offer a contemplative theory of appreciation, we must present its other characteristics as well.

Secondly, Bullough's antinomy between emotional indulgence and psychic distance and his recommendation that we ought to indulge up to the point of the elimination of psychic distance are unnecessary. The basic premise — that our appreciation of art depends in part upon our immediate participation in the emotions presented — is not true on factual grounds. One can appreciate art without this participation, by understanding the emotions (expressive properties, we call them), as they unfold in relation to the other constituents of the work of art. In fact, in our appreciation of any work of art in which there is great emotional complexity, it is not possible, psychologically, to indulge in the emotions presented, because to indulge at all would demand our seeing the complexity from one or at most a few points of view, provided the emotions were not contradictory. To appreciate any really emotionally complex work of art, we must assume a detached, completely spectatorial, point of view, if we wish to see it wholly. An excellent example of this complexity which demands complete withdrawal from the indulgence in the emotions presented in order to appreciate them in their complexity is Bullough's own, *Othello*. Consider the third scene of the fourth act:

> *Emilia.* How goes it now? He looks gentler than he did.
> *Desdemona.* He says he will return incontinent;
> And hath commanded me to go to bed,
> And bid me to dismiss you.
> *Emilia.* Dismiss me!

Desdemona. It was his bidding; Therefore, good Emilia,
Give me my nightly wearing, and adieu.
We must not now displease him.

Emilia. I would you had never seen him!

Desdemona. So would not I. My love doth so approve him,
That even his stubbornness, his checks, his frowns, —
Prithee, unpin me, — have grace and favour in them.

Emilia. I have laid those sheets you bade me on the bed.

Desdemona. All's one. Good faith, how foolish are our minds!
If I do die before thee, prithee, shroud me
In one of those same sheets.

Emilia. Come, come, you talk.

Desdemona. My mother had a maid call'd Barbary;
She was in love, and he she lov'd prov'd mad
And did forsake her. She had a song of "Willow";
An old thing 'twas, but it express'd her fortune,
And she died singing it. That song to-night
Will not go from my mind; I have much to do
But to go hang my head all at one side
And sing it like poor Barbary. Prithee, dispatch.

Emilia. Shall I go fetch your nightgown?

Desdemona. No, unpin me here.
This Lodovico is a proper man.

Emilia. A very handsome man.

Desdemona. He speaks well.

Emilia. I know a lady in Venice would have walk'd barefoot
to Palestine for a touch of his nether lip.

Desdemona. [*Singing.*]
"The poor soul sat sighing by a sycamore tree,
　　Sing all a green willow;
　Her hand on her bosom, her head on her knee,
　　Sing willow, willow, willow.
　The fresh streams ran by her and murmur'd her moans;
　　Sing willow, willow, willow;
　Her salt tears fell from her, and soft'ned the stones.
　　Sing willow, willow, willow;"
Lay by these: —

[*Singing.*] "Willow, willow;" —
Prithee, hie thee; he'll come anon; —
[*Singing.*]   "Sing all a green willow must be my garland.
                Let nobody blame him; his scorn I approve," —
Nay, that's not next. — Hark! who is't that knocks?
  Emilia. It's the wind.
  Desdemona. [*Singing.*]
"I call'd my love false love; but what said he then?
      Sing willow, willow, willow.
  If I court moe women, you'll couch with moe men." —
So, get thee gone; good-night. Mine eyes do itch;
Doth that bode weeping?
  Emilia. 'Tis neither here nor there.
  Desdemona. I have heard it said so. O, these men, these men!
Dost thou in conscience think, — tell me, Emilia, —
That there be women do abuse their husbands
In such gross kind?
  Emilia. There be some such, no question.
  Desdemona. Wouldst thou do such a deed for all the world?
  Emilia. Why, would not you?
  Desdemona. No, by this heavenly light!
  Emilia. Nor I neither by this heavenly light;
I might do't as well i' th' dark.
  Desdemona. Wouldst thou do such a deed for all the world?
  Emilia. The world's a huge thing; it is a great price for a small
vice.
  Desdemona. In troth, I think thou wouldst not.
  Emilia. In troth, I think I should; and undo't when I had done.
Marry, I would not do such a thing for a joint-ring, not for
measures of lawn, nor for gowns, petticoats, nor caps, nor any
petty exhibition; but, for all the whole world, — 'ud's pity,
who would not make her husband a cuckold to make him a mon-
arch? I should venture purgatory for't.
  Desdemona. Beshrew me, if I would do such a wrong
For the whole world.
  Emilia. Why, the wrong is but a wrong i' th' world; and

having the world for your labour, 'tis a wrong in your own
world, and you might quickly make it right.

    Desdemona. I do not think there is any such woman.

    Emilia. Yes, a dozen; and as many to th' vantage as would
store the world they play'd for.
But I do think it is their husbands' faults
If wives do fall. Say that they slack their duties
And pour our treasures into foreign laps,
Or else break out in peevish jealousies,
Throwing restraint upon us; or say they strike us,
Or scant our former having in despite;
Why, we have galls, and though we have some grace,
Yet have we some revenge. Let husbands know
Their wives have sense like them; they see, and smell,
And have their palates both for sweet and sour
As husbands have. What is it that they do
When they change us for others? Is it sport?
I think it is. And doth affection breed it?
I think it doth. Is't frailty that thus errs?
It is so too. And have not we affections,
Desires for sport, and frailty, as men have?
Then let them use us well; else let them know,
The ills we do, their ills instruct us so.

    Desdemona. Good-night, good-night. Heaven me such uses
send,
Not to pick bad from bad, but by bad mend!   (*Exeunt.*)

This is, even with all of its many threads, a relatively simple
emotional pattern so far as the arts are concerned; and yet its
complexity is evident: The simultaneous unfolding of the comic
and the tragic, in which death and adultery are united through the
medium of a lowly pun; the dramatic playing off against each
other of the childlike acquiescence of Desdemona and the sophisticated assertiveness of Emilia; and the reference to Lodovico,
made in innocence by Desdemona and charged with impending
disaster because of the earlier references to him in the play.

How can we indulge in all of this? It is psychologically impossible. At most, we can indulge in one of the portrayed emotions, Desdemona's pathetic state, let us say. But should we really do so, we cannot help but resent the verbal horseplay of the nurse. In real life, this resentment would be proper, but in the experience of art it is not, since it misses the whole point of this kind of activity, that it can transcend the narrow limits of our ordinary experiences. It is in this way that the aesthetic experience is richer than our ordinary experiences, because it gives us the opportunity to see life as a kind of whole, in which we are not called upon to choose sides and look at it from our chosen side.

It is only the person who does not participate in the emotions exhibited in this scene but who remains detached from them and watches them unfold in all of their humanly devastating complexity and relates them to the language, the metrics, the allusions, and the other scenes of the play, who really appreciates *the play* in all its manifold fullness. Art can demand nothing less than this total apprehension.

Contemplation: Defense of the Theory of Bell and Fry

During the present chapter we have been dealing with a number of theories in an attempt to clarify the differences between the descriptive and the normative approaches to appreciation and, if possible, to arrive at a more adequate theory of our own. Throughout our discussion, there has emerged one doctrine above all others that these different theories share. Whether descriptive or normative, each of these views on the nature of appreciation has accepted what we may call the *functional* approach. That is to say, they have assumed that the problem of appreciation of art is solvable only in terms of our understanding the nature of the art object. To know how we do or how we ought to respond to a work of art, we must first find out the nature of a work of art. Thus, Ducasse tells us that we ought to "listen to" the emotions of art when we appreciate it because art is fundamentally the embodiment of emotions. Tolstoy proclaims that we do and ought to indulge in the emotions of the art object because art is essentially an instrument of evocative communication. Parker asserts that appreciation is primarily a satisfaction of desire in the imagination because the art object is basically the embodiment of imaginatively satisfied desires. And, finally, Richards insists that we ought to give no heed to the truth claims of art because art is not a referential language. It can be seen that in all of these theories, even if it is true that in none of them is this functional notion developed at all, it is the nature of the work of art which determines the way we do and ought to appreciate the work.

The fact that aestheticians have accepted the functional approach — and it would be difficult to repudiate it without denying the very existence of art and its intrinsic character — is important because it provides us with an objective, publicly accepted criterion for judging the adequacy of a theory of appreciation: that theory is best which best takes into account the actual nature of a work of art. Now, if our hypothesis of the nature of art is correct, art objects are expressively organic wholes presented in sensuous media like words or sounds or canvas, which may contain many different constituents, including subjects, meanings and symbols, and truth claims. An adequate theory of appreciation, therefore, must be one that allows for a response to the totality of the work and to the totality of historical and contemporary artistic expression. Throughout our entire essay, we have accepted this as one of the ruling ideas of an adequate aesthetic theory, whether it pertain to the art object, to creation, or now to appreciation. There is no final proof of the validity of this assumption; it seems to me to be one of those self-evident truths, at least in this sense, that should it be denied, it would destroy the very being of the aesthetic experience as an intrinsic thing and reduce it to something else, like moral, religious, or scientific experience. But even if this principle is conceived as no more than a postulate, all aes-

theticians who are interested in the aesthetic experience and regard it as good in itself, not merely as good because it satisfies
some social or religious or metaphysical doctrine, accept it, and
this fact makes it possible to arrive at an answer to the question
of an adequate theory of appreciation. Let the best theory of appreciation be that which enables us best to attend to all the constituents of all works of art. We can then evaluate each specific
theory in terms of this fundamental postulate or principle. This,
of course, is precisely what we have been doing in this chapter;
and because we have found each of these theories to be inadequate, either in the sense of being simply false or else of constituting an arbitrary limitation on the kinds of value that art may
incorporate, we have rejected them all. The only theory that meets
this ultimate requirement is the normative theory of contemplation as it has been suggested by Bell and Fry and as it must be
supplemented by certain ideas that are derived from an enriched
understanding of the nature of art.

We have already dealt extensively with Bell's and Fry's theory
of appreciation in our first chapter, so we need do no more than
summarize their views here. Their fundamental notion regarding
appreciation is that of pure appreciation. Pure appreciation is a
function of the art object and is achieved through an analysis of
the nature of the art object. They conceive the art object as significant form; to appreciate art we must respond to this significant
form. To do otherwise or more is to misuse the art object, to treat
it as an object of history or science or morality. The best way to
respond to significant form is to contemplate it: to analyze and
to synthesize its various constituents in order to intuit them as an
integrated expressive whole. In other words, if we are to appreciate
art, we ought to contemplate its essence, its significant form. This
is the normative aspect of their theory.

Descriptively, now, once we do react to significant form in this
contemplative manner, we find that we are engaging in an activity
which is essentially exalted, ecstatic, isolated, hedonic, and which

is quite unlike and unrelated to our everyday experiences. The combination of these characteristics they call the "unique aesthetic emotion."

This view has been severely criticized by many aestheticians but, so far as I can see, the main criticism and the most serious one is that the theory forces too discontinuous a distinction between ordinary and artistic experiences. Art, their critics say, *is* related to life and the difference between art and nonartistic experiences is at most one of degree.

This criticism is a cogent one, I think, but it does not call for a rejection of the whole of the theory of Bell and Fry, only a modification of it. Of course art is rooted in normal, ordinary experiences, and there is no need to deny it. But granted this, we may still affirm with Bell and Fry that appreciation of art ought to be the contemplation of the essence of the art object, and that once this contemplation is attained, it *is* the rather unique affair they consider it to be.

Our expanded view, then, is this: art is essentially an expressive organic complex of different constituents. To appreciate it, we ought to attend to all of these constituents as they play their roles in relation to each other. And this means that we must be able to comprehend the emotional or expressive elements in art, too. But we cannot do all of this unless we become detached, emotionally and morally, from the work of art. It is difficult but we must strive for this contemplative attitude if we wish to appreciate the complete work of art and also the fullness of the divergences of expression in the history of art. The alternative to the contemplative theory is one that inevitably imposes some sort of limitation on the range of artistic expression.

Once we do arrive at the contemplative attitude toward art, we shall find, I think, with Bell and Fry, that we have secured a unique experience for ourselves, and one which includes an emotional richness all its own that is not related to or caused by an indulgence in the emotions of the art object but by the contemplative experience itself. It is in this sense that appreciation is a legitimate emotional experience. The adherence to the contemplative attitude offers its own emotional rewards which are even richer than the emotional experiences we would have if we capitulated to the emotions of the art object; they are richer because they are rarer and can be gotten only from this one experience of contemplating the organic unfolding of a work of art. The joy and rapture that come from perceiving the expressive quality of a certain element in a work of art and relating it to others are experiences that cannot be secured except in the contemplative aesthetic experience. The recognition of the juxtaposition of death and adultery and the comprehension of them in relation to the other constituents of *Othello*, for example, give rise to an emotional experience which is as exciting as any indulgence in one or other of the actual emotions being portrayed in the play.

Many spectators, who are not aware of it, I think, have had this combined contemplative-emotive experience. The spiritual uplift of witnessing a great tragedy is not always due to indulgence or even purgation, but sometimes to the contemplation (perhaps even unwittingly on the part of the spectator) of the unfolding of the complexity of experience exhibited and the spiritual joy that accompanies such contemplation. In other words, people who do not hold to the contemplative theory often mistake the emotional excitation that they get from just such a contemplation with what they take to be indulgence in or purgation of portrayed emotions. This, of course, means that the contemplative attitude, although it needs no support from any empirical generalization about the way people actually do respond to art, since it is completely a normative theory in its fundamental claim, is not as strange to most of us as we might like to think.[26]

Aesthetic contemplation has other characteristics, too, besides those of attending to the unfolding of the constituents of a work of art and the accompanying emotions such attending offers. As others have frequently stressed, it is detached, disinterested, non-

practical and hedonic. Also, it is voluntaristic, that is, the satisfying of desire, not, however, as Freud or Parker has argued, those
desires that are frustrated in ordinary activities, but, as Fry perceived long ago, the satisfying of the desire to see the world from
the spectatorial or contemplative point of view. It is in this sense
that art and the contemplation of it provide us with an enrichment of our spiritual life.

The Problem of Criticism

We come finally to the relation between appreciation and criticism of works of art. The whole problem of criticism is in difficult
straits today. For one thing, so many different kinds of activity
pass for criticism: historical scholarship, textual analysis, sociological exegesis, etc. About these activities, there can be no dispute
over their making empirically meaningful and verifiable statements. The real problem begins when aesthetic *evaluations* are
made and called into question by dissenting critics.

Sometimes these disputes can be settled by an appeal to certain
standards that both parties adhere to. For example, suppose someone objects to a certain metaphor in a poem on the grounds that
it is out of place, that it does not contribute anything. Another
person may show him that the metaphor is not out of place, but
essential to the total meaning of the poem. This is the sort of
thing that is constantly occurring in literary criticism. Disagree-
ments are constantly being resolved in this way, by pointing out
that the objectionable ingredient is precisely the kind of thing
that the objector values. In this example, of course, both parties
are appealing to the same standard, namely, that every constituent
should play a contributory role in the total work, and both are
satisfied as critics if the argument over the aesthetic worth of the
work of art is carried on in terms of this criterion.

But the real problem comes in when someone calls into question
the *status* of these standards. And this is what has happened in

our day, not only in art criticism but in all fields where value judgments are made. Probably at no time has the dictum, *de gustibus non est disputandum,* been more vigorously championed. The impact of anthropological and psychological data has rocked the foundations of absolutism in the arts; and the general implications of positivism, which reduces all value judgments to mere emotional ejaculation, seem to have shattered the foundations altogether.

In contemporary aesthetic theory Ducasse, intent upon formulating a "Declaration of Independence of Taste" in the arts, promotes a theory of criticism that exhibits the extreme subjectivism characteristic of our age. He writes:

> The critic's evaluations . . . ultimately are just as purely matters of his individual taste as are those of the unsophisticated amateur. The great difference . . . is . . . that the naïve amateur is pleased or displeased without knowing exactly why, whereas the critic does know what specific features are responsible for his own pleasure or displeasure in a given work of art. But in both cases the situation is in the end just the same as with, let us say, the taste of pineapple. Some persons like it, and others dislike it; but it would be absurd to say that it is *really* good, although some dislike it, or *really* bad, although some like it. For when the values concerned are not instrumental values but immediate values — whether of odors, of tastes, of sounds, of plastic qualities, or of facial expressions — then individual likes and dislikes constitute the only meaning of good and bad.
>
> A person's tastes, thus — whether he be sophisticated critic or simple amateur — are ultimately at once incapable of justification and self-justifying.[27]

This is an extremely bold statement and one wonders whether its author realizes just how bold it is. For, in the first place, it is most certainly *no* declaration of independence at all, but an invitation to a kind of anarchy in criticism. The essence of a declaration of independence is that it is founded upon certain objective principles, as, for example, our own American Declaration of Independence.

Secondly, on Ducasse's view, suppose a dispute should arise over whether the *Eroica* is better than, say, Beethoven's *Fourth Symphony*. The phrase "better than" is interpreted as having reference to certain standards; and this is as it should be. But these standards are further conceived as expressions of preferences; that is, they are construed as emotive utterances which are neither true nor false in any objective sense. Therefore, if I should say, for example, that the *Eroica* is better than the *Fourth* of Beethoven, and should offer in defense of my judgment the fact that the *Eroica* makes me laugh harder, which fact I take as my ultimate criterion for evaluating music, then on Ducasse's view that will be as legitimate an aesthetic judgment as another's contention that the *Eroica* is better than the *Fourth* because the musical materials are more profound, more imaginatively developed, more integrated in the one than in the other!

I do not mean to be saying now that Ducasse is wrong in his subjectivism. Rather, like the positivist in ethics who claims that he is freeing mankind from the trammels of dogmatism by demonstrating the nonreferential nature of ethical judgments — for example, "democracy is better than Fascism" or "kindness is better than wanton cruelty and sadism" — but who is really promulgating an extreme form of nihilism, Ducasse should be made aware of the *implications* of his position.

Perhaps, in the end, all standards are subjective or emotive grunts and groans, and there is no refutation of positivism. But in art, at least, there seem to be good reasons for believing that some standards, e.g., the integration of materials, are *more relevant* than others, e.g., the ability of a work of art to make me laugh hard. These standards are difficult to ascertain but we can get some insight into them by understanding the nature and purpose of the arts in human experience. Ducasse, himself, believes that this can be done, as his discussion of the normative character of appreciation reveals.

The basic difficulty with Ducasse's position seems to be his identification of critical standards with preferences and tastes. It would be absurd, he claims, to say that a work of art is good even though one does not like it or really bad if one does like it. I cannot see that either of these statements is absurd at all. In fact, one encounters them all the time in museums, theaters, and concert halls. "I like Gershwin, although I know he is not really good," or "I know *The Iceman Cometh* is really good, but I don't like plays like that." It simply is a fact that people, amateurs and critics alike, do distinguish between their preferences and their evaluations. It may be that they ought not to do so, and perhaps this is Ducasse's real point, but that they do make the distinction and are ready to act on it cannot be denied. The big difference between the amateur and the critic, therefore, lies not in the fact that the one is interested, and the other is not, in the causes of his pleasure or displeasure, but that the critic — provided, of course, that he is a real critic, not merely a reporter — tries to seek out within the work of art *what* it is that makes it good, whereas the amateur is willing to accept his reactions with no such curiosity.

However, this is no satisfactory reply to Ducasse's basic rejection of objective standards. If he (or his fellow positivists) sustains his attack against us, he can show that any ultimate criterion in evaluation is an emotive preference, and not something referential and objective. I know of no refutation of this claim except to point out that it is tantamount to utter nihilism, that is, to a situation in which *any* value judgment is as cogent as any other. Nihilism in aesthetics or ethics is like solipsism in the theory of knowledge, irrefutable but totally unacceptable to the demands of human experience.[28]

In contrast to this extreme subjectivism in criticism, which reduces evaluation in the arts to a sophisticated form of verbal drooling, the organic theory, like many others, offers a philosophy of criticism that is based upon certain objective criteria. These are derived from a consideration of the nature of the art object and from certain reflections concerning the nature of the aesthetic in relation to other experiences.

The first of these criteria is this. The aesthetic value of any work of art does not reside in any one constituent, like a particular color or melody or metaphor or piece of good acting in a play. Rather it inheres in the total integration of constituents: for example, the colors working with the lines; these working with the space, design and subject; and the complete work of art functioning as an expressive whole.

The expressive character of any constituent is in part determined by the other constituents. The expressiveness, that is, the emotional import, of a single color or an area of color, for instance, depends upon the total context. This is a kind of *Gestalt* of the expressive. Dali's purple, in his "Palladio's Corridor of Thalia," for example, is not the eerie color that it is *all* by itself; its full expressiveness is derived from the other colors, the space, and the subjects. And yet, of course, the eeriness is *also* dependent upon the initial purple; the specific expressiveness could not have been obtained with an extremely warm yellow.

Further, factors like the ineffective use of color, inadequate feeling for space, insufficient design, are, in part, relationally determined. So is the effectiveness of a melody, the convincingness of a scene, the delineation of a character.

Brooks and Warren, as we have seen, show why Shelley's "Death" fails — because there is no integration, no working together of theme and metrics. But we cannot say that jigging metrics by itself is never effectively expressive or that the theme of death is always profoundly expressive. The doctrine that it is always effective is as obsolete as the eighteenth-century doctrine that there are certain elements which are "poetic" in themselves and others that are just as uniquely "unpoetic."

These two authors employ this same criterion in all their critical analyses. In their discussion of Keats's "Ode to a Nightingale," for example, they point out that, great as the poem is, it suffers from the nonfunctional character of much of its imagery, which exists in the poem only as precious ornamentation.[29] And it is important to realize that if someone were to show that the imagery *is* functional throughout by, let us say, a new and valid interpretation of one of the elements of the poem, Brooks and Warren would withdraw their reservations about the poem and regard it as being *better* than they originally considered it.

An enormous amount of legitimate critical evaluation is of this sort. Throughout our many analyses, some partial, others rather complete, like our analysis of "Prufrock," we have accepted as one criterion of objective, evaluative criticism the principle of organic unity. In "Prufrock," for example, the fact that the image of the etherized patient *does* tie up with the other elements of the poem, adding to their expressiveness, makes it a better poem than it would be if there were no such relation. Or, in our discussion of Rouault's "Christ Mocked by Soldiers," we assumed — and quite legitimately, too, I think — that because the chunkiness of texture, with its sense of brute power, *does* relate effectively to the humility of Christ's face, it is consequently a better picture than it would be if there were no working relation at all between them. One last example. In Thomas Wolfe's *You Can't Go Home Again* there is present in the first half of the novel a fascinating character who becomes the hero's mistress. The affair is followed until a great fire in the apartment building where she lives. The hero then leaves his mistress and throughout the rest of the novel there is no mention of her again. She is left stranded aesthetically, so to speak; her absence is not worked out in dramatic terms. Many readers have felt this to be a defect in the novel and rightly so, I think, because Wolfe has not utilized his materials as effectively as he might have done.

One objective criterion of good art, then, according to the organic theory, is this principle of integration: the working together of all the elements is aesthetically good and the working against each other of some or all of the elements is aesthetically bad. Part of the reason some art is good is that it integrates its many elements; and part of the function of evaluative criticism is to determine what the elements or constituents are and whether or not they do work together. A critical judgment that is based upon this criterion is aesthetically more cogent than one that is founded upon, let us say, the criterion of the duration or the cost of an art work. It is objective in the sense that no evaluative criticism is possible without it. The alternative to the acceptance of this sort of principle as at least one aesthetic, critical principle is the denial of evaluative criticism altogether, from which it follows, as we have seen, that any criterion (the ability of a work to put me to sleep or to keep me from scratching myself or to get me to think about the valleys on the other side of the moon) is as aesthetically valid as any other.

But, many will say, it is not enough that a work of art be integrated in order that it may be good or great art. It must also communicate important expressive qualities of human experience. Art is fundamentally the embodiment of the expressive; and the *quality* or *kind* of expressive that is embodied makes a difference to the aesthetic merit of the work and our evaluative critical judgments of it.[30] The fact that Picasso's "Guernica" deals with the expressive quality of horrendous destruction is part of what makes it a great work of art. The fact that Rouault's "Christ Mocked by Soldiers" embodies the expressive quality of the conflict between force and humility enters into the total fact of its greatness as a work of art. On the other hand, the fact that Matisse's work on the whole seems to concern itself mainly with the expressive quality of the gay and decorative and not with the thunderous and

demonic in human experience renders it for many critics inferior
to works like the "Guernica." In other words, there does seem to
be in criticism some criterion of the aesthetic worth of any particular work of art which is based upon the specific quality of the
expressive and not upon the working together of the various constituents of the work of art. What the use of this criterion reveals,
of course, is that aesthetic, evaluative criticism, that is, *critical
appreciation*, involves itself in certain standards that are derived
from our total philosophies of life. Some people regard the dramatic, the tense, the demonic, and the powerful as the controlling
forces of human destiny and prefer these in their art. Others focus
upon the lyrical, the tender, the warm, and the pleasurable in
human experiences and desire these in their art. Still others enjoy
the sentimental, even the saccharine in life and consequently look
for these in their artistic experiences. There is no gainsaying this;
it is simply a fact that many of us do allow and, moreover, think
it justifiable, that our nonaesthetic preferences shall determine in
part our critical evaluations of art.

It is here that one should seek out the relativism, and even
subjectivism, in the critical enterprise. Suppose someone were to
challenge the rather widely accepted evaluation of Matisse in
relation to Picasso and were to affirm his preference for Matisse.
How would we solve such a dispute? Of course, the easiest way
would be to deny that there is a dispute in any sense in which a
dispute is something that is solvable by an appeal to ascertainable
standards. In effect, this would *resolve* the dispute by pointing
out that there really is none to begin with. But this would satisfy
neither party. And it should not, for it is like telling a Fascist and
a believer in democracy to stop arguing about the merits of their
respective causes since they are not really arguing, only articulating
their emotional preferences.

There is a more sophisticated way to deal with this problem
which, strangely enough, resembles the above resolution. It is to
point out that in the realm of the aesthetic, if we wish to preserve

its intrinsic character (if we do not, all of this is irrelevant and the only thing that is relevant is whether a philosophy of values that reduces the aesthetic experience to something else, like morality or religion or metaphysics, is a defensible one; and if it is, which it may very well be, what such a philosophy of values entails so far as the range of experiences is concerned), then we must accept the principle that there is no *aesthetic* difference between the kinds of expressive characteristic. That is, in art, the gay, the lyrical, the pleasurable, the comic, if you will, count for as much as the dramatic, the demonic, the tense, or the tragic. In other words, a mature theory of criticism recognizes the role of the nonaesthetic in practical criticism but insists upon the inclusion of all values in art and the equal aesthetic weight of each, so far as our evaluations are concerned. It is true that aesthetic criticism is rooted in part in a philosophy of values but, on the principle that the aesthetic experience is beholden to no other (and is like science or religion in this respect), it is incumbent upon an adequate philosophy of values to give free and impartial scope to the expressive qualities of the different works of art. To ask if Matisse is better than Picasso, or vice versa, in the sense that we wish to know if the one is better than the other because of the nature of the expressive in each, is, therefore, to ask an immature question. Like Plato's little children, we shall reply when asked which is better, "Give us both."

It will not, of course, satisfy the Fascist or the democrat to resolve their dispute in this way; and it should not because their dispute is not an aesthetic, but a political one. And political disputes have different standards of solution from aesthetic ones. In politics we cannot accept both Fascism and democracy. But in art we can allow for such contraries, even for contradictories; and it is this that constitutes one of the great differences between art and politics as human activities. Art, unlike politics, or most activities, for that matter, comprises the realm of *possibilities* for human understanding and action. It is a kind of Platonic realm of emotional universals, the very contemplation of which is good for its own sake. It is this which renders the experience of art unique in the total realm of human experience and provides us with the ultimate fact about art to which any adequate philosophy of values must bow.

In ordinary activities, certain values do become more important than others to all of us; and since people differ on what they regard as most important, there will naturally be relativism in our basic philosophies of life. But, and this has been our main point, whatever our philosophy of life, if we wish to preserve the integrity of the aesthetic experience, we must not apply our specific value hierarchies to our critical judgments of art. Art can free us from our narrow province of chosen value and provide us passage to the whole realm of human experience.

But what about the sentimental and the saccharine in art? Do these count for as much as the gay or the demonic? Aside from all considerations of the working together of constituents, is a work like *The Sorrows of Werther* as aesthetically good as *Hamlet*? Is it not the case that the characters, plot, and theme, with their individual and total expressive properties, in *Hamlet* are aesthetically better than the characters, plot, and theme, with all of their individual and total expressive characteristics, of *Werther*? Does not the fact that *Werther* is essentially sentimental in its expressive qualities and *Hamlet* is not make *Hamlet* a better work of art for those who prefer the tragic to the sentimental?

Further, is there not some cogency in the fact that in some art the richness of a character or the profundity of a theme enters into our evaluation of the work and may come to balance or even overbalance any deficiencies of organic unity? Here, all over again, is the problem that concerned Véron, except that we have generalized it, from how important is the subject? to how important is the specific quality of the expressive? One may easily grant our point that in art *some* qualities ought not to count for more than others — for example, the tender or lyrical as against the demonic or tense. But this principle of tolerance, it may be argued, should not allow that *any* quality is as aesthetically good as any other, the sentimental or saccharine as important as the tender *or* the tense.

In my opinion, it is here that we encounter ultimate relativism or subjectivism in evaluative criticism. What makes one theme more profound than another, one character richer than another, or one expressive quality more important than another depends upon our basic philosophies of life and reality. While it is true that most of us in the Western tradition would accept certain expressive qualities — we call them themes but they are larger than themes — as more important than others, suffering, love, hate, tragedy, compassion, for example, there is no way, so far as I can see, to demonstrate to the satisfaction of anyone who might question whether these are more important than the sentimental, that they are. If our root value be that of sentimentalism and if we regard it as the highest value for artistic communication, then no critical evaluation that implicitly or explicitly repudiates this philosophy can effectively refute it. There is no absolute standard to which we can appeal in order to prove that the experience of compassion or love or hate or the tense is more profound than the experience of pure sentimentality. Most of us may regard the sentimentalist as being inferior to ourselves so far as total human personality is concerned, but there is no way to show this to his satisfaction, or even to the satisfaction of a nonsentimentalist who assumes a skeptical attitude toward fundamental axiology.

The most we can ask of the sentimentalist is that he not limit the range of the aesthetically acceptable to his preferred value, but that he accept all other values as aesthetically equal and that his critical evaluations not be based upon the fact that the expressive qualities of the work of art happen to add up to sentimentalism. He will differ from us in the extent of his tolerance, but not in his being tolerant, provided he wishes to preserve

the integrity of the aesthetic experience and not to make it subordinate to anything else.

Criticism, to sum up our discussion, is based upon two fundamental criteria, one gathered from reflections on the nature of
the art object, the other from considerations of the nature of
human choices among different kinds of experience. At least two
objective criteria emerge from these deliberations: (1) one work
of art is better than another if its constituents work together
more effectively to form a total unity; and (2) it is impossible
to have a work of art in which there are no expressive characteristics, but the specific characteristic does not determine the
aesthetic merit of the work. An evaluative critic is one, therefore,
who does more than set out the reasons for his pleasure or displeasure. He enumerates the various elements of the work of art,
their relations to each other, and their individual and collective
expressive qualities. He may then inquire into the extra-aesthetic
bearing of the expressive characteristics of the work, even show
their general importance to all or some of us, but he cannot allow
his or even any or all of our choices to determine his evaluations
in the sense in which he wishes to maintain that his evaluations
are indisputable. The critic can go no further, unless he is prepared to demonstrate the philosophical priority of one value or
set of values over another.

Defense of the Doctrine of Art for Art's Sake

There are certain implications of our aesthetic theory in regard
to the whole problem of the function of art and I should like to
conclude this essay with a statement of one of these implications,
the defense of that unpopular heresy, the doctrine of art for art's
sake.

The functions of art have been much discussed in aesthetic
theory and in the general philosophy of values. Many divergent
views have been formulated. If there is a dominant one today,

it is, I suppose, some kind of instrumentalism. The Marxists, humanists, Thomists, and pragmatists, perhaps quite inadvertently, have joined forces in the condemnation of any doctrine of art for art's sake. Art is good not at all intrinsically, for its own sake, but instrumentally, for the sake of something else, either its promotion of progressive social action or its revelation of certain moral and metaphysical truths. The doctrine of the intrinsic character of art, that it is good for its own sake, is regarded as effete and reactionary, and the art that it sponsors is evaluated as sick and decadent.

Our whole book challenges such a verdict on the doctrine of art for art's sake. There is no denying the defects of the doctrine, especially as it has been formulated at various times, but its essential claim, I think, is sound. The aesthetic experience is intrinsically good. It is not good only because it promotes social welfare or embodies moral and metaphysical truth. It is good also in the way that the activity of searching for scientific truth is good or having a religious experience is good, that is, in the sense that it is not beholden to any other kind of experience either for its standards of evaluation or for its *raison d'être*.

Art is the embodiment of the expressive — of values, as many philosophers have declared. The creation and the appreciation of this realm of the expressive are good in the way that any other intrinsic activity is good. The advocate of the doctrine of art for art's sake need affirm no more than this, for it is sufficient to refute instrumentalism of this stamp. He need not assert that art (creation, object, or appreciation) is better than anything else or that everything else is good only in so far as it contributes to art ("life for art's sake"), even though these views have often been associated with art for art's sake.

The insistence upon the doctrine that art creation and appreciation are good in themselves in no way militates against the instrumental functions of art. Art creation may serve to realize a number of values. It may assuage the tensions of the artist;

it may provide him with satisfactions of desires that he cannot get in other ways; it may even further his social action. So too with appreciation; it may eventuate in all kinds of experiences and values. Through the contemplation of the possibilities open to human experience which are presented in the arts, we may come to enlarge our understanding of and activity in human values. Our appreciation of art may result in our becoming better instruments of social action and may help us promote a more progressive society. In fact, the effects of the aesthetic experience may be even more important to the total personality than the actual experience itself. There is no contradiction in the view that art is a good in itself and yet is not the most important good. What we must not do, however, if we wish to preserve the integrity of art, is to reduce the aesthetic experience to the status of an instrumental good because we shall then begin to apply all sorts of nonaesthetic standards, like the promotion of social action or the enhancement of sensibilities, to the arts, and this application invariably has led to the moral, metaphysical, or social dissolution of the aesthetic experience.

The advocate of the doctrine of art for art's sake, then, like the theoretical physicist in relation to the construction of his mathematical formulations, or the religious mystic in relation to his God, wishes only to call attention to the initially and primarily intrinsic character of his experience with art. He wishes to distinguish sharply between art as an end and art as a means; and he wishes to affirm that whatever experiences there are that are intrinsic, the aesthetic is among them. It is in this sense that he wishes to say that art either exists for its own sake or not at all, for without the recognition and acceptance of this intrinsic dimension of art, it becomes a handmaiden of something else and in that way is destroyed as an independent activity.

NOTES

NOTES

CHAPTER 1. AESTHETIC FORMALISM

[1] Clive Bell, *Art*, p. 6.
[2] *Ibid.*, p. 9. See also his *Since Cézanne*, chap. xv.
[3] *Art*, pp. 12–16.
[4] Bell's contention may be borne out by the following experiment. Present Picasso's "Portrait of a Lady" and "Woman in White" to a group of spectators. No one will say that the first, which is rather satirical, even grotesque in character, is beautiful, although many will not hesitate to designate the second as beautiful because the object represented is rather attractive as a woman.
[5] *Art*, p. 25.
[6] *Ibid.*, pp. 224–225.
[7] *Ibid.*, p. 68. Also see *Since Cézanne*, pp. 40–48.
[8] *Art*, p. 34.
[9] *Ibid.*, p. 25.
[10] *Ibid.*, pp. 29–30.
[11] *Ibid.*, p. 68.
[12] *Ibid.*, pp. 70–71.
[13] *Ibid.*, pp. 25–26. Cf. Bertrand Russell's *The Problems of Philosophy*, which was published in 1912, about the same time as *Art* (1914), for similar views.
[14] *Art*, pp. 26–27.
[15] *Ibid.*, p. 82.
[16] *Ibid.*, p. 25. Also "A knowledge of life can help no one to an understanding of art" (p. 286). Again "To appreciate fully a work of art we require nothing but sensibility. To those that can hear Art speaks for itself: facts and dates do not . . . To appreciate a man's art I need know nothing whatever about the artist . . ." (pp. 98–99).
[17] *Landmarks in Nineteenth-Century Painting*, p. vi.
[18] *Since Cézanne*, p. 154.
[19] *Art*, pp. 51–53. Of Cézanne, e.g., for whom he has the highest regard, Bell writes: "For, gazing at the familiar landscape, Cézanne came to understand it, not as a mode of light, nor yet as a player in the game of human life, but as an end in itself and an object of intense emotion. Every great artist has seen landscape as an end in itself — as pure form, that is to say; Cézanne has made a generation of artists feel that compared with its significance as an end in itself all else about a landscape is negligible" (pp. 208–209).

[20] *Ibid.*, p. 49.

[21] *Ibid.*, pp. 31–33.

[22] "The 'Difference' of Literature," *New Republic*, Nov. 29, 1922, pp. 18–19.

[23] *Art*, p. 158; see also p. 153.

[24] *Ibid.*, p. 292.

[25] *Ibid.*, p. 241.

[26] R. E. Fry, "An Essay in Aesthetics," *Vision and Design*, pp. 23–24.

[27] Fry, *The Artist and Psycho-Analysis*, pp. 3–4.

[28] "Retrospect," *Vision and Design*, p. 237.

[29] *Ibid.*; also "An Essay in Aesthetics," *op. cit.*, pp. 36–37.

[30] "Some Questions in Esthetics," *Transformations*, pp. 3–5.

[31] There is reason to believe that, had he lived beyond 1934, Fry might have given up this third view for a less stringent one in which qualities other than the compositional would be aesthetically legitimate; see his *Last Lectures*, chaps. 2 and 3.

[32] "Retrospect," *Vision and Design*, p. 237.

[33] *The Artist and Psycho-Analysis*, p. 16. See also "Some Questions in Esthetics," *Transformations*, pp. 3–5.

[34] "Retrospect," *Vision and Design*, e.g., "I conceived the form of the work of art to be its most essential quality, but I believed this form to be the direct outcome of an apprehension of some emotion of actual life by the artist, although, no doubt, that apprehension was of a special and peculiar kind and implied a certain detachment," p. 237.

[35] *Ibid.*, pp. 237–238.

[36] *Ibid.*, pp. 239–240. In "Some Questions in Esthetics," Fry reaffirms this technique of analyzing paintings into their form and content. Form is still the spatial relationships and content the representations. In *The Artist and Psycho-Analysis*, pp. 16–17, Fry states unequivocally that the essence of art is the form; and this is taken to be the manner of treating the subject: "Now I venture to say that no one who has a real understanding of the art of painting attaches any importance to what we call the subject of a picture — what is represented. To one who feels the language of pictorial form all depends on *how* it is presented, *nothing* on what," (italics in original). See also Fry's *Reflections on British Painting*, p. 49, for the same point of view: "He [Reynolds] tried to show that the deepest spiritual experiences which art can communicate are only to be expressed by formal relations, by the manner of painting, and not by what is painted."

[37] "Retrospect," *Vision and Design*; see also "Giotto," *Vision and Design*.

[38] I. A. Richards, *Principles of Literary Criticism*, chap. ii.

[39] "Some Questions in Esthetics," *Transformations*, pp. 15–16.

[40] *Ibid.*, pp. 16–18.

[41] *Ibid.*, pp. 18–20.

[42] *Ibid.*, p. 23.

[43] *Ibid.*, p. 27.

[44] *Ibid.*, p. 3.

[45] *Ibid.*, p. 10. And in *The Artist and Psycho-Analysis*, p. 12, Fry writes: Great novels "note the inexorable sequence in life of cause and effect, they mark the total indifference of fate to all human desires, and they endeavour to derive precisely from that inexorability of fate an altogether different kind

of pleasure — the pleasure which consists in the recognition of *inevitable sequences*" (italics in original).

In passing, we may note at least two serious internal difficulties with this theory: (1) it deals only with tragedy, hence is incomplete; (2) in making inevitability the essence of literature and that to which we are to respond in true appreciation, it reduces literature to the instinctual level of experience, from which it of course follows that there can be no aesthetic emotion so far as our response to literature is concerned.

⁴⁶ Quoted from Richards, *Principles of Literary Criticism*, p. 16, in "Some Questions in Esthetics," *Transformations*, p. 2.

⁴⁷ *Ibid.*, pp. 5–6.

CHAPTER 2. THE CRITIQUE OF FORMALISM

¹ DeWitt Parker, *The Analysis of Art*, pp. 2–3; "Aesthetics," in D. D. Runes (ed.), *Twentieth Century Philosophy*, pp. 42–47.

² "Aesthetics," pp. 43–44.

³ *The Analysis of Art*, pp. 3 ff; also "Wish Fulfillment and Intuition in Art," *Proceedings of the Sixth International Congress of Philosophy*, reprinted in M. M. Rader (ed.), *A Modern Book of Esthetics*, pp. 73–74.

⁴ *The Analysis of Art*, p. 21.

⁵ *Ibid.*, p. 29.

⁶ *Ibid.*, chap. ii.

⁷ *Ibid.*, pp. 73 ff; cf. D. W. Prall, *Aesthetic Judgment*, chap. v and *Aesthetic Analysis*, chaps. i and ii.

⁸ *The Analysis of Art*, p. 79.

⁹ *Ibid.*, p. 93.

¹⁰ *Ibid.*, pp. 96–97.

¹¹ *Ibid.*, pp. 29–30; see also pp. 32–33.

¹² In "Retrospect," *Vision and Design*, pp. 239–240.

¹³ In Chapter 3, we shall return to Parker's sense of form; and we shall there show that he means by it certain "second-order" properties.

¹⁴ C. J. Ducasse, *Art, the Critics, and You*, pp. 52–53.

¹⁵ Ducasse, *Philosophy of Art*, p. 202 (italics in original).

¹⁶ *Philosophy of Art*, pp. 203 ff; and *Art, the Critics, and You*, pp. 54–55.

¹⁷ *Art, the Critics, and You*, pp. 55–56 (italics in original); see also *Philosophy of Art*, pp. 214 ff.

¹⁸ Eugene Véron, "Art as the Expression of Emotion," *Aesthetics*, reprinted in Rader, *A Modern Book of Esthetics*, p. 86.

¹⁹ "The [decorative], solely devoted to the gratification of eye and ear, affords no measure of its success beyond the pleasure which it gives. The [expressive], whose chief object is to express the feelings and ideas, and, through them, to manifest the power of conception and expansion possessed by the artist, must obviously be estimated, partly at least, by the moral or other value of the ideas and sentiments in question. And, as the value of a work depends directly upon the capability of its author, and as many artists have been about equal in their technical ability, we must be ready to acknowledge that moral and intellectual superiority is a real superiority, and is

naturally marked by the possession of an instinctive and spontaneous power of sympathy." *Ibid.*, p. 95.

²⁰ Laurence Buermeyer has made the same sort of criticism of Bell and Fry; see his essays, "Pattern and Plastic Form," and "The Aesthetics of Roger Fry," in John Dewey and others, *Art and Education*.

²¹ Jacques Maritain, *Art and Scholasticism*, esp. chaps. iv–vii.

²² Cf. Georgi V. Plekhanov, *Art and Society*. "There is no such thing as a work of art completely devoid of ideological content, and also . . . not every idea can serve as a theme for a work of art, or truly inspire the artist. Only that which promotes communion between men can be the basis of a work of art. The possible limits of such a communion are determined not by the artist alone but by the cultural level of the social group to which he belongs, and in a society divided into classes, the extent of this communion is still further conditioned at any given time by the mutual relations of these classes and their degree of development" (p. 65). Also: "*The modern artist will not find inspiration in a sound idea if he seeks to defend the bourgeoisie in its struggle against the proletariat*" (p. 74; italics in original).

The literature on Marxist philosophy and aesthetics is vast, but, in the main, the above account is derived from Marx's "Preface" to *A Contribution to the Critique of Political Economy*, especially the following: "The general result at which I arrived and which, once won, served as a guiding thread for my studies, can be briefly formulated as follows: In the social production which men carry on they enter into definite relations that are indispensable and independent of their will; these relations of production correspond to a definite stage of development of their material forces of production. The sum total of these relations of production constitutes the economic structure of society — the real foundation, on which rises a legal and political superstructure and to which correspond definite forms of social consciousness. The mode of production in material life determines the social, political and intellectual life processes in general. It is not the consciousness of men that determines their being, but, on the contrary, their social being that determines their consciousness. At a certain stage of their development, the material forces of production in society come in conflict with the existing relations of production, or — what is but a legal expression for the same thing — with the property relations within which they have been at work before. From forms of development of the forces of production these relations turn into their fetters. Then begins an epoch of social revolution. With the change of the economic foundations the immense superstructure is more or less rapidly transformed." (This translation is from Karl Marx: *Selected Works*, vol. I, p. 356).

²³ F. J. Klingender, in his pamphlet, *Marxism and Modern Art*, which is the only work I know in which Bell and Fry are criticized specifically from the Marxist point of view, offers this as the fundamental objection to formalism; see esp. pp. 5–16.

²⁴ Bell, *Since Cézanne*, p. 102.

²⁵ Ducasse, in *Philosophy of Art*, "Appendix"; Buermeyer, "Pattern and Plastic Form," in *Art and Education*; and John Hospers, *Meaning and Truth in the Arts*, pp. 98 ff, make this same criticism.

²⁶ See Chapter 4 for a consideration of these qualities.

CHAPTER 3. RESOLUTION: THE ORGANIC THEORY

[1] Bertrand Russell, *Our Knowledge of the External World*, p. 45 (italics in original); see also his *Introduction to Mathematical Philosophy*, p. 199.

[2] See, e.g., Moore's essay, "The Sculptor's Aims," in Herbert Read (ed.), *Unit One*, reprinted in *Henry Moore: Sculpture and Drawings*; and Calder's painting, "The Alphabet of Forms."

[3] A. E. Housman, *The Name and Nature of Poetry*, pp. 35 ff; and Ducasse, *Art, the Critics, and You*, esp. pp. 42–43. This usage is at least as old as Cicero; see his *On the Character of the Orator*, bk. I, chap. xiv.

[4] This is certainly *one* way in which aestheticians have interpreted formalism. See, e.g., A. C. Bradley, "Poetry for Poetry's Sake," *Oxford Lectures on Poetry*, pp. 7–8. Also, Ducasse, *Art, the Critics, and You*, p. 81.

[5] Ducasse, *Philosophy of Art*, p. 202 (italics in original).

[6] Eduard Hanslick, *The Beautiful in Music*, pp. 166–167.

[7] Erwin Panofsky, the great exponent of Iconology in the study of the history of art, also unwittingly commits himself to a theory which, because of his initial acceptance of the form — content distinction, entails the view that there are works of art with all form and no content. He does this by distinguishing between form and meaning. By meaning Panofsky understands representational meanings, like objects in nature or stories or allegories; and by form, certain elements like lines and colors in configurations. Such a distinction will work so long as we are dealing with nonabstract art, but it breaks down when we apply it to abstract art — for example, one of Kandinsky's "Improvisations" — unless we offer an extended theory of artistic meaning or representation (which, of course, Panofsky does not do) in which lines and colors have meanings just as surely as representations of natural objects or historical events. And the reason the distinction breaks down, and especially for Panofsky, when we apply it to abstract art, is that, on his assumptions, it makes of that art one in which there is all form and no content, i.e., meanings; which makes of Iconology a science that cannot, upon its stated principles, encompass the whole history of art. Iconologists, of course, do deal with modern art, and one might add, rather brilliantly, too, but they do so by transcending the semantical foundations of their discipline as these have been set forth by Panofsky. See *Studies in Iconology: Humanistic Themes in the Art of the Renaissance*, chap. i.

[8] For an analysis and justification of real definition as against nominal or contextual, see my "Analysis and the Unity of Russell's Philosophy," P. A. Schilpp (ed.), *The Philosophy of Bertrand Russell*, pp. 110–121.

[9] A. C. Bradley, "Poetry for Poetry's Sake," *Oxford Lectures on Poetry*, pp. 9 ff.

[10] No Platonic theory is intended, necessarily. The main point is that nominalism cannot explain communication and that universals are not mere words or "legisigns." Charles Peirce recognized this long ago in his conception of "thirdness" or "law" as essential to communication, although some of his supposed followers have forgotten it.

That nominalism cannot deal adequately with the facts of communication was demonstrated by Russell in 1912, in *The Problems of Philosophy*, chap. ix. His arguments are still cogent.

[11] See, e.g., Freud's *Leonardo da Vinci; a Psychosexual Study of an Infantile Reminiscence.*

[12] Cf. A. C. Bradley, "Poetry for Poetry's Sake," p. 12.

[13] *Ibid.*

[14] A. C. Barnes, *The Art in Painting*, bk. II, chap. ii.

[15] John Dewey, *Art as Experience*, p. 110.

[16] Cf. Cleanth Brooks, "The New Criticism: A Brief for the Defense," *The American Scholar*, XIII (Summer 1944), No. 3, pp. 294–295.

[17] DeWitt Parker, *The Analysis of Art*, chap. iii, esp. pp. 93–94.

[18] A second-order property is one that is a function of a first-order property. For example, if Napoleon was brave, cunning, quick, etc., then he had all the characteristics of a great general. "Having all the characteristics of a great general" is a second-order property of Napoleon, being a function of his first-order characteristics: being brave, being cunning, etc. See A. N. Whitehead and Bertrand Russell, *Principia Mathematica*, vol. I, chap. ii.

[19] A. C. Barnes, *The Art in Painting*, bk. II, chap. ii.

[20] *Ibid.*

[21] Cf. Bertrand Russell, *Principles of Mathematics*, pp. 211–224, and "Logical Atomism," *Contemporary British Philosophy*, First Series, pp. 374–375. Russell means by an externally related system one in which the relations cannot be reduced to predicates of the terms or the whole complex. I agree with him that organic systems, as we have conceived them, are externally related ones, in *his* sense; but his sense does not distinguish between systems in which constituents make a difference to each other's nature and systems in which they do not. And this distinction between *internal* and *external constituency* necessitates our division into mechanical and organic.

[22] My own view is that a good frame is one that neither enhances nor detracts from the plastic elements but tends to neutralize itself.

[23] Henri Matisse, *Notes d'un Peintre*, quoted in John Dewey, *Art as Experience*, p. 136 (italics mine).

[24] Cleanth Brooks and R. P. Warren, *Understanding Poetry*, pp. 18–19 (their italics). The authors offer excellent examples of the organic principle in poetry throughout their book. One effective example is Shelley's "Death." This is their comment: "Here, in 'Death' . . . we have a case in which the specific feeling stimulated by the jigging rhythm, tends to contradict the response suggested by the ideas, images, etc. of the poem. The poem is an unsuccessful poem because the parts do not work together — they are not properly related" (pp. 219–220). See also their analyses of some of the poems of Shakespeare, Davenant, Burns, and Keats (pp. 19–21, 409–415, and 488). Their entire book is an excellent example of practical criticism as founded upon an organic theory of art.

[25] See especially L. A. Reid, *A Study in Aesthetics*, chap. ii; and John Hospers, *Meaning and Truth in the Arts*, chap. iii.

[26] By sign we mean what most semioticians mean: *a* is a sign if it means, stands for, designates, denotes *b* to some interpreter.

[27] Cf. Parker, "Aesthetics," *op. cit.*, p. 46; and Prall, *Aesthetic Analysis*, chap. i.

[28] "A is a representative of B"; "A represents B"; "A means B"; and "A denotes B" are all synonymous in this usage, which is a rather common one.

[29] Carroll Pratt, *The Meaning of Music*, pt. ii, sec. 13.

[30] Laurence Buermeyer, in his "Pattern and Plastic Form," has shown brilliantly how art can integrate plastic and nonplastic values. "In every great painter the presence of pattern can easily be demonstrated by an analysis of his pictures. In Giotto, for example, the rhythm and sequence of line, distribution of masses, and contrast and harmony of color, have an immediate and obvious decorative effect, but the expression proper (not of course merely facial expression but imaginative insight) goes far beyond decoration. It resides in the restraint and dignity with which the figures are conceived, in the mystical quality conveyed largely by a pervasive, transfiguring color-glow and by a convincing spatiousness, attained by few and, in themselves, rather schematic indications of perspective. These things enter also into the pattern, but it is in their service in revealing a world which only Giotto was capable of seeing that their most moving aesthetic effect resides." (John Dewey and others, *Art and Education*, pp. 98–99.)

[31] A. C. Bradley, "Poetry for Poetry's Sake," p. 7.

[32] In their *Understanding Poetry* (p. 488), Brooks and Warren offer an excellent illustration of the identity of the how and the what in poetry. They present (but with no analysis) two versions of the "Tomorrow and tomorrow" soliloquy of *Macbeth*, the original Shakespearian and an "improved" rewriting by Sir William Davenant, who was intent upon removing certain "defects" from the original in the interests of reasonableness and logic. Here are the two versions:

(Shakespeare's)

Tomorrow, and tomorrow, and tomorrow
Creeps in this petty pace from day to day
To the last syllable of recorded time;
And all our yesterdays have lighted fools
The way to dusty death. Out, out, brief candle!
Life's but a walking shadow, a poor player
That struts and frets his hour upon the stage
And then is heard no more. It is a tale
Told by an idiot, full of sound and fury,
Signifying nothing.

(Davenant's)

Tomorrow and tomorrow and tomorrow
Creeps in a stealing pace from day to day,
To the last minute of recorded time,
And all our yesterdays have lighted fools
To their eternal homes; out, out, that candle!
Etc.

Our first reaction to these two versions is to say that their content, their "whatness," is the same; and that their form, their "howness," is different. But this is an entirely incorrect view, as the slightest analysis of these two versions reveals. In Shakespeare's version, the general expressive quality is one of the *earthiness albeit meaninglessness* of human experience. Davenant, in his "corrected" edition, offers, among his substitutions, "stealing" for "petty" and "eternal homes" for "dusty death." Both of these substitutions, but especially the second, destroy the general effect aimed at in the passage. Actually, Davenant's version, in spite of his attempt to render Shakespeare "logical," is self-contradictory, since the whole connotation of "eternal homes" is that life is not *meaningless* but has its purpose in something beyond it!

These two versions, therefore, do not share the same content. With a change in *how* something is expressed, in Davenant, the *what* changes so radically as to render the passage unintelligent. In art, how = what!

CHAPTER 4. THE ARTS: PAINTING

[1] A. C. Barnes, *The Art in Painting*, p. 82.
[2] Cf. Kate Gordon, *Esthetics*, p. 162.
[3] Cf. A. R. Chandler, *Beauty and Human Nature*, chap. iv.
[4] Cf. A. C. Barnes, *The Art in Painting*, bk. II, chap. iii.
[5] John Dewey, *Art as Experience*, pp. 116–117.
[6] A. C. Barnes, *The Art in Painting*, p. 77.
[7] *Ibid.*, p. 115.
[8] *Ibid.*, bk. II, chap. v.
[9] Sheldon Cheney, *Expressionism in Art*, chaps. vi–vii.
[10] A. H. Barr, Jr., *Picasso: Fifty Years of His Art*, p. 202.
[11] Kandinsky distinguishes between "Impressions," "Improvisations," and "Compositions." The first two types contain subjects; only the third is without any subject.
[12] Cf. J. J. Sweeney, "Piet Mondrian," *The Museum of Modern Art Bulletin*, XII (Spring 1945), No. 4, p. 9.
[13] A black-and-white reproduction of the picture and the above quotation are in Sidney Janis, *Abstract and Surrealist Art in America*, p. 65 (italics in original).

CHAPTER 5. THE ARTS: POETRY

[1] Cf. Cleanth Brooks and R. P. Warren, *Understanding Poetry*, p. 591. I am deeply indebted to their analysis of "Prufrock," although I disagree with many of their essential points.
[2] Cf. F. H. Bradley, *Appearance and Reality*, with its insistence upon the degrees of reality. It is worth noting here that Eliot is a great admirer of Bradley; see Eliot's "Francis Herbert Bradley," *Selected Essays*, pp. 358–368.
[3] The term is Parker's; see his *Principles of Aesthetics* (second edition), p. 32.
[4] Cleanth Brooks, *The Well Wrought Urn*, p. 182.
[5] The term is Philip Wheelright's; see his "On the Semantics of Poetry," *The Kenyon Review*, Summer, 1940, pp. 266–270. Cf. William Empson, *Seven Types of Ambiguity*, Ch. I.
[6] Cleanth Brooks, *Modern Poetry and the Tradition*, Ch. I, esp. pp. 15–17.

CHAPTER 6. THE ARTS: MUSIC

[1] Thus Hanslick writes: "Seeing then how easy it is to deduce from the inherent nature of sound the inability of music to represent definite emotions, it seems almost incredible that our every-day experience should, nevertheless, have failed to firmly establish this fact. Let those who, when listening to some instrumental composition, imagine the strings to quiver with a profusion of feeling, clearly show *what* feeling is the subject of the music." *The Beautiful in Music*, p. 40 (italics in original).

Again, let the advocate of program music listen to the themes of the great masters. "Who would be bold enough to point out a definite feeling as the subject of any of these themes? One will say 'love.' He may be right. Another thinks it is 'longing.' Perhaps so. A third feels it to be 'religious fervor.' Who can contradict him? Now, how can we talk of a definite feeling being *represented*, when nobody really knows *what* is represented?" *Ibid.*, p. 44 (italics in original).

Also: "But no instrumental composition can describe the ideas of love, wrath, or fear, since there is no *causal nexus* between these ideas and certain combinations of sounds." *Ibid.*, p. 38 (italics in original).

[2] Max Schoen, *The Understanding of Music*, pp. 103–104.

[3] He writes, for example: " 'Meaning' may be defined as those qualities which reveal no correspondence with the physical properties of the stimulus . . . Meanings are those qualities which have been acquired by an object through association and suggestion." *The Meaning of Music*, pp. 9–10; see also the whole of Part III.

[4] *Ibid.*, p. 238.

[5] Eduard Hanslick, *The Beautiful in Music*, p. 67 (his italics).

[6] Consider these statements as proof of this interpretation of Hanslick:

(1) "A certain class of *ideas*, however, is quite susceptible of being adequately expressed by means which unquestionably belong to the sphere of music proper. This class comprises all ideas which, consistently with the organ to which they appeal, are associated with audible changes of strength, motion, and ratio: the ideas of intensity waxing and diminishing; of motion hastening and lingering; of ingeniously complex and simple progression, &c. The aesthetic expression of music may be described by terms such as graceful, gentle, violent, vigorous, elegant, fresh; all these ideas being expressible by corresponding modifications of sound. We may, therefore, use those adjectives as directly describing *musical* phenomena . . ." *Ibid.*, pp. 35–36 (italics in original).

(2) "We are perfectly justified in calling a musical theme grand, graceful, warm, hollow, vulgar; but all these terms are exclusively suggestive of the *musical* character of the particular passage." *Ibid.*, p. 74 (italics in original).

(3) "The aesthetic enquirer . . . will, therefore, without knowing the name or the biography of the author, detect in Beethoven's symphonies impetuousness and struggling, an unsatisfied longing and a defiance, supported by a consciousness of strength." *Ibid.*, pp. 87–88.

(4) "Every musical note having its individual complexion, the prominent characteristics of the composer, such as sentimentality, energy, cheerfulness,

&c., may through the preference given by him to certain keys, rhythms, and modulations be traced in those *general* phenomena which music is capable of reproducing." *Ibid.*, p. 102 (italics in original).

[7] J. W. N. Sullivan, in his inspired book, *Beethoven: His Spiritual Development*, has made this point in a brilliant fashion, that ordinary languages are simply inadequate to describe the "meanings" of music.

[8] S. K. Langer, *Philosophy in a New Key*, pp. 228–229.

CHAPTER 7. THE ARTS: THE MEDIUM

[1] Bernard Bosanquet, *Three Lectures on Aesthetic*, Lecture II, but esp. pp. 67 ff.

[2] Quoted in H.-R. Hitchcock, *Modern Architecture*, p. 175.

[3] The phrase is Le Corbusier's.

[4] Henry Moore, *Sculpture and Drawings*, p. xxxix.

[5] S. M. Eisenstein, *The Film Sense*, esp. Ch. I.

[6] Erwin Panofsky, "Style and Medium in the Motion Pictures," *Critique* (January-February 1947), p. 8.

[7] E. S. Selden, *The Dancer's Quest*, p. 22.

[8] *Ibid.*, p. 112.

[9] C. J. Ducasse, *Art, the Critics, and You*, p. 56.

[10] Philipp Spitta, in his classic work, *Johann Sebastian Bach*, has shown in detail the integration of the text of the mass and the musical materials that Bach used; see vol. III, bk. vi, chap. ii.

CHAPTER 8. ART, LANGUAGE AND TRUTH

[1] DeWitt Parker, "Aesthetics," *op. cit.*, pp. 42–45.

[2] C. J. Ducasse, *Art, the Critics, and You*, pp. 52–53 (italics in original).

[3] C. K. Ogden and I. A. Richards, *The Meaning of Meaning*, esp. pp. 123–126; 147–151; 227–229; and 230–236.

[4] Rudolf Carnap, *Philosophy and Logical Syntax*, chap. i.

[5] T. M. Greene, *The Arts and the Art of Criticism*, chap. xxiii; B. C. Heyl, *New Bearings in Esthetics and Art Criticism*, chap. iii; and John Hospers, *Meaning and Truth in the Arts*, chaps. v–vi.

[6] John Hospers, *Meaning and Truth in the Arts*, p. 160 (italics in original).

[7] DeWitt Parker, *The Principles of Aesthetics*, p. 32.

[8] This example and its analysis constitute a revision of my articles, "Does Art Tell the Truth?" and "The Logic of Art," *Philosophy and Phenomenological Research*, III (March 1943), no. 3; and V (March 1945), no. 3.

[9] Richard Wright, *Native Son*, p. 358; reprinted by courtesy of the publishers, Harper and Bros.

[10] P. A. Schilpp, ed., *The Philosophy of G. E. Moore*, p. 542 (italics in original).

[11] A. J. Ayer, *Language, Truth and Logic*, pp. 37–39.

[12] Erwin Panofsky, "Et in Arcadia Ego," in Raymond Klibansky and H. J. Paton, ed., *Philosophy and History, Essays Presented to Ernst Cassirer*, p. 240.

[13] *Ibid.*, p. 242.

[14] *Ibid.*, pp. 247–248.

[15] We follow Sheffer and Lewis in distinguishing between propositions and assertions, and in regarding truth and falsity as attributes of assertions, not of propositions. See C. I. Lewis, *An Analysis of Knowledge and Valuation*, pp. 48 ff.

CHAPTER 9. THE APPRECIATION OF ART

[1] Konrad Lange, "Art as Play," reprinted in M. M. Rader (ed.), *A Modern Book of Esthetics*, p. 35.

[2] DeWitt Parker, *The Analysis of Art*, pp. 4–5.

[3] T. S. Eliot, *The Use of Poetry and the Use of Criticism*, p. 82.

[4] I. A. Richards, *Science and Poetry*, pp. 34–35 (italics in original).

[5] *Ibid.*, p. 49.

[6] Eliot, "Dante," *Selected Essays*, pp. 229–231 (italics in original).

[7] Eliot, "Shelley and Keats," *The Use of Poetry and the Use of Criticism*, p. 82.

[8] *Ibid.*, p. 87.

[9] Cleanth Brooks, *The Well Wrought Urn*, esp. pp. 182, 184, 186, 194, and 230 for his main views on the nature of poetry.

[10] *Ibid.*, p. 228.

[11] *Ibid.*, p. 229.

[12] Throughout this discussion of Freud, I am deeply indebted to Dr. Richard Sterba. His paper, "The Problem of Art in Freud's Writings," *The Psychoanalytic Quarterly*, IX, no. 2 (April 1940), is the best exposition of Freud's aesthetics with which I am acquainted.

[13] R. E. Fry, *The Artist and Psycho-Analysis*, p. 18 (italics in original).

[14] Ducasse, *The Philosophy of Art*, chap. iv.

[15] Leo Tolstoy, *What Is Art?* (World's Classics ed.), p. 123.

[16] *Ibid.*, p. 235.

[17] *Ibid.*, pp. 221 ff and 249. It is important to recognize that Tolstoy was willing to throw out the whole of instrumental music on the grounds that it contains no feelings, hence no humanitarian feelings. This consequence of his views should be sufficient to dismiss his general aesthetics.

[18] R. E. Fry, "An Essay in Aesthetics," *Vision and Design*, pp. 30–32.

[19] Yrjö Hirn, *The Origins of Art*, chaps. ii, viii–ix.

[20] See, for example, Ducasse's brilliant refutation of empathy in *The Philosophy of Art*, chap. x.

[21] Ducasse, *Art, the Critics, and You*, chap. iii; and *The Philosophy of Art*, chap. xi.

[22] *Art, the Critics, and You*, p. 73 (italics in original).

[23] *Ibid.*, p. 74.

[24] *Ibid.*, p. 79.

[25] Edward Bullough, " 'Psychical Distance' as a Factor in Art and an Esthetic Principle," *British Journal of Psychology*, V (1912–13), reprinted in M. M. Rader (ed.), *A Modern Book of Esthetics*, pp. 315–342.

[26] Perhaps it should be emphasized again that there is no insistence upon the correctness of the psychological or descriptive aspects of the contemplative

theory; it may be that we have distorted or even missed some of the facts. It is for each of us to articulate the characteristics we find in our contemplative appreciation of art. The only thing we do insist upon is the normative aspect of the contemplative theory, namely, that contemplation is the only way we ought to respond to art.

[27] *Art, the Critics, and You*, pp. 120–121 (italics in original).
[28] Cf. A. C. Ewing, *The Definition of Good*, Chaps. I–II.
[29] Cleanth Brooks and R. P. Warren, *Understanding Poetry*, p. 413.
[30] Cf. Stephen Pepper, *The Basis of Criticism in the Arts*, pp. 79 ff.

BIBLIOGRAPHY

(Articles are not listed here, since the full facts of their publications are given in the notes.)

Abell, Walter, *Representation and Form*. New York: C. Scribner's Sons, 1936.

Arnheim, Rudolf, *Film*. London: Faber and Faber, 1933.

Ayer, A. J., *Language, Truth and Logic*. New York: Oxford University Press, 1936.

Barnes, A. C., *The Art in Painting*. New York: Harcourt, Brace and Co., 1937.

Barr, A. H., Jr., *Picasso: Fifty Years of his Art*. New York: The Museum of Modern Art, 1946.

Bell, Clive, *Art*. London: Chatto and Windus, 1914.

————— *Enjoying Pictures*. New York: Harcourt, Brace and Co., 1934.

————— *Landmarks in Nineteenth-Century Painting*. London: Chatto and Windus, 1927.

————— *Proust*. London: L. and V. Woolf, 1928.

————— *Since Cézanne*. London: Chatto and Windus, 1922.

Birkhoff, G. D., *Aesthetic Measure*. Cambridge: Harvard University Press, 1933.

Blackmur, R. P., *The Double Agent*. New York: Arrow Editions, 1935.

————— *The Expense of Greatness*. New York: Arrow Editions, 1940.

Bosanquet, Bernard, *Three Lectures on Aesthetic*. London: Macmillan and Co., Ltd., 1923.

Bradley, A. C., *Oxford Lectures on Poetry*. London: Macmillan and Co., Ltd., 1909.

Bradley, F. H., *Appearance and Reality*. London: S. Sonnenschein and Co., 1902.

Brooks, Cleanth, *Modern Poetry and the Tradition*. Chapel Hill: University of North Carolina Press, 1939.

—— *The Well Wrought Urn*. New York: Reynal and Hitchcock, 1947.

—— and R. P. Warren, *Understanding Poetry*. New York: Henry Holt and Co., 1938.

Buermeyer, Laurence, *The Esthetic Experience*. Merion, Pa.: Barnes Foundation, 1924.

Burke, Kenneth, *A Grammar of Motives*. New York: Prentice-Hall, Inc., 1945.

—— *The Philosophy of Literary Form*. Baton Rouge: Louisiana State University Press, 1941.

Carnap, Rudolf, *Philosophy and Logical Syntax*. London: K. Paul, Trench, Trubner and Co., 1935.

Cassirer, Ernst, *An Essay on Man*. New Haven: Yale University Press, 1945.

—— *Language and Myth*. New York: Harper and Bros., 1946.

Chandler, A. R., *A Bibliography of Experimental Aesthetics, 1865–1932*. Columbus: The Ohio State University Press, 1933.

—— *Beauty and Human Nature*. New York and London: D. Appleton-Century Co., Inc., 1934.

Cheney, Sheldon, *A Primer of Modern Art*. New York: Tudor Publishing Co., 1939.

—— *Expressionism in Art*. New York: Liveright Publishing Corporation, 1934.

—— *The New World Architecture*. London and New York: Longmans, Green and Co., 1930.

Cicero, *On the Character of the Orator*. London: Bohn's Classical Library, 1855.

Le Corbusier (Jeanneret-Gris, C. E.), *Towards a New Architecture*. New York: Payson and Clarke, Ltd., 1927.

Croce, Benedetto, *Aesthetic*. London: Macmillan and Co., 1929.

—— *The Essence of Aesthetic*. London: W. Heinemann, 1921.

Dewey, John, *Art as Experience*. New York: Minton, Balch and Co., 1934.

—— and others, *Art and Education*. Merion, Pa.: Barnes Foundation, 1929.

Ducasse, C. J., *Art, the Critics, and You*. New York: Oskar Piest, 1944.

—— *The Philosophy of Art*. New York: L. Mac Veagh, The Dial Press, 1929.

Eastman, Max, *The Literary Mind*. New York: C. Scribner's Sons, 1931.

Eisenstein, S. M., *The Film Sense*. New York: Harcourt, Brace and Co., 1942.

Eliot, T. S., *Collected Poems, 1909–1935*. New York: Harcourt, Brace and Co., 1936.

—— *Selected Essays, 1917–1932*. New York: Harcourt, Brace and Co., 1932.

—— *The Sacred Wood*. London: Methuen and Co., Ltd., 1932.

—— *The Use of Poetry and the Use of Criticism*. Cambridge: Harvard University Press, 1933.

Empson, William, *Seven Types of Ambiguity*. London: Chatto and Windus, 1930.

Ewing, A. C., *The Definition of Good*. New York: The Macmillan Company, 1947.

Freud, Sigmund, *Civilisation and its Discontents*. London: L. and V. Woolf, at the Hogarth Press, 1930.

—— *A General Introduction to Psycho-Analysis*. Garden City: Garden City Publishing Co., Inc., 1943.

—— *Leonardo da Vinci: A Psychosexual Study of an Infantile Reminiscence*. New York: Moffat, Yard and Co., 1916.

—— *New Introductory Lectures*. New York: W. W. Norton and Co., Inc., 1933.

—— *Psychoanalytische Studien an Werken der Dichtung und Kunst*. Leipsig, Wien, Zürich: Internationaler Psychoanalytischer Verlag, 1924.

—— *The Basic Writings*. New York: The Modern Library, 1938.

Fry, R. E., *Art and Commerce*. London: L. and V. Woolf, 1926.

—— *Art-History as an Academic Study*. Cambridge: The University Press, 1933.

—— *Cézanne*. New York: The Macmillan Co., 1927.

———— *Characteristics of French Art*. London: Chatto and Windus, 1932.

———— *Flemish Art*. New York: Brentano's, 1927.

———— *Giovanni Bellini*. London: At the Sign of the Unicorn, 1899.

———— *Henri-Matisse*. New York: E. Weyhe, 1930.

———— *Last Lectures*. Cambridge: The University Press, 1939.

———— *Reflections on British Painting*. New York: The Macmillan Co., 1934.

———— *The Artist and Psycho-Analysis*. London: L. and V. Woolf, 1924.

———— *The Arts of Painting and Sculpture*. London: V. Gollancz, 1932.

———— *Transformations*. London: Chatto and Windus, 1926.

———— *Vision and Design*. London: Chatto and Windus, 1920.

———— and others, *Chinese Art*. London: B. T. Batsford, Ltd., 1925.

———— and others, *Georgian Art* (1760–1820). London: B. T. Batsford, Ltd., 1929.

Giedion, Sigfried, *Space, Time and Architecture*. Cambridge: Harvard University Press, 1941.

Gilbert, K. E., and Helmut Kuhn, *A History of Esthetics*. New York: The Macmillan Co., 1939.

Gordon, Kate, *Esthetics*. New York: Henry Holt and Co., 1909.

Greene, T. M., *The Arts and the Art of Criticism*. Princeton: Princeton University Press, 1940.

Gropius, Walter, *The New Architecture and the Bauhaus*. London: Faber and Faber, 1935.

Gurney, Edmund, *The Power of Sound*. London: Smith, Elder, and Co., 1880.

Hanslick, Eduard, *The Beautiful in Music*. New York: Novello, Ewer and Co., 1891.

H'Doubler, M. N., *The Dance and its Place in Education*. New York: Harcourt, Brace and Co., 1925.

Heyl, B. C., *New Bearings in Esthetics and Art Criticism*. New Haven: Yale University Press, 1943.

Hirn, Yrjö, *The Origins of Art*. New York: The Macmillan Co., 1931.

Hitchcock, H.-R., Jr., *In the Nature of Materials*. New York: Duell, Sloan and Pearce, 1942.

—— *Modern Architecture*. New York: Payson and Clarke, Ltd., 1929.

—— and Philip Johnson, *The International Style*. New York: W. W. Norton and Co., 1932.

Hospers, John, *Meaning and Truth in the Arts*. Chapel Hill: University of North Carolina Press, 1946.

Housman, A. E., *The Name and Nature of Poetry*. Cambridge: The University Press, 1933.

Janis, Sidney, *Abstract and Surrealist Art in America*. New York: Reynal and Hitchcock, 1944.

Kandinsky, Wassily, *The Art of Spiritual Harmony*. London: Constable and Co., Ltd., 1914.

Klibansky, Raymond, and H. J. Paton, *Philosophy and History: Essays Presented to Ernst Cassirer*. Oxford: The Clarendon Press, 1936.

Klingender, F. J., *Marxism and Modern Art*. New York: International Publishers, 1945.

Langer, S. K., *Philosophy in a New Key*. Cambridge: Harvard University Press, 1942.

Lee, Vernon (Violet Paget), *The Beautiful*. Cambridge: The University Press, 1913.

Lewis, C. I., *An Analysis of Knowledge and Valuation*. La Salle: The Open Court Publishing Co., 1946.

Listowel, Earl of, *A Critical History of Modern Aesthetics*. London: G. Allen and Unwin, 1933.

Maritain, Jacques, *Art and Scholasticism*. New York: C. Scribner's Sons, 1930.

Martin, John, *The Dance*. New York: Tudor Publishing Co., 1947.

Marx, Karl, *Selected Works*. New York: International Publishers, 1936.

Mauron, Charles, *Aesthetics and Psychology*. London: Hogarth Press, 1935.

Morris, C. W., *Foundations of the Theory of Signs*. (*International Encyclopedia of Unified Science*, Vol. 1, no. 2). Chicago: The University of Chicago Press, 1938.

—— *Signs, Language and Behavior.* New York: Prentice-Hall, Inc., 1946.

Moore, Henry, *Sculpture and Drawings.* New York: Curt Valentin, 1944.

Muirhead, J. H., ed., *Contemporary British Philosophy.* 2 Vols. New York: The Macmillan Co., 1924–25.

Mumford, Lewis, *Sticks and Stones: A Study of American Architecture and Civilization.* New York: Boni and Liveright, 1924.

—— *Technics and Civilization.* New York: Harcourt, Brace and Co., 1934.

—— *The Culture of Cities.* New York: Harcourt, Brace and Co., 1938.

Ogden, C. K., and I. A. Richards, *The Meaning of Meaning.* New York: Harcourt, Brace and Co., 1923.

Panofsky, Erwin, *Studies in Iconology: Humanistic Themes in the Art of the Renaissance.* New York: Oxford University Press, 1939.

Parker, DeWitt, *The Analysis of Art.* New Haven: Yale University Press, 1926.

—— *The Principles of Aesthetics.* Second edition. New York: F. S. Crofts and Co., 1946.

Pepper, Stephen, *Esthetic Quality.* New York: C. Scribner's Sons, 1938.

—— *The Basis of Criticism in the Arts.* Cambridge: Harvard University Press, 1945.

Plekhanov, Georgĭ, *Art and Society.* New York: Critics Group, 1936.

Prall, D. W., *Esthetic Analysis.* New York: Thomas Y. Crowell Co., 1936.

—— *Esthetic Judgment.* New York: Thomas Y. Crowell Co., 1929.

Pratt, Carroll, *The Meaning of Music.* New York, London: McGraw-Hill Book Co., Inc., 1931.

Pudovkin, V. I., *On Film Technique.* London: V. Gollancz, Ltd., 1929.

Rader, M. M., ed., *A Modern Book of Esthetics.* New York: Henry Holt and Co., 1935.

Reid, L. A., A Study in Aesthetics. New York: The Macmillan Co., 1931.

Richards, I. A., Coleridge on Imagination. London: K. Paul, Trench, Trubner and Co., Ltd., 1934.

—— Practical Criticism. New York: Harcourt, Brace and Co., 1929.

—— Principles of Literary Criticism. New York: Harcourt, Brace and Co., 1926.

—— Science and Poetry. London: K. Paul, Trench, Trubner and Co., Ltd., 1926.

—— and others, The Foundations of Aesthetics. New York: International Publishers, 1929.

Rotha, Paul, The Film Till Now. London: J. Cape, 1931.

Runes, D. D., ed., Twentieth Century Philosophy. New York: Philosophical Library, 1943.

—— and H. G. Schrickel, eds., Encyclopedia of the Arts. New York: Philosophical Library, 1946.

Russell, Bertrand, Introduction to Mathematical Philosophy. London: George Allen and Unwin, Ltd., 1919.

—— Our Knowledge of the External World. New York: W. W. Norton and Co., Inc., 1929.

—— The Principles of Mathematics. Second edition. New York: W. W. Norton and Co., Inc., 1937.

—— The Problems of Philosophy. New York: Henry Holt and Co., 1912.

—— and A. N. Whitehead, Principia Mathematica. 3 Vols. Cambridge: The University Press, 1910–13.

Santayana, George, The Sense of Beauty. New York: C. Scribner's Sons, 1896.

Schilpp, P. A., ed., The Philosophy of Bertrand Russell. Evanston and Chicago: Northwestern University Press, 1944.

—— The Philosophy of G. E. Moore. Evanston and Chicago: Northwestern University Press, 1942.

Schoen, Max, The Effects of Music. New York: Harcourt, Brace and Co., 1927.

—— The Understanding of Music. New York: Harper and Bros., 1945.

Selden, E. S., *The Dancer's Quest*. Berkeley: University of California Press, 1935.

Spitta, Philipp, *Johann Sebastian Bach*. 3 Vols. New York: H. W. Gray and Co., 1899.

Sullivan, J. W. N., *Beethoven: His Spiritual Development*. New York: A. A. Knopf, 1927.

Tolstoy, Leo, *What Is Art?* (Oxford's The World Classics' edition). New York: Oxford University Press, 1930.

Tyler, Parker, *Magic and Myth of the Movies*. New York: Henry Holt and Co., 1947.

Woolf, Virginia, *Roger Fry*. New York: Harcourt, Brace and Co., 1940.

Wright, F. L., *An Autobiography*. New York: Duell, Sloan and Pearce, 1943.

—— *The Disappearing City*. New York: W. F. Payson, 1932.

—— *An Organic Architecture: The Architecture of Democracy*. London: Lund, Humphries and Co., Ltd., 1939.

INDEX